SECRETS
OF THE
GEM TRADE

Secrets Of The Gem Trade

THE CONNOISSEUR'S GUIDE TO PRECIOUS GEMSTONES

Richard W. Wise

BRUNSWICK HOUSE PRESS

Lenox, Massachuttes

1st Special Jewelry Television Edition 2006

Publisher's Cataloging-in-Publication

(Provided by Quality Books, Inc.)

Wise, Richard W.
   Secrets of the gem trade : the connoisseur's guide to precious gemstones / by Richard W. Wise
   p. cm.
   Includes bibliographical references and index.
   LCCN 2003103774
   ISBN 0-9728223-7-2

   1. Gems--Collectors and collecting--Handbooks, manuals, etc. 2.Precious stones--Collection and preservation--Handbooks, manuals, etc. I. Title

NK5530.W57 2003   736'.2'075
                         QB103-200285

Copy editing by Sarah Novak and Rebekah V. Wise
Cover, book design and graphics by Harry Bernard
Drawings by Joseph Sparaco

Published by Brunswick House Press
81 Church Street, Lenox, Massachusetts 01240
Fax: (413) 637-8275
Email: sage@secretsofthegemtrade.com
Website: www.secretsofthegemtrade.com

SAN:255-1365

to Rebekah, wife,
partner and companion
in all my travels
with love and admiration

CONTENTS

LIFTING THE VEIL

The gemstone trade is an old and venerable one. Evidence of its existence dates back at least seven thousand years. Since medieval times, a few ethnic minorities have dominated the gem business — the Indians on the Asian subcontinent, the ethnic Chinese in Thailand, and the Jews in Europe. The Jewish people, for example, endured discrimination all across Europe. In some countries they were denied membership in the craft guilds, which regulated and determined who could work in a specific trade. People denied a livelihood found other means to earn a living. The gem trade was in many respects a natural one for these restless peoples. Secrecy was essential: gemstones are rare and so are good sources. Given the political conditions in Europe at that time, to reveal the inner workings of the business would have been both a tactical and strategic error. Secrecy was not simply a necessity of business; it was a matter of self-preservation. Thus the gem trade became a closed fraternity, its wisdom passed orally from father to son. Secrecy became a habit, one that has persisted until the present day.

I was not born into the trade, but came to it in my early thirties, after pursuing other interests for a number of years. Gems, however, have always fascinated me. When I was a child and my friends collected baseball cards, I collected gems and shells. Oh, not real gems, of course, just rhinestones and paste. Some were given to me; others were pried out of discarded pieces of costume jewelry. In those days, Providence, Rhode Island, the town where I grew up, was the center of the costume jewelry industry. A number of adults I knew made a living working at Coro and other factories making costume pieces. They were the source of a number of my treasures.

I began my career in the jewelry business as a craftsman, an apprentice goldsmith. Like many people who matured politically in the 1960s, I graduated from college with a burning desire to right the world's wrongs. I spent several years as a political activist. Also, like many others, I eventually grew disillusioned with social activism. Learning to make jewelry was a sort of therapy, something interesting to do while I sorted out my life and thought about my next step.

In the tiny shop where I worked we used a lot of stones, cabochons mostly: jasper, agate, and turquoise. This was the late seventies, the tail end of the second Arts and Crafts Movement.[1] Precious materials, including platinum and ruby, were considered politically incorrect. "Honest materials" such as sterling silver and turquoise were the materials of choice. What else would you wear with a work shirt and jeans? I enjoyed working with these gemstones, but I can't say that they really moved me. During this time I found myself a partner in a retail craft-jewelry shop.

As the eighties dawned the business began to receive more and more requests for pieces made of gold, and along with that, a renewed interest in diamonds, sapphires, and other faceted gems. My own appetite stimulated, and, seeing an opportunity for profit, I decided to learn all I could about gemstones.

My years in college and graduate school and the time spent in community organizing had prepared me, I thought, with the necessary research tools to begin my studies. I began searching for books and asking questions of the gem dealers who, with increasing frequency, called at our shop. "Why," I asked, "was one green tourmaline more expensive than another? What are the parameters used to define quality?" I visited museums and attended previews at some of the big auction houses in New York, where I saw magnificent jewels. I could not understand why the much smaller gemstones offered me by dealers were not as beautiful. Why couldn't I purchase smaller gems comparable to the large ones I had seen at the major auction houses? The larger stones were, after all, much rarer. The dealers I asked fended off my queries. Their answers were either illogical or just plain evasive. Either they didn't have the answers or they simply

[1]. It is interesting to note that the rediscovery of handcrafts reached its peak in the 1970s, almost exactly one hundred years after the heyday of the Arts and Crafts Movement of the late nineteenth century. The two movements shared much of the same folk ideology — the celebration of handwork and the use of nontraditional materials.

were not going to tell me. Later, I found out, it was a little bit of both.

The books I read did little to clarify the issue. The authors had a great deal to say about history, lore, sources, and the physical characteristics of gemstones, but almost nothing to say about quality, connoisseurship, or beauty. I was frustrated, but determined that I would force this trade to yield up its secrets.

I then made three decisions that put me on the right track. First, I enrolled, by correspondence, in the Graduate Gemology program offered by the Gemological Institute of America. Second, I took a subscription to *Gems & Gemology*, the journal of the institute. Third, and most importantly, I decided to take my questions to the source. I had always had a yen to travel, and the romance of the exotic entrepôts of Asia had taken hold of my imagination.

My first trip took me to Thailand, the ancient center of the ruby and sapphire trade. A friend and colleague with a number of years in the gem business provided me with introductions. I visited the mining centers of Chantaburi and Trat, and the great trading city of Bangkok. That first trip marked the beginning of my real education. Other trips followed: I visited the pearl farms of Tahiti, the opal mines of the Queensland outback, the mining districts of Brazil, Tanzania, and Burma — observing, always observing, and asking questions.

Still, the quest was not an easy one, and it is far from over. It may surprise the reader to know that much of the information contained in this book has never been available before. A trade that has kept its secrets for thousands of years does not yield up its wisdom simply for the asking. Sources must be protected and contacts safeguarded. However, this is the age of information, and excessive secrecy does the trade a disservice. The public distrusts what it does not understand. It is no coincidence that the expanded interest in gemstones, specifically colored gemstones, coincides with the opening up of the trade by an intrepid band of young gem cutters and entrepreneurs who were part of the crafts movement of the 1970s. Also, many of the stones included here are fairly new discoveries, and I am among the first to consider them seriously from a purely aesthetic point of view.

My gemology studies provided some of the connoisseur's tools, but by no means all. Much of what I have learned has been gleaned by asking questions and by comparing one gem to another and interpreting what I saw.

I began writing early in my travels. It provided a legitimate reason for asking questions, and helped me to organize and reinforce the information I was able to glean from my sources. During a visit to the black pearl farms of the Tuamotu Archipelago, on a pier overlooking the lagoon on Manihi Atoll, I wrote the first draft of my very first article. This effort was followed by many more.

In the course of my travels I have been tutored by some of the world's great experts. To those who have patiently answered my questions, I am profoundly grateful.

One of the most important things I have learned is to trust my own eye. Some of my best acquisitions have been newly discovered stones or unusual examples of well-known gems that have been disparaged by veteran dealers. The gem trade is deeply conservative, and will often dismiss newly discovered stones (or new sources of traditional gems) whose characteristics differ from those of traditional sources. The passage of time between a gem's discovery and its grudging acceptance by the trade is ripe with opportunity for one who views the gem with an educated but unprejudiced eye.

Another great lesson learned about acquiring gems — if you see it and can afford it, grab it! Gems are often found in large concentrations or pockets, so a large number of stones will appear on the market at a given time. This gives the false impression that the particular gemstone is in plentiful supply. It is, but the supply is fleeting. Once the initial find has stimulated the market's appetite and supply slows, prices will rise. In many cases the source pipeline quickly dries up; the best stones are snapped up, the price rises, and an opportunity to acquire a beautiful stone at a reasonable price has passed, perhaps forever.

Acknowledgments

Many people have aided me in my quest for knowledge; some willingly, some not so. I would like to thank the following: C.R. "Cap" Beesley, whose "short" courses in gemstones, together with numerous conversations provided many insights. Barry Hodgin, my first dealer in Thailand, showed much patience early on. Ronald Sage of Papeete introduced me to the world of the black pearl. Sidney Soriano provided me with introductions on my first trip to Asia, overcame his natural reluctance, and answered many of my questions about pearls. The late Don Thompson was a true adventurer and good friend. Nittin and Jaswin Pattni took me under their wing on my first trip to Africa. Campbell Bridges proved a patient guide; David Stanley Epstein is a fellow truth-seeker and expert on all things Brazilian. My good friend Joseph Belmont showed me the best in ruby and was my companion in Burma. The late Vince Evert was my guide to the Queensland outback. I would also like to thank Charlie McGovern, my first dealer; Dr. N.R. Barot, a learned colleague; Joe Crescenji, a fine cutter; Stephen Hofer and Nick Hale, who taught me much about color; and Mongol Perdicci, Si and Ann Fraser, Lou Wackler, Bernd Munsteiner, Michael Dyber, Fuji Voll, the Elawar family, and Paulo Zonari.

I would like to thank the following for their help in preparing the manuscript: Fred Ward, who warned me that I needed a good editor and then became one; my wife and companion in many travels, Rebekah, who read, reread, then read it over again; and Stephen Hofer, Henri Masliah, Gloria Lieberman, David Wilson, Dr. Edward Gibson, Peter Kaplan, Damien Cody, and David Epstein for their suggestions and editorial comments.

PART I

BECOMING A CONNOISSEUR: ESSENTIALS

The beginning of man's lust for the glittering beauty of gemstones is lost somewhere along the dusty corridors of time. Like a moth transfixed by the flame, our interest in these curious and beautiful na tural creations seems instinctive. The first gem may have been a transparent pebble plucked from a stream or a glint of crystal caught in the firelight and pried from the wall of a cave. Perhaps in the search for flint to knap into tools or weapons, a particularly beautiful piece of agate caught a young girl's fancy. Man's desire to adorn also seems instinctive. The first known jewelry was found in a Paleolithic gravesite dating back over 45,000 years.

© R.W. Wise

From earliest times we have been charmed, intrigued, and awed by the natural beauty of gems. These water-worn natural topaz crystals were found in a stream just outside the Brazilian town of Rodrigo Silva, Minas Gerais.

© R.W. Wise

Primordial eye candy! A close-up view of one of the finer crystals shown in the previous photo, a topaz with an exceptionally pure golden yellow color.

The first gems were curiosities appreciated for their beauty and their unusual form. There were no preconceived notions of preciousness. Perhaps a handful of crystals was pried from the side of a cliff; some had more pronounced color, were clearer, or possessed greater perfection of form. The standards were gut level. Even today, an untrained person shown a box containing several exceptional stones of the same variety will, in the vast majority of cases, instantly select the finest stone. The affinity is immediate. The basic principles of connoisseurship can be deduced from a thoughtful contemplation of a single fine gemstone.

The trick, of course, is in the preselection: I have presented this test to clients many times, after first narrowing the field by choosing only finer quality gemstones. In a jeweler's office one can see hundreds, at a gem show it is possible to see thousands of stones. Under such circumstances, the eye is dazzled and the mind soon goes numb. Without a thorough understanding of principles the budding but inexperienced connoisseur is like the proverbial fatted lamb, ripe and primed for the slaughter.

Chapter 1

Precious Gems: The History of a Concept

The clumsy modern category of "precious" stones has little relevance when applied to the ancient world.

Jack Ogden, 1982

reciousness: ancient concept or modern prejudice?

The idea that a given material is, by nature, precious, is a relatively recent one. The idea that one material was precious while another was merely semi-precious simply did not exist in ancient times.[2] The idea of dividing gemstones into the categories of precious and semi-precious is a relatively modern idea. The word *semi-precious* itself entered the English lexicon only in the nineteenth century.

For example, in ancient Egypt, color, not type of material, was evidently the primary criterion of value. Egyptian taste in jewelry favored solid bars of vivid color, particularly blue and orange. Opaque and semi-translucent gems such as lapis lazuli, coral, turquoise, carnelian, and sard were highly valued. Masterpieces of ancient jewelry, such as those made for the boy king Tutankhamen, were beautifully worked in gold by skilled craftsmen. These pieces included gems such as turquoise and carnelian alternated with stones of faience[3] (a ceramic glass of melted feldspar) dyed to resemble a specific gemstone; in short, a fake! Was this due to a rarity of materials? It was obviously not a question of price. Were the Egyptian craftsmen misled by clever

© 2001 Christie's Images

Ancient fake! Egyptian engraved faience (glass) bead from the reign of Amenhotep III, 1391-1353 BC, dyed to resemble lapis lazuli. Faience beads have been found in many fine pieces of ancient jewelry, often with natural gemstones such as turquoise and coral.

forgeries? Doubtful! The Egyptians simply placed a higher value on visual beauty than on the pedigree of the materials themselves.

This seems odd to us today with our preconceived notions of what is precious and what is not. Would Cartier or Tiffany consider offering gold jewelry set with glass, plastic, or synthetic gems? Yet the glassmakers of ancient Egypt enjoyed royal patronage.[4] The point is that preciousness

2. Jack Ogden, *Jewellery of the Ancient World* (New York: Rizzoli International, 1982), p. 90.

3. Lois S. Dubin, *The History of Beads: From 30,000 BC to the Present* (New York: Harry N. Abrams, 1987), p. 42.

4. Dubin, *History of Beads*, p. 43.

was not an idea tied to the use of gemstones that today are called precious. The popularity of gem materials has waxed and waned over the millennia. The truth of this becomes clear when we consider that much of the gem wealth found buried with the pharaohs of Egypt, at Babylon, and in the royal tombs of ancient Sumer is what many today still label as semi-precious.[5]

Descriptions in the Bible also clearly demonstrate that the ideas of the ancients concerning the hierarchy of precious materials differed markedly from our modern view. In Revelation (21: 9-21) an angel describes the heavenly city of Jerusalem as "having the glory of God; and her light was like a stone most precious, even like a jasper stone clear as crystal. . . . And the foundations of the wall of the city were garnished with all manner of precious stones. The first foundation was jasper; the second, sapphire; the third, chalcedony; the fourth, emerald; the fifth, sardonyx; the sixth, sardius; the seventh, crysolite (topaz); the eighth, beryl. . . ." Of the twelve gems named, only emerald and sapphire figure as precious today, and although emerald was known to the ancient world, we know that sapphire was almost certainly the ancient name for lapis lazuli.[6]

It is important to keep in mind that beauty was not the sole reason gems were valued in the ancient world. From earliest times gems have been esteemed as religious symbols, as talismans, as symbols of rank and status, and for their purported medicinal value.

In the Egypt of the pharaohs, carnelian

© Christie's Images

Roman carnelian cameo circa the second century AD. One of the most coveted gems of antiquity, today carnelian is consigned to the semi-precious backwaters.

symbolized blood. In ancient Sumer lapis lazuli represented the heavens. In classical Greece a man supposedly could drink his fill and remain sober if he drank his wine from a cup made of amethyst. To avoid eyestrain, the Roman emperor Nero reputedly viewed gladiatorial contests through a lens made of emerald.

In ancient China, badges made of gem materials were used to denote rank. Mandarins of the first rank wore red stones such as ruby and red or pink tourmaline;

5. Ibid.

6. Although the ancient Egyptians, from whom the Hebrews no doubt derived their notions of gemstones, knew emerald, some distinguished scholars believe that "emerald" (*bareketh*) was the name given to light green serpentine. George Frederick Kunz, *The Curious Lore of Precious Stones* (1913; reprint ed., New York: Dover Editions, 1971) pp. 292-301.

coral and garnet were reserved for bureaucrats of the second rank. Blue stones such as lapis lazuli and aquamarine symbolized the third rank. Mandarins of the fourth rank wore rock crystal. Other white stones indicated the fifth rank. Here again, color, not gemstone type, seems to have been the defining criterion.[7]

Gems were also valued as much for their talismanic or medicinal value as for their beauty. These arcane beliefs and associations persist today, but they no longer have any effect on value or preciousness of gemstones, particularly as judged in the marketplace.

Seal stone engraving: value added

The carving of gems became an important art in ancient times with the introduction

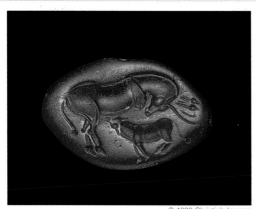

© 1999 Christie's Images

Minoan/Mycenaean carnelian seal stone (1450-1300 BC) shows a cow suckling her calf. In early times, the use of seals was limited to the aristocracy. This masterwork of the engraver's art demonstrates that exceptional craftsmanship was often applied to mediocre gem material (carnelian).

(circa 3500 BC) of seal stone engraving by the Babylonians. Gemstones were engraved intaglios with mythical scenes which appeared in relief when the stones were impressed in clay tablets. These engraved gems became the official signatures of kings, nobles, and high-ranking officials of the court. In ancient Mycenae, seal engraving reached a high degree of sophistication by the late Bronze Age. A group of seals recovered from Mycenaean shaft graves at Dendra (on the Greek mainland) shows a mastery of technique as well as a lyric sensibility equaled only by the Greek masters of the classical period and never since.[8]

Seals were first made of relatively soft stones such as serpentine and steatite; these stones could be carved using bronze tools. However, by the twelfth century BC, hard stones such as agate became the gems of choice. Engraving these stones (over six on the Mohs scale of hardness) required a more sophisticated technique: even iron, the hardest metal then known, was too soft to carve hard stones such as carnelian.

Carnelian, the eighth stone of the breastplate of the Tabernacle's high priest described in the Biblical book of Exodus, was the gem of choice for engravers from the Bronze Age until late Roman times. Fully fifty percent of Greek seals and more than ninety percent of Roman intaglios were carved of carnelian. Today the stone barely makes the semi-precious list, but carnelian was unquestionably one of the precious stones of antiquity.

7. Kunz, *Curious Lore*, p. 256.

8. K. Demakopoulou, ed., *The Aidonia Treasure* (Athens: National Archaeological Museum, 1996), p. 51.

9. (SEE NEXT PAGE) Greek philospher Theophrastus, in his treatise on gemstones, written toward the end of the fourth century BC, uses the word *perittotera,* which Calley and Richards translate

as "precious." See E.R. Calley and J.C. Richards, *Theophrastus on Stones* (Columbus, Ohio: Ohio State University Press, 1956), p. 45. Other translators, notably Eichholz, translate *perittotera* as meaning

"unusual." Professor C.J. Fuqua of Williams College states that Theophrastus uses the term in the sense of *more unusual,* not *more precious.* Theophrastus does not use the superlative degree, "most

By classical times seals were in use throughout the lands bordering the Inland Sea. Experts in this craft enjoyed high status. Some of the best quality gem material is found in Mycenaean gems unearthed at Aidonia on the Greek mainland. These are carved in the finest translucent layered carnelian. They are the exception: by Roman times, some of the finest masterworks of the engraver's art were executed in relatively mundane pieces of carnelian and sard, demonstrating that the beauty of the material itself was at best of secondary importance. The real preciousness of the gem lay in the artistry and the quality of execution.[9]

The Middle Ages: shifting values

In medieval Europe, superstitions about the religious, talismanic, and medicinal properties of gemstones were accepted without question. Many of these beliefs had been passed down from ancient times in the writings of the Roman scholar Pliny and repeated in the works of the seventh century bishop Isidore of Seville. The medieval mind, obsessed as it was with questions of life and death, proved fertile ground for the growth and dissemination of such beliefs.

In those times, each gem was valued for its ability to protect its wearer from evils both physical and spiritual. "Coral, which for twenty centuries or more was classed among the precious stones," cured madness and assured wisdom. [10] Emerald was considered to protect the wearer against all manner of enchantments. Carnelian drove out evil and protected the wearer from envy.

Lapis lazuli was a sure cure for quartan fever. Sapphire also offered protection from envy and was thought to attract divine favor. Chrysoprase protected the thief from hanging.

So universal was the belief in the magical and medicinal qualities of gem materials in the Middle Ages, that it is impossible to discuss the value of gemstones without reference to them. Was the emerald sought after for its beauty, or for its supposed value as a treatment for diseases of the eye?

Diamond: the invincible

Diamond's fluctuating popularity on the gemstone hit parade further illustrates the point. Diamond was unquestionably the preeminent gemstone in India from as early as the fifth century BC. India in those far-off times was the only source of diamond, and had a flourishing gem-trading industry. The Romans, too, placed diamond at the very pinnacle of preciousness. By early medieval times in the West, however, diamond had fallen to number seventeen on the bestseller list. As late as the sixteenth century, the celebrated Italian goldsmith Benvenuto Cellini placed diamond third after ruby and emerald, with a price of only one eighth of what a ruby would bring. Writing in 1565, Garcia ab Horto, an early European traveler who described his trip to the gem fields of India, placed diamond at number three, but considered emerald, not ruby, to be the most precious gem of all.

One prominent scholar, Godeherd Lenzen, maintains that diamond's early popularity in

unusual," in this passage. There is no hierarchy involved with *perittotera*. (C.J. Fuqua, personal communication, 1999.)

10. Kunz, *Curious Lore*, p. 69.

11. Godeherd Lenzen, *The History of Diamond Production and the Diamond Trade* (London: Barrie & Jenkins, 1970), pp. 18-19. *The Arthashastra of Kautilya*, written sometime between the fifth and sixth

centuries BC, characterizes a good diamond as one that is "regular in shape, capable of . . . reflecting light brilliantly in all directions." Some scholars have held that this is a description of a cut diamond, and

conclude that diamonds were cut in India as early as the fifth century BC. Lenzen maintains that the diamond described here is a perfectly formed natural crystal, and that such rare crystals were greatly desired in

Natural bipyramidal diamond crystals. In earliest times before the technology existed to cut and polish diamonds these natural six-pointed crystals were highly sought after for their perfect form, transparency and brilliance.

the western world was based not on its beauty, but on its durability and hardness. The characteristics that make diamond so desirable today — brilliance, dispersion, and transparency — are qualities that occur naturally only in perfectly formed diamond crystals. In Roman times, the technology did not exist to fashion or polish diamonds.

Transparent well-formed crystals either were retained and sold in India (where they were highly valued) or bought up along the trade route before they reached Rome. Thus, due to the rarity and desirability of fine crystals and the length of the trade route between India and Rome, the uncut rough stones that

India and never found their way as far as Europe. According to Lenzen, the diamond crystals familiar to the Romans would have been gray, misshapen, barely translucent, and not at all beautiful. See also

Kautilya, *The Arthashastra*, ed. and trans. L.N. Rangarajan (India: Penguin Books, 1992), p. 775. The second century BC writer Damigeron states that "the best diamonds are found in India, second best in

Arabia and the rest in Cyprus." Lenzen, a scholar, not a trader, would perhaps not be aware that a stone might be purchased in Arabia but not necessarily remain there if a better price could be obtained in

Rome. Damigeron, *The Virtues of Stones*, trans. Patricia Tahil (Seattle: Ars Obscura, 1989), p. 10.

made their way to the ancient Mediterranean were of inferior quality; the attributes of beauty which make the diamond so avidly sought after today were necessarily unknown to the ancient Romans.[11] Therefore, Lenzen argues, diamonds could not have been valued for beauty at all, but must have had some other attraction. The Greeks named diamond adamas, a word that means invincible. This obviously relates to the gem's legendary hardness, a virtue much admired in imperial times. Was it diamond's "invincibility" that made it so attractive and valuable to the Romans?

To be fair, diamond regained its preeminent position in the gem world by the close of the seventeenth century. The Portuguese subjugation of Goa in west-central India opened up more direct trade routes, increasing the flow of finer diamond rough to the West. The necessary technology for revealing the diamond's

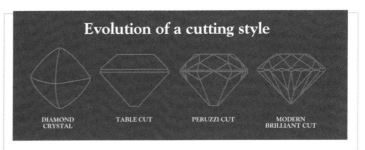

Evolution of a cutting style

DIAMOND CRYSTAL   TABLE CUT   PERUZZI CUT   MODERN BRILLIANT CUT

Moving from left to right: The bipyramidal habit of the natural diamond crystal suggests the outline of the table cut, one of the earliest styles. The table cut was little more than a polished crystal with the top cut off to make a table and the bottom point cut off to form the culet. The Peruzzi cut is the next logical step and an early attempt to manipulate light by adding facets. The modern brilliant cut shows a subtle change in proportions and 58 precisely arranged facets.

unique beauty — polishing, cutting, and cleaving — was in place in Europe by the middle part of the century.[12] Diamond's return to preeminence is also a direct result of the development in the late seventeenth century of the Peruzzi cut, the precursor of the modern brilliant cut. This important technological advance in gem cutting unleashed, for the first time, diamond's full potential — the astonishing brilliance and fire for which the gem is justly revered.

12. Lenzen, *History of Diamond Production*, p. 105. Although the crude process of faceting — by rubbing one diamond against another to wear each stone down — was known as early as the fourteenth century, the technology for cleaving and sawing was not developed until the seventeenth century.

Chapter 2

Preciousness Redefined:
The Modern Concept of a Gem

Man's first and instinctive appreciation was the truest, and it has required centuries of enlightenment to bring us back to this love of precious stones for their esthetic beauty alone.

G.F. Kunz, 1908

As medieval times passed to modern, the relative importance of external concerns about the medicinal or talismanic significance of gemstones slowly begins to recede. The innate beauty of the gemstone becomes central. Today few people seek out an emerald to cure disease, an agate to use as a shield against the evil eye, or the amethyst to ward off drunkenness. In developing connoisseurship in gemstones, beauty has become the defining criterion.

The dawning of our modern age brought little in the way of unanimity on the issues of which gems were precious and which were not, unsurprisingly. The great gemologist Max Bauer, writing in 1904, maintains: "Minerals which combine the highest degrees of beauty, hardness, durability, and rarity — diamond, ruby, sapphire, and emerald, for example — are by common consent placed among the foremost rank of gems." Bauer further states that "it is impossible to draw a hard and fast line between precious and semi-precious stones," and that "the minerals that must be reckoned as precious stones are by no means fixed in number." Why? Because, says the great mineralogist, it depends largely on "the fashion of the day." Bauer includes as precious most transparent stones (except amethyst) and two translucent gems, opal and pearl.[13]

The English gemologist G-F Herbert Smith, writing twenty years later, includes among the precious gems diamond, ruby, sapphire, and all forms of beryl (emerald, aquamarine, morganite), excluding all others.[14] Other writers have made different lists. All have included the "big four" but most have agreed on little else.[15]

Grading standards: the market

One barrier to developing connoisseurship in gemstones is that many experts, mainly dealers, maintain that there are no objective standards of judgment in the appreciation of gemstones. Beauty is, after all, in the eye of the beholder. The aficionado will hear that phrase repeated *ad nauseam*. If there are no standards, then the stone that the dealer across the counter is trying to sell is obviously the best choice.

The fact is that there are very definite standards for the grading and valuing of all gemstones in the world market. The market is the place where all the sophistry and all the nonsense about beauty and the eye of the beholder get swallowed up and vanish without a trace. The same experts who contend that collectors in the West prefer

13. Max Bauer, *Precious Stones*, trans. L.J. Spencer (1904; reprint ed., New York: Dover Editions, 1968) pp. 1-3.

14. G-F Herbert Smith, *Gemstones* (London: Methuen & Company,

1940), pp. xi-xii. This book was originally published in 1912.

15. Edwin W. Streeter, *Precious Stones and Gems* (London: Chapman & Hall, 1879), pp. 17-21. Streeter, a famous nineteenth-

century English jeweler, uses much the same criteria as Bauer regarding beauty and durability but reduces the list to diamond, ruby, sapphire, and emerald, plus cat's-eyes (chrysoberyl), turquoise, and

star stones. Oddly enough, he excludes aquamarine, another beryl that has the same physical properties as emerald.

opals with more blue, and Asian buyers prefer red (and that value is all in what you like), will admit that the red stone may cost four times as much as the one with a predominant blue play of color. Why? A

© R.W. Wise

Portrait of a disappointment! Young girl panning for rubies and sapphires in a stream in Chantaburi Province, central Thailand.

combination of rarity, beauty, supply, and demand! Red stones are rarer, and demand exceeds supply; therefore reds will cost more. Obviously, the market enforces universal standards.

For example, one excellent quality grading system, *ColorScan*, developed by the American Gemological Laboratories, identifies sixty different color combinations of hue/tone in blue sapphire. Each of these is associated with a specific market price. *The Guide*, an important industry pricing

publication, identifies eleven different quality-pricing grids for blue sapphire, and cautions that even these do not cover the entire range of available qualities.[16]

A very stringent standard exists for the grading of colorless diamond. This standard, developed in the 1950s by the Gemological Institute of America has, with modification, become accepted worldwide.[17]

Precious versus semi-precious: a distinction without a difference

The question "Is it a precious or semi-precious stone?" is an expression of pure market snobbery. As has been already shown, the term "preciousness" has had different meanings at different periods in different cultures. In earliest times, it had no meaning at all. The term *semi-precious* is today as meaningless as the term *semi-pregnant* or *semi-deceased*. That this term is still in general usage points only to the fact that many of the gemstones described here still lack a degree of market acceptance, and still may be purchased at relatively low prices.

Several gem species and varieties discussed in Part II of this book are fairly recent discoveries: tsavorite garnet, tanzanite, and malaya garnet were completely unknown just fifty years ago. In many cases these new precious gemstones are rarer and more beautiful than those gems that have traditionally been called precious.

16. *The Guide* (Northbrook, Illinois: Gemworld International, Inc., 2002). *The Guide* is a prominent wholesale price list published for the trade.

17. In fact, GIA codified and adopted the traditional grading system that can be traced at least as far back as the fourth century BC.

The Arthashastra of Kautilya describes good diamonds as "regular in shape and reflecting light brilliantly in all directions . . .

which have the whiteness of a shell or of rock crystal . . . unblemished, smooth, heavy, lustrous, transparent. . . ." Rangarajan, *The*

To the astute aficionado "semi-precious" should translate as "buying opportunity." The true lover of gemstones looks at the object without regard for the verbal baggage it may carry along with it. If the foregoing discussion has demonstrated anything, it is that the whole idea of preciousness is fluid. In the world of gemstones, if it is rare and beautiful, and if demand is strong, it is precious.

Beauty versus pedigree: the question of origin

Each time a new pocket of gemstones is unearthed, stones from the new location are compared with those produced by traditional sources — usually to the detriment of the newer source. This is a crutch and yet another manifestation of the innate conservatism of the gem market, one controlled by professional dealers. From the connoisseur's perspective this misses the point entirely. The point is to look at the stone. The most conservative dealer will always fall back on a stone's pedigree. These traders are often those who have prospered, have well-heeled clients, and can pay the highest prices.

In the gem marketplace, a fine stone with a famous pedigree will command an extraordinary premium. A natural sapphire from Burma will often sell for twice the price of a comparable gem from Sri Lanka (Ceylon). A very fine but comparable natural Kashmir, a sapphire discovered on one side of a stony hillock in colonial India, will bring at least one and a half times that! These premium prices are based solely on the stone's geographic origin. Astronomical prices are regularly paid for stones that carry this kind of pedigree. Depending on the local geology, a given gemstone will have slightly different visual characteristics than examples from another location. This is usually the result of the mix of minerals specific to a particular geographic setting. For example, the iron-rich environment of the central Thai provinces of Chantaburi and Trat lends ruby from this area a distinctly brownish cast, whereas ruby from the iron-poor soil of northern Burma generally lacks a brownish color. Burmese ruby is *better,* generally speaking, because it looks better than ruby from Thailand, and it looks better because the physical environment is more favorable.

As a result of these localized differences, gemstones from different areas develop reputations based on the general look of the stones from that specific source. This has led to marked price differentials for stones just because they come from a specific area or country. In the marketplace, Burma ruby, Kashmir sapphire, and Paraiba tourmaline will command premium prices simply because they hail from the specific areas named. This is not a scam but it is a snare! The aficionado is interested in a beautiful gem. Each gemstone is an individual with a distinct personality. A given stone from Burma very well may be inferior to a given gem from Thailand, and not worthy of the premium asked. The Thai stone, by contrast, may be a particularly fine example and worth collecting despite the general reputation of Thai ruby.

Arthashastra, pp. 775-778. The Arab scholar Ahmad ibn Yusuf al Tifaschi writing around AD 1250 divided diamond qualities into two categories: *zayti*, those with a slight yellow body color, and *billawri,* those that are colorless like rock crystal. Tifaschi held that the former were of the highest value. See Samar Najm Abul Huda, *Arab Roots of Gemology: Ahmad ibn Yusuf al Tifaschi's Best Thoughts on the Best of Stones* (London: The Scarecrow Press, 1998), p. 118.

© R.W. Wise

Traditional mining in the ancient "Valley of the Serpents," Mogok, Burma. This age-old mining method consists of a twinlun, a hand-dug vertical shaft which drops forty feet to the gem-bearing layer, or byon, where a narrow horizontal shaft is dug into the gem gravel. The gravel is raised by bucket and sorted.

price?" The answer generally may be yes, if the best stones from the area in question are truly the best of their kind. However, it is important to stay focused. The aficionado collects gems, not generalizations. The gem under consideration must be judged for what it is: its beauty, not its geographic origin.

The rarity factor

The relationship between beauty and price is, at best, problematic. People have preferences. In the gemstone market preference creates demand, which is a primary determinant of price. Are yellow stones intrinsically more or less desirable, more or less beautiful, than blue? Obviously not! Such partiality is clearly subjective. All colors are created equal. Yet a fine blue sapphire commands a much higher price than a fine yellow sapphire. This is purely a function of subjective preference, which manifests itself as market demand.

In the gem world, beauty drives demand and rarity drives price.[18] This is a catchy little phrase, but what does it mean? More to the point, what weight should the connoisseur give to the rarity factor when deciding on an acquisition?

Here lies the snare! The connoisseur must ask, "Does the beauty of *this* stone from this source justify paying a premium

There are two categories of rarity, *actual* and *apparent*. Some gem varieties are found in very small numbers and can be classed

18. The sole exception to this rule is fancy color diamonds. See the Introduction to Color Diamonds.

as *actually* rare. Other varieties are in such high demand that though relatively numerous they are very difficult to find in the marketplace. Gems that fit into this second category are *apparently* rare. Another name might be market rarity. Of the two types, apparent (market rarity) is the more important. Unless the item is in demand, then its actual rarity doesn't matter very much. Fine amethyst is actually quite rare, yet due to relatively lackluster demand its price remains relatively low. Things really get interesting when a gem is both *apparently* and *actually* rare. These are stones that are in short supply and also in high demand. Alexandrite and blue diamond are good examples of gems that are both *apparently* and *actually* rare. Gems that fall into this category will command the very highest prices.

It is fair to say that, with the exception of colorless diamonds of less than ten carats, the finest examples of all gem species and varieties are, at least, apparently rare and difficult to find in the marketplace. From the connoisseur's viewpoint the very finest examples of any gemstone are rare and difficult to obtain. Amethyst is an excellent example. Amethyst is a type of quartz, one of the earth's most abundant minerals. Even so, the deep Siberian quality described in Chapter 9 is extraordinarily difficult to find. The author has sorted through thousands of parcels of cut and rough amethyst at the source in Brazil and Africa and come away with out a

single example of the finest quality of this relatively common gem.

Harold and Erica Van Pelt: Courtesy of Kalil Elawar

Natural Brazilian alexandrite crystal.

In almost all cases rarity increases with size (tanzanite is perhaps the sole exception). Fairly large examples of the very finest quality tanzanite are relatively more available than smaller gems. A one-carat gem-quality tanzanite is much rarer than a twenty-carat stone.

Before the eighteenth century, diamonds came mainly from India, and were extremely rare, especially in Europe. The Indian sources, chiefly the Golconda mines in the Indian province of Hyderabad, were essentially already mined out when diamonds were discovered in Brazil in

19. This is the traditional date given by most sources. The first date mentioned in the literature is 1714. J.P. Cassedenne, "Diamonds in Brazil," *Mineralogical Record*, vol. 20 (1986), pp. 325-335.

20. Lenzen, *History of Diamond Production*, pp. 50, 126. DeBeers was not the first syndicate to control the market. The diamond market was saved by the simple expedient of monopolistic practices on the part of the Antwerp Diamond Cutters Guild, which controlled prices in the eighteenth century to such a degree that lower prices for rough were not passed on to the jeweler and consumer as lower prices for cut stones. Cut stone prices remained stable.

1725.[19] Diamond exports from Brazil from 1730 to 1787 increased total world diamond supplies as much as twenty-fold. Due to this abundance, between 1730 and 1735 the diamond market went into freefall and rough diamond prices dropped seventy-five percent.[20]

With the discovery in the late nineteenth century of vast diamond reserves in southern Africa, huge supplies of diamonds began to enter the market. Newer discoveries in Russia, Australia, and, most recently, Canada have kept supply strong. These discoveries, coupled with improvements in prospecting and recovery methods, have created a glut of colorless diamonds.

In 1992 it was estimated that if all diamonds produced by Indian and Brazilian sources from antiquity to that date were totaled, that number would be equal to just twenty-two percent of the total world production of the previous five years. In fact, the annual production from Australia's Argyle Mine in the early 1990s was approximately equal to the total amount of diamonds produced in India and Brazil from antiquity to 1869.[21] In the past two decades, cut diamond production has increased from fifty million carats (gem quality) to approximately one hundred twenty million carats annually. It is estimated that perhaps eight hundred million cut stones, of all sizes, enter the market every year.

In the case of diamond, an *apparent* rarity, maintaining the price structure is created by high demand coupled with a carefully controlled distribution system. The monopolizing organization, variously called the cartel, the syndicate, or simply DeBeers, took control of the diamond market in 1889.[22] Diamonds are not *actually* rare, but the syndicate (through selective distribution and a careful hoarding of reserves) insures that supply does not exceed demand.[23] Thus the price of diamonds, as with all other gems, is based on beauty — plus supply and demand. The difference is that demand for diamonds is mightily stimulated by advertising, and supply is, or at least has been, ruthlessly controlled by the DeBeers cartel.

As the new century dawns, the iron control formerly exercised by DeBeers has begun to slip. In fact, the syndicate claims that it is no longer trying to control the market. New diamond strikes in Australia and northern Canada (which are outside the syndicate's control) have reduced its influence. From a high of eighty-five percent a decade ago, currently no more than sixty percent of the world's diamonds pass through the cartel's hands.[24] Thus far, the main effect of this has been a squeezing of wholesale and retail profit margins. What does it bode for the future? Unless new marketing strategies can stimulate demand, the effect of the diamond glut must inevitably lead to lower prices.

21. A.A. Levinson et al., "Diamond Sources and Production: Past, Present and Future," *Gems & Gemology*, Winter 1992, p. 236.

22. Stefan Kanfer, *The Last Empire: De Beers, Diamonds, and the World* (New York: Noonday Press, 1993), p. 106.

23. Kanfer, *The Last Empire*, p. 339.

24. In spite of its public statements, the DeBeers cartel is not standing by idly on the sidelines while its market share erodes. As of this writing (2003) only one Canadian diamond mine, Ekati, is in

production. A consortium of companies not connected with DeBeers owns Ekati. A second mine, Daivik, also outside the cartel's control, should begin production in 2003. However, of the four "advanced projects" which could begin production in the next

decade, two are wholly owed by DeBeers and it owns controlling interest in the third. Only one of the five, Jericho, is currently outside DeBeer's control. See B.A. Kjarsgaard and A.A. Levinson, "Diamonds in Canada," *Gems & Gemology*, Fall 2002, p. 234.

Chapter 3

Connoisseurship: Rethinking the Four Cs

In selecting precious stones you must mentally ask yourself the following questions: Is their transparency conspicuous? Are they like a dew-drop hanging from a damask rose leaf; that is, are they of pure water and do they possess the power of refraction to a high degree? Or, are they transparent and colored; and, if the latter, have they a play of color? Lastly, have they notable imperfections?

E.W. Streeter, 1879

Over the centuries experts have developed a series of criteria for judging the objective aspects of beauty in gemstones. Lately these criteria have been given a catchy title, *the four* Cs. Although something of an oversimplification, these categories — *color, cut, clarity,* and *carat* weight — are useful. The traditional four Cs, or at least the first three Cs (weight has nothing to do with quality), can be used as criteria for evaluation of the beauty and quality of all gemstones. However, I propose to omit carat weight and substitute, or rather reintroduce, a neglected, almost forgotten, but necessary criterion, *crystal.—Crystal* is, as will be demonstrated in the following chapter, the true fourth C of gemstone connoisseurship.

Beauty is a question of balance. C*olor,* c*larity, cut,* and c*rystal* are the four factors— abstractions, really —that are used to analyze and discuss the beauty of a gemstone. None of these criteria is sufficient in itself to make a beautiful gem. All four are necessary conditions, without which the stone will simply not make the grade. Of the four factors, cut is most quantifiable, and the only one which depends completely on the ingenuity of man.

© R.W. Wise

Gem cutting the old-fashioned way. This Thai gem cutter estimates facet angles by eye and cuts freehand, in Bo Rai, Trat Province, central Thailand.

The idea of the *four Cs* is useful. The concept would be more useful still if each C were of equal relative importance in the connoisseurship of all species and varieties of gemstones. Unfortunately, they are not. *Color* is of primary importance in the appreciation of colored gemstones. *Cut* is the primary criterion in the evaluation of colorless diamonds. *Crystal,* as we will see, is the key to connoisseurship in the appreciation of translucent cabochon-cut gemstones.

Quality and connoisseurship in colored stones, by far the broadest class, will be discussed first, followed by phenomenal stones (stars and cat's-eyes), diamonds, and the pearl. Opal exists in a world of its own and will be dealt with in detail in Part II.

COLOR: FIRST AMONG EQUALS

> *By convention there is color, but in reality there are only atoms and space.*
>
> Democritus, 460 BC

Common perceptions

In the 1960s a group of cultural anthropologists conducted a worldwide survey to determine how the world's cultures defined color. Representatives of each society surveyed were shown a specially prepared color chart containing all colors — some 329 different hues.

The anthropologists studied the color terms native to twenty languages. The most primitive cultures surveyed had only two concepts, or two words that they used to describe all the colors on the chart: *black* and *white* or *light* and *dark,* what we would call *tones.* Interestingly enough, all the

cultures with two concepts had the same two concepts. Other slightly more "advanced" societies had three words: *light*, *dark*, and *red*. Still more advanced cultures added a word that meant *green or yellow*. Those cultures that had a fifth word had a term for *yellow* and one for *green*. Languages that contained a sixth term added *blue*; those with seven added *brown*. Cultures whose language included eight or more terms contained words for—*purple*, *pink*, *orange*, *grey*, or some combination of these colors.[25]

By way of conclusion, the anthropologists determined that all human societies share (at most) just eleven basic color concepts: *red*, *orange*, *yellow*, *green*, *blue*, *violet*, *purple*, *white*, *gray*, and *black and brown*.[26] Although we may categorize and amplify these basic color concepts in different ways, adding sophisticated variations such as *umber* and *chartreuse* to describe mixed hues, the fact remains that all the gemstones discussed in this book can and will be described using these same eleven words.

All human beings share the same perceptual apparatus. We receive raw data through our senses, and our perceptual apparatus refines and orders this data for us. The German philosopher Immanuel Kant called this apparatus "the faculty of apperception." The philosopher was seeking a method of explaining how it is that human beings perceive and understand what they see.

All that we see, feel, and taste is processed through the funnel of our sensory

25. Brent Berlin and Paul Kay, *Basic Evolution* (Los Angeles: University *Color Terms, Their Universality and* of California Press, 1969), pp. 2-3.

26. Ibid.

apparatus. Sense data, then, assumes the shape of that funnel. According to Kant, the human mind impresses certain categories upon the data the senses deliver to the brain. He called these mental filters *a priori categories*.[27] *Space* and *time*, for example, were types of *a priori* categories that did not exist in the world at all, but only in the mind. Odd though this may seem at first, did you ever see an animal, aside from Alice's white rabbit, that seemed to have any concept of time? How is it that all societies share just eleven basic color concepts? Kant's faculty of apperception explains it very well. "The eleven basic color concepts" — in fact, color itself — is an *a priori* category.

Blessed with color vision, humans see the world much differently from other species. The family dog, for example, cannot perceive colors; his world exists solely in black and white. By contrast, this same dog, with his superior hearing, perceives sounds that we humans cannot hear at all. We are different species, and the machinery of our perception is different. Luckily, humans, as members of the same species, possess an identical sensory apparatus.

Human beings differ from the family pet in other ways. We have the faculty of judgment. We make qualitative decisions about the raw data our sense organs deliver to us. The eye is a part of the brain. We see colors, but are free to prefer the color blue to yellow, pink to red, etc. Because we have similar faculties, we often have similar tastes. Opinions, however, are personal and subject to change. In the gemstone marketplace, price differentials represent the current opinion expressed as market demand.

The perception of color

Color has many interesting properties. Colors can be pure, intense, warm, dark, or cool. Colored objects can appear large, small, close, or distant. The brighter the color the larger the object appears. Yellow is the "largest," most highly saturated color, followed by orange, red, green, and blue.

In the fine arts, specifically painting, color alone can be used to create the illusion of depth. Warm colors come forward; cool colors recede. In modern art, cubist and constructivist painters fomented an artistic revolution by using the visual laws of color to create, on their canvases, a sense of depth without the use of perspective.

Color has direct physiological and psychological effects on the viewer. Red causes the lens of the eye to thicken, blue flattens the lens.[28] Wassily Kandinsky, the first artist to paint totally abstract pictures, believed that the use of certain colors alone could induce specific emotional states in the viewer.

Demonstrating the proof of Kandinsky's thesis is the idea that colors have connotations that have remained constant over the centuries. Red is the hot color of blood and the color of war. To become angry is to see red. Blue is the color of the heavens. When a person is depressed he has the blues.

27. Immanuel Kant, *The Critique of Pure Reason*, trans. Norman Kemp Smith (London: St. Martins Press, 1964), pp. 65-74. *A priori* refers to categories that exist before sense data, and through which the data of the senses passes and is understood. Color itself, or at least our manner of perceiving it, is an *a priori* category impressed by the mind upon the raw data of the senses.

28. L. Moholy-Nagy, *Vision in Motion* (Chicago: Paul Theobold, 1947), p. 155.

In art class we learned that the color wheel divides into primary and secondary colors. Red, blue, and yellow are primary in the sense that they are irreducible, unmixed pure hues. Secondary colors are those created by mixing two or more primaries. For example, mixing yellow and blue makes green. However, the rules of the color wheel have to do with paint and pigments. The rules change when color and light are considered. When two colored slides are projected on a screen, green and red light will mix and create yellow. A similar mixture of paints would yield a dirty olive brown.[29] Colored light contains eight chromatic hues: red, orange, yellow, green, blue, violet, pink, and purple. The first six hues are called *primary spectral hues*: the colors of the rainbow or the colors seen when white light is refracted through a prism. The last two, purple and pink, are *modified spectral hues*: purple is the hue that lies halfway between red and blue on the color wheel, and pink is a lighter-toned hue of red. Any of the eight hues can play the part of the primary or secondary hue in a gemstone.

Color as it is applied to connoisseurship in gemstones requires further definition. Color is divided into three components: *hue*, *saturation*, and *tone*. These categories are relatively common in color science where they are called variously hue, value, and chroma; or hue, intensity, and tone.

Hue

Hue is the technical equivalent of "color" as that term is used in normal speech: What color is it? In gemstone parlance, color is a general term; red and blue are *hues*. Nature exhibits relatively few pure hues. The colors that we see in objects are a mixture of hues. Thus, for technical precision in describing color it is necessary to divide hues into primary, secondary, and occasionally tertiary categories. Primary is used in the sense of dominant, the majority hue. A sapphire that is greenish blue has a primary hue of blue and a secondary hue of green. Just as in language, the term greenish is an adjective modifying the noun blue; green is a secondary hue modifying the primary or dominant hue, in this case blue.

A royal blue sapphire has a primary blue hue. The term royal is simply a more poetic way of describing the combination of the primary blue with the secondary hue, which in this case is purple. Put more precisely, the hue may be described in percentages. In the above example, royal blue sapphire is mostly blue, perhaps eighty-five percent, with an admixture of about fifteen percent purple. The color of a royal blue sapphire is more precisely described as a slightly purplish blue and even more precisely as having an eighty-five percent primary blue hue with a fifteen percent secondary purple hue. Both of these descriptions are useful. The use of percentages is, however, more precise.

Faceted gemstones exhibit two types of color, reflected color and refracted color. When a beam of light is directed toward the top, or crown, of a faceted gem, some of that light will enter the gem, reflect internally, and be refracted back to the eye. The color of that refracted light is called the *key color*.

29. Ibid., p. 159.

This is the color of the sparkle or brilliance. The color of the gem is evaluated by observing the *key color*. This is a vital point. *Body color* results from light that is transmitted through the gem. The quality of these phenomena, *body color* and *key color*, almost always differ at least in darkness or lightness — the component of color that is called *tone*.

The key color is the color used to evaluate faceted stones, except colorless diamond, which is judged by its own unique set of rules (see Chapter 5). This distinction may be confusing at first. To differentiate between key and body color, the gem is turned table or face down under a light source. A gemstone is designed to generate brilliance in the face-up position. Face down the gem will not sparkle, it will glow. The color seen is the body color. The gem can then be turned over and viewed face up. In this position the color of the sparkle may be observed and the differences in hue (key versus body color) will become apparent.

Key color is often lighter in tone and paler in saturation than the gem's body color. Body color can be particularly seductive in lighter-toned highly crystalline gems such as aquamarine. Take care! If the eye becomes lazy, the result can be costly.

Saturation

Saturation, the second of the three components of color, refers to the brightness of the hue or the *quantity* of color. The greater the quantity of color the brighter it will be. Saturation may be described as *vivid* or *dull* or somewhere in between. Although some hues are brighter than others, pure hues are always vivid! International orange, the color used in buoys and life jackets, and the red of a stop sign are examples of particularly vivid hues. "Day-Glo" colors are vivid hues. In this system of evaluation, the neutral, non-spectral colors gray and brown are not classified as hues; they are considered to be saturation modifiers or masks.

Like a splash of mud on a Hawaiian shirt, the addition of gray and brown dulls the hue. Some gem varieties have a tendency toward brown, some toward gray, rarely both. Blue sapphire may be grayish, but rarely brownish, whereas red tourmaline will often have a brown modifier. A grayish greenish blue sapphire is a dull greenish blue sapphire. A brownish red tourmaline is a muddy-looking red tourmaline.

Gray or brown *masks* are often like a light film that is itself of low saturation and very light tone, and is difficult to see. The effect — *dullness* or *muddiness* — is visible and, since pure hues are always bright, we infer from this that a gray or brown mask is present. A trained eye and careful observation are often necessary to see the mask. Another clue which may help is that brown gives the impression of warmth, whereas gray is cool. If the hue appears dull and cool, the mask present is probably gray. If the hue seems to be dull and warm, the mask is likely brown.

Saturation modifiers:
from minus to plus

What good are rules if there are no exceptions? Life would be so much simpler, consistent, and boring. When gray and brown are themselves highly saturated and dark enough to be dominant, they too begin to act the part of a hue. This is particularly true of brown. Thus dark-toned gray and brown, if they are dominant, become hues, whereas grays and browns that modify, or dull, a spectral hue (such as blue) are *saturation modifiers* or *masks*. Orange, when it is dark toned, appears brown. To sum up: brown and gray are not generally considered to be hues, but are classed as saturation modifiers or masks, unless the stone is either brown or gray; then they are

Tino Hammid

Amethyst: Tonal range of purple hue. From right to left, tonal percentages graduate in approximately ten percent increments from ten percent tone to eighty percent tone. Darker tone yields a richer and more vivid hue.

considered hues, and may even have spectral hues as modifiers — for example, reddish brown. Examples of beautiful brown-hued stones include fancy color diamond, sapphire, and tourmaline.

Tone

Tone — that is, lightness and darkness — is the third component of color. It can best be described as the addition of black or white to a hue. A dollop of black paint added to a bucket of robin's egg blue yields a darker blue. The more black that is mixed in, the darker the tone: first sky blue, then royal blue, then midnight blue, and finally enough black is added to overcome the color, turning the paint completely black. White added to a color has the opposite effect.

For the sake of analysis, tone is described as a percentage. A transparent quartz crystal or a windowpane is zero tone. No tone means no color. A lump of coal or a crow's wing is one hundred percent tone. One hundred percent tone is always black. Too much tone snuffs out both hue and saturation. When this occurs the stone is *overcolor*. Tone refers to the key color of the gem, not the body color. Dark areas in the body of the gem are extinguished; the phenomenon is called *extinction* and is the result of off-axis reflection. Light refracting out of the interior of the gem but away from the eye is the cause. Extinction is achromatic; that is, shows an absence of color, like a shadow that is gray to black in appearance. A refracted hue (key color) which is dark in tone but still contains some color cannot be and should not be confused

with *extinction,* which is, by definition, gray to black.

Jeff Scovil

Extinction: This pink sapphire shows some refracted pink scattered about the face but most of the gem shows an unattractive achromatic dark gray body color. Extinction is always achromatic (without color) in tones from gray to black. The effect is caused by a phenomenon known as off-axis reflection. Too much extinction, as in this photo, classifies the stone as undesirable.

In gemstones the beauty of the color is a balance of *hue*, *saturation*, and *tone*. For each color the optimum percentages differ. If the tonal levels are too high the stone is described as being overcolor, or too dark. If the key color is too light in tone the hue appears pale and washed out.

The two attributes of *saturation* and *tone* function together to define the beauty of the hue. Color scientists have long recognized

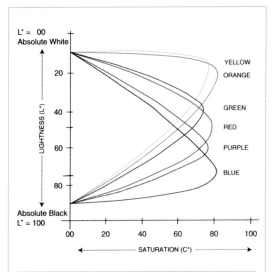

Stephen Hofer, *Collecting and Classifying Coloured Diamonds*

Color gamut limits: The graph illustrates the point at which saturation and tone combine to produce the most vivid hue. Note that yellow and orange achieve maximum brightness at relatively light tones (twenty to thirty percent). Above these tonal values, saturation (brightness) of the hue rapidly diminishes. Blue and purple require fairly dark tones (sixty to eighty percent) to achieve maximum saturation; one hundred percent would appear as absolute black and totally opaque. Tonal values below these gamut limits begin to look washed out. The most desirable combinations of saturation and tone in gems of these hues follow these curves fairly closely; e.g., the finest yellow diamond is fairly light and bright; the finest blue sapphire, deep and rich. This graph objectively demonstrates the very simple dictum that, in almost every case, the brighter the hue of a gemstone, the more beautiful it is and the more desirable it will be in the marketplace.

that there is an optimum combination of saturation and tone for each hue. This is the point at which saturation and tone produce the most vivid hue. These points are called *gamut limits*.[30] For example, the most vivid tone for yellow is twenty percent, while the most vivid tone in blue is about eighty-five percent, red eighty percent, and green seventy-five percent.[31] Beyond these limits, as the hue darkens, it loses saturation.

Not surprisingly, desirability in the market exactly parallels these *gamut limits* for gems that occur in these primary hues. The optimum tone for ruby is eighty percent, sapphire and tanzanite eighty-five percent, and emerald and tsavorite seventy-five percent. The rule must be applied somewhat gingerly because gemstones never occur in an absolutely pure hue. Purple gems can be something of an exception. Amethyst, for example, reaches its peak saturation at approximately eighty percent tone. The gamut limit graph demonstrates that the hue purple achieves its *gamut limit* at a much lighter sixty percent tone. This means, reduced to simplest terms, the brighter the hue the better the hue. In the case of purple gems such as amethyst it means that a richer hue is generally preferred over a brighter hue.

The color of a gemstone can be accurately described using this terminology. For example, a fine bright, dark, violetish red ruby is better described as a ruby with a ninety percent vivid primary red hue, and a ten percent purple secondary hue of eighty percent tone (with little or no gray mask present).

30. Nick Hale, personal communication, 2002.

31. Stephen C. Hofer, *Collecting and Classifying Coloured Diamonds* (New York: Ashland Press, 1998), p. 172, fig. 13-3. The chart pictured above shows saturation gamuts for opaque color pigments; however, gamut limits for transparent media are higher, although the relative saturation between different hues remains the same.

CUT: THE GEOMETRY OF BEAUTY

The faceted gem

Traditionally, the relative importance given each of the four Cs has differed depending on whether it was applied to colored gemstones or colorless diamonds. In colored gemstones the most important criteria is, of course, color. In diamond, which has no color, it is brilliance, or life, which is a function of cut, and is of first importance.

The refinement of the lapidary art and the invention of faceting in fifteenth-century Europe ushered in the modern period of gem appreciation. Proper cutting and polishing are required to achieve a gem's full potential. By the end of the sixteenth century, beauty became the primary criteria in the evaluation of gemstones.[32] Before then, as we have seen, religious, talismanic, and medicinal uses of gemstones were at least as important and often of greater importance than beauty in the value equation.

Although the shaping of gems, mostly as cabochons, had reached a high degree of sophistication in the Middle East by the third millennium BC, faceting was not developed until the Renaissance and it was a European invention. Even today, cutting as a grading criterion is emphasized a great deal more in the West than in the East. In Asia, color is by far the predominant factor in grading gemstones; the perfection of cut, what we call "make," is at best a secondary consideration.

The outward form of the gem crystals themselves suggested the first cutting styles. Diamond, for example, normally occurs as a bipyramidal crystal; i.e., its normal form, what crystallographers call its "habit," looks like two pyramids joined together at the base. Before the invention of faceting in the fifteenth century, uncut diamond crystals were often set into jewelry. Knock the point off one end of a well-formed diamond crystal, polish the sloping sides, and presto! a fine example of the first faceting style, known as the table cut (see p.8). Viewed in profile the table cut retains the same basic outline of the natural crystal. A few more modifications and the table cut evolves into the cushion and old mine cuts and, finally, into the modern round brilliant, the cutting style that graces the engagement finger of millions of young women . Other cutting styles have a similar history: the

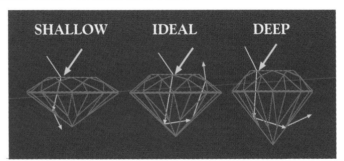

As the illustration shows, it is proportions (width to depth), not number or placement of facets, that will dictate the amount of brilliance and dispersion a gem will produce.

23

32. Lenzen, *History of Diamond Production*, p. 110.

hexagonal profile of the emerald crystal suggests the basic outline of the emerald cut. The cabochon, perhaps the oldest cut of all, is little more than a stream pebble that has been flattened on one side and polished.

As technology developed, cutting gradually achieved greater importance. Today fine cutting must be considered a necessary factor in the connoisseurship equation. That is, a well-cut stone may not necessarily be fine, but a fine stone must always be well cut.

Natural uncut gem material, commonly called *rough*, is found in all sorts of shapes and sizes. The crystals may have grown together or in distorted shapes. Other minerals, sometimes other crystals, may have formed and been trapped within them. In the millions of years since its formation, the rough may have been cracked by landslides, broken by earthquakes, or pulverized by glacial action. Rough gem material may have been displaced from the place of its formation by erosion, tumbled down mountain streams, or ground into pebbles by the action of ocean tides.

The shape and size of the cut gemstone is dictated in part by the size, shape, and clarity of the piece of raw material placed before the lapidary. Rough is expensive and is sold by weight. The objective of the lapidary is twofold: first, to create a beautiful gem; second, to maximize the yield in carat weight from the rough material and thereby maximize the price. Bigger and heavier translate into more profit, particularly when fudging the proportions makes the difference between "holding the carat" or cutting a sub-carat gem. This is particularly true in Asia. In Bangkok the asking price for a one-carat (1.00+) blue sapphire may be four times that asked for a similar 0.85-carat stone.[33] Little surprise that the choice between maximizing beauty or maximizing profit often tilts in the direction of commerce. In many cases the loss of weight necessary to create a beautiful stone is unacceptable to the dealer.

Beauty versus profit! These two objectives are often at odds. If the dealer's wares are criticized for poor cut, he will often shrug and use the term *native cut* implying that the gems were fashioned by technologically challenged primitives. This is both an ethnic slur and a very convenient bit of misinformation. Cutters in Asia, Africa, and South America are very familiar with their indigenous materials and are exceptionally skilled. For example, I have seen lapidaries in upper Burma produce precisely cut sapphire using primitive foot-operated cutting wheels with buffalo horn fittings. Poor cutting is almost always the result of a well thought out weight-retention strategy. There is no excuse for poor cutting. The aficionado should remember that a poorly cut gem is the result of a conscious decision made before the rough is put on to the cutter's wheel.

For four hundred years the major preoccupation of the lapidary arts has been the development of proportions and facet patterns that would maximize the brilliance, or life, of a gemstone. Cutting is all about brilliance. Brilliance is defined as the total

33. The modern metric carat is one fifth of a gram. The carat is divided into one hundred points. A half- carat is written 0.50. The carat was originally based on the weight of the carob bean.

amount of reflected light reaching the eye from the internal and external surfaces of the facets. The color of the refracted light, the color coming from inside the gem, is what is called the key color of the gem.

Viewed face up, a faceted gemstone is far from uniform in appearance. It is a complex mosaic, a chromatic jigsaw puzzle, a shifting crazy quilt of color. On close examination, some facets appear bright, others dull; some one color, some another. Faceted gemstones are designed so that light enters through the crown of the stone, bends, or refracts into, and reflects within the gemstone, and returns through the crown to the eye. Jewelers sometimes talk about gems gathering light from the back and sides. They will even suggest that prong settings, particularly high ones, will improve the stone's brilliance. This is a misunderstanding of the geometry of light and the objective of the lapidary. In a properly cut gem, light is not gathered from the sides or back of the stone; it enters through the top or crown of the stone, is reflected internally, and is refracted back out of the crown. As we will see, only a poorly cut stone can derive any real benefit from an open setting.

Brilliance is partly a result of faceting but more directly a result of the gem being cut to the proper proportions. Proportions refer to the ratio between the length or width

© The Gemological Institute of America

of the stone and the depth. Light bends when entering a substance; this is called refraction. The angle of the bend depends on the density of the substance and is different for every gemstone species. The angle of refraction can be measured and is called the refractive index. If the gem is properly proportioned (length-width to depth), most of the light entering the crown will be bent so that it reflects several times within the stone and exits through the crown, causing the gem to dance in the light.

Window, fish-eye, or belly

Three basic cutting strategies are used to maximize the size and/or weight of a gemstone. One strategy which maximizes the weight as well as optimizes the size of the gem is called cutting a "window." In this case, the lapidary cuts a stone that is both wider and shallower than it should be. This gives the illusion that the stone is actually bigger because it has a greater diameter. Unfortunately, the depth-to-width ratio is too small and the pavilion is too shallow. As a result, light, instead of refracting back through the crown to the eye, passes right through the middle of the stone and causes a lens effect or "window" beneath the table of the stone. If a windowed stone is placed over a sheet of printing, the words printed on the page will be visible. In a properly cut gemstone, the words on the page would not be visible because the light entering the gem through the crown is bouncing off the internal sides of the pavilion, returning the way it came, and exiting through the crown. A lens effect, on the other hand, allows light to move in both directions, resulting in a loss of brilliance. The larger the window in the stone, the greater will be the loss of brilliance.

If the stone has been cut in such a way that the face or diameter is fifty percent larger than normal, but is so shallow that it loses fifty percent of its brilliance, where is the net gain? When the stone is viewed at a distance, it is the light return, or brilliance (not the diameter of the stone) that is most apparent. Sometimes a window will be cut in a gem that is overcolor or has poor crystal;

i.e., the stone is too dark to sparkle. By cutting a lens, the craftsman can assure that some color, primarily transmitted or body color, will be observed in the face-up gem.

Unfortunately, in our culture, bigger often translates as better. Thus, a dealer or jeweler can often entice a buyer to purchase a stone with a larger diameter simply because it is of a more impressive size, particularly if all the stones the buyer sees are poorly cut. If the stone has a window, light can enter through the back in a sort of lens. This is precisely the type of cut that, to use the old jeweler's phrase, "gathers the light." Windowed gems benefit from an open setting; in a closed setting the window naturally appears dark. A small amount of windowing is difficult to avoid. The connoisseur will be offered many windowed gems. As with any grading criterion, the question is how much does the effect disturb the eye and detract from the beauty of the gem? A bit of a window may be acceptable. But by any standard, badly windowed gems should be judged as de facto cabochons; unless the collector is looking for a cabochon, badly windowed gems are poor bargains and should be avoided.[34]

Another strategy used by the cutter to preserve weight is to cut the stone overly deep, or too deep for its width. In this case, some of the light entering the gem will bounce around the inside of the stone and exit through the side of the pavilion rather than exiting through the crown, causing the gem to seem dark toward the center. In trade parlance, this is referred to as a "fish-eye," meaning that the center of the stone,

34. Cabochon, from the French meaning "little head," is a facetless round-topped gem that looks like a gumdrop. It is little more than a natural stream pebble that has been polished. Cabochons, or "cabs," are normally cut from badly flawed rough and, although they can be quite beautiful, sell at discounts of as much as seventy-five percent less than faceted gems of similar color. Opaque gems such as turquoise and lapis lazuli are normally cut en cabochon.

35. Each gem species— tourmaline, spinel, tanzanite, etc.— has a

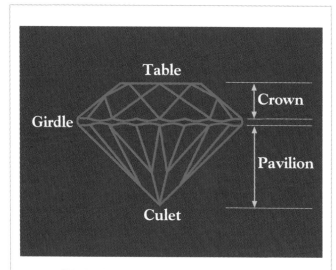

This drawing illustrates the basic parts of a faceted gemstone. Although the gem pictured is a round brilliant cut, almost all cutting styles: oval, pear shaped or square have a table, crown, girdle, pavilion, and culet. For exceptions see "New Cutters, New Rules": pp. 31-33

percent of the total weight, whereas the pavilion is sixty percent. A well-cut stone viewed in profile will look similar to the illustration at left. The face is measured at the girdle. A stone with a little fat around the belly will show a bulbous, rounded profile between the girdle and the bottom tip of the stone (or culet). The additional fat adds nothing to the beauty of the gem. Stones cut in this manner have a smaller face for its weight class than a properly cut stone.

Most ruby and sapphire are bellied. Two one-carat size sapphires may have markedly different faces. One may measure 6mm at the girdle; another only 5.5mm. The additional weight will usually be found encircling the pavilion just below the girdle. Any additional weight above what is necessary should not be considered in the evaluation and pricing of the gem; e.g., a 5.5mm round sapphire should weigh approximately 0.87 carats and this should be considered as part of the desirability equation. The optimum dimensions of a perfectly cut stone will differ for each gem species.[35] In the author's view, up to twelve percent extra weight is acceptable in a rare stone.

In some gem species, color is not distributed uniformly throughout the gem. This is particularly true of ruby and sapphire. These two gem varieties can be exceptions to the rules that govern most gemstones. Bands of color alternating with zones of

under the table, is dark like the iris of a fish's eye, with some brilliance from the crown surrounding it like a halo. The term *extinction*, on the other hand, refers to the part of the gem that is dark.

Stones cut with a rounded or bulbous profile below the girdle are referred to as "bellied." Cutting bellied stones is another common practice used to retain weight. Such stones may show no defect in brilliance, but like an overweight man with a spare tire around his middle, they are simply out of proportion. Since the largest percentage of a stone's weight is centered at the girdle, bellying a stone can increase its weight by a surprisingly large degree.

As a rule of thumb, the crown in a well-made faceted stone is approximately forty

different density or specific gravity (s.g.). Carat is a unit of weight equal to one fifth of a gram. The higher the specific gravity, the

denser the substance and the smaller it will be per carat. Some gems weigh more than others. A perfectly cut round one-carat ruby

has a specific gravity of 4.00 and an optimum dimension of 6mm. A 6mm round tourmaline, by contrast, has a specific gravity of 3.06 and

perfectly cut will weigh only 0.87 carats, thirteen percent less.

colorlessness are common in both gems. Often the cutter must sacrifice something in proportion and symmetry to mix the color so that it will appear uniform when the gem is viewed in the face-up position. This can lead to overly deep or bellied stones, off-center culets, odd facet patterns, and unusual or asymmetrical shapes. These are all faults, but they are more acceptable in gems with color banding, such as ruby and sapphire. Banding can usually be seen by viewing the stone through the side or by placing it face down on a white surface. The relative importance of these faults depends very much on how they affect the overall beauty of the stone when viewed face up. A stone with a striated or blotchy color appearance face up is far less desirable than one with odd proportions.

In a perfectly cut stone, over ninety percent of the light entering through the crown bounces off the pavilion facets and is returned to the eye. In practical terms, the greater the percentage of a gem's crown that refracts and reflects light, the more successful the cut and the more beautiful the stone.

Performing the test

The *quantity* or percentage of brilliance that a gemstone exhibits can be measured by a straightforward test. Hold the stone face up directly under an overhead light. Diffused fluorescent light is best. For this test, the kelvin temperature of the light is not important. Stones that are not perfectly round or square should be held along the long axis with a pair of gem tweezers. Then

tilt the stone toward you to a forty-five degree angle toward the perpendicular.[36] This will allow viewing of the gemstone without your shadow intruding between the eye and the light source.

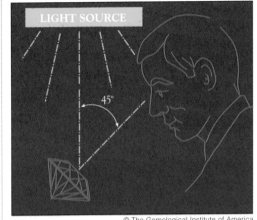

© The Gemological Institute of America

The correct viewing angle for evaluating brilliance of a gem. At this angle, the lower half of the gem's face is evaluated, then the stone is rotated 180 degrees and the percentage of brilliance exhibited by the other half is measured. The sum of the two numbers equals the total brilliance of the gem.

This procedure will allow you to observe the brilliance of the bottom half of the stone. At this viewing angle, the upper half of the stone usually will not exhibit brilliance, but if it does, ignore it. Look at the bottom half of the stone: if half of the bottom half of the stone is reflecting light, it is twenty-five percent brilliant. To view the brilliance of the other half, rotate the stone one hundred eighty degrees with the bottom half again tilted toward you. Again mentally draw a horizontal line dividing the face of the gem in half. Divide the total brilliance of the other

36. Cabochon cut stones, including opal and phenomenal stones (stars, cat's-eyes, moonstones), must be viewed face up *directly* beneath the light source. As discussed in Chapter 5, the phenomena (star, cat's-eye) will not be completely visible if the stone is tilted toward the viewer.

half in half and add the two figures together. The sum derived is the total brilliance of the gemstone. If the second half reflects light from one third of the surface, that is added to the initial figure (25 percent + 16.6 percent = 41.6 percent) which yields the total brilliance of the gem. The remaining fifty-eight percent of the gem shows extinction; that is, that portion appears gray to black and exhibits no brilliance. This part of the face-up gem has no life; it is, in short, dead.

As a supplementary test of the stone's liveliness, rock the gem back and forth directly under the light source. Hold it just as you would if it was set in a ring. When mounted in jewelry and worn, gems move relative to the light. Next, place the stone between the first and index fingers. Placing the stone between the fingers simulates the effect of prong-setting the gem. This procedure should give you an idea of how the gem will act when mounted. If the stone is windowed, it will likely darken toward the center.

As previously mentioned, the lapidary sometimes purposely cuts a slight window in the center of a dark-toned gem, usually ruby or sapphire. A stone cut this way will look livelier in a jeweler's parcel that contains a number of gems; viewing the stone between the fingers simulates the effect of setting the stone and closing the window. The gem should be wiped thoroughly with a gem cloth before, during, and after this procedure. Slight amounts of dirt or grease from the skin on the stone's pavilion will materially diminish the liveliness of the gem.

When viewing a stone, avoid direct sunlight. Very few gemstones hold up well in direct sun and the glare caused by light reflecting from the surface of the facets makes it difficult to evaluate either the cut or the color. If natural light is used, turn the back to allow the light to diffuse around the body and hold the stone with the table of the gem at an angle directly perpendicular to the sun's angle and far enough away from the body to allow the brilliance to be observed. This alternative method allows one hundred percent of the face of the stone to be viewed at one time. For the mathematically challenged, it also eliminates the need to use arithmetic to calculate the total brilliance.

The gem photograph: viewer beware

One way to educate the eye is to view photographs of rare and exceptional gems. The techniques of gem photography have improved markedly over the past two decades. Master photographers specializing in gem and mineral photography took the gemstone photographs in this book. However, the stones pictured rarely look the same to an observer using the viewing techniques described above, which rely on a single normal everyday light source. To achieve the photographic effects in this book, the photographer used high intensity lighting and multiple light sources.[37] Each photograph shows the entire stone illuminated at one time. This almost never happens under normal conditions, if only because the viewer's head intrudes between the gem and the light source, casting a

37. For the reader interested in gemstone photographic techniques, I recommend the very excellent book by Jeffrey A. Scovil,'*Photographing Minerals, Fossils and Lapidary Materials* (Tucson, Arizona: Geoscience Press, 1996).

shadow and causing the light to diffuse around the head.

Digital technology now makes it possible to enhance photographs in a number of ways. The photographs in this book are meant to aid the reader in developing a connoisseur's eye. Therefore, other than as stated above, they have not been improved in any way. This is not necessarily true of other gem books. The photographer's objective is to show the gem under optimum conditions. These days that may mean blasting the stone with ten thousand watts of high intensity light at precisely the moment the film is exposed. Photographs are useful but they are not a substitute for the real thing. The following principle is a good rule of thumb when looking at pictures of gemstones: if it looks too good to be true, it probably is too good to be true. Viewer beware!

Proportion and symmetry

Two other cut factors not directly related to brilliance affect the overall desirability of a gem. These factors are *proportion* and *symmetry* and they refer to the eye appeal and craftsmanship of the cut stone. The outline of the stone should be symmetrical. The facets should be symmetrical and evenly distributed. The girdle should not be noticeably thick.

The most important symmetry issues are those that are visible when the stone is viewed in the face-up position. In most cases, faults below the girdle are hidden when the stone is set. For this reason, odd proportions or cutting faults between the girdle and crown have more effect on the overall desirability of the gem than those that occur on the pavilion, below the girdle of the stone.

In the market, certain length-width ratios are preferred, affecting the value in some gemstones. In diamond, for example, the ideal length-width ratio for an emerald cut is 1.5-1.75. Stones with length-to-width ratios over 2.00 are considered to be "lean" looking, and those with of 1.25 to 1.10 are called "squarish."

Tourmaline and topaz are normally cut with length-to-width ratios of five to one and more. This is because the rough crystals are themselves long and narrow. Such stones are strikingly beautiful in part because of their long narrow outline. In these cases the extended shape has no effect on value. On the other hand, if the stone is supposed to be round and it looks more like a flat tire, this is not pleasing to the eye and will have a definite and dramatic effect on value. Symmetry faults are for the most part more detrimental than odd proportions.

Certain shapes will command a premium within specific gemstone species. For example, ruby and sapphire are normally cut as ovals, cushions, and pear shapes simply because the outline of the rough lends itself to these shapes. Round shapes are rare, potentially more brilliant, and command a premium in most gems. Emeralds, a notable exception, are usually shaped in the octagonal step cut, also called the classic emerald cut, not only to retain maximum yield from the rough, but also because many connoisseurs rightly believe that this shape maximizes the satiny beauty of emerald (as will be seen in Part II). Round emeralds actually sell at a discount.

Gems cut to standard sizes often are priced at a premium for reasons unrelated to the beauty of the gem. Such stones are referred to as calibrated. Calibrated gems fit in standard-size jewelry mountings and are, therefore, in great demand by commercial jewelers. A collector can often find an uncalibrated stone at a much more attractive price simply because it will not fit into a standard commercial setting. Non-calibrated stones present a buying opportunity for the collector. Non-standard stones can be set by a skilled goldsmith at a price somewhat higher than that of setting calibrated stones. Moreover, handmade settings can be a good investment. In many cases the skilled craftsman will make a setting that actually enhances the beauty of the stone.

To summarize, the total area above the crown viewed in overhead lighting constitutes one hundred percent of the gem for the purpose of measuring brilliance. The percentage of the gem that is dark, or shows a window or lens effect, is deducted from the equation to arrive at the total brilliance of the stone. Barring truly disturbing faults in symmetry and proportion, a colored gem that exhibits brilliance over eighty percent of the crown is a one hundred percent success. As a standard of judgment, fifty percent brilliance is acceptable and over eighty is exceptional. Total brilliance under fifty percent classifies the gem as undesirable.

Finely cut stones do command a premium. Though poorly cut gems are of little or no interest to the connoisseur, the price of a colored gem will normally be discounted ten percent for a gem that exhibits less than sixty percent brilliance. Stones with brilliance less than forty percent are discounted fifteen percent and more. Colored gems that show more than eighty percent brilliance will command a ten to fifteen percent premium.[38] Price differentials for cut in colorless diamonds can vary as much as seventy percent between fine and poorly cut stones. A detailed discussion of diamond cutting is in Chapter 5.

New cutters, new rules

For the last four hundred years, the major preoccupation of the lapidary arts has been the pursuit of faceting designs which produce more and more brilliance. This has led to a sort of tunnel vision, continually narrowing, so that by the beginning of our own century, the lapidary was concerned almost exclusively with the cutting of the four basic symmetrical shapes: round, oval, step cut, and pear.

In the early 1980s, the German master lapidary Bernd Munsteiner introduced a new style of gem cutting in the United States. Immediately dubbed "Munsteiners" or "fantasy cuts," these gemstones were fashioned with asymmetrical outlines and faceting patterns that were more reminiscent of optical sculpture than traditional gemstones. Though ridiculed by conservatives, innovative jewelry designers and consumers

38. Ted Themelis, *Mogok: Valley of Rubies and Sapphires* (Los Angeles: A&T Publishing, 2000), p. 213. Themelis refers specifically to premiums charged for ruby and sapphire by the gem dealers of Mogok, Burma; that is, in the oldest gem market on earth. The range described in this book is more general and based on average premiums charged around the world.

embraced Munsteiner's fantasy cuts. After four centuries, the market was hungry for something new. Though little noted at the

Helen Constantine Shull: Courtesy: Larry Winn

Not just about brilliance! With unconventional techniques such as concave and negative faceting, holographic effects can be induced into the gemstone. This 57-carat Brazilian aquamarine gem sculpture was cut by Larry Winn. (see footnote#39)

time, a revolution had begun, a lapidary renaissance, and the only major change in gem-cutting philosophy since the cabochon gave way to the point cut.

In the past decade a whole generation of new cutters has emerged. The term "new cutters" is used simply for lack of a better one. These are lapidary artists, mostly Germans and Americans, whose chief interest is not just cutting a well-made brilliant, but creating a tiny work of art.

Given recent history it is natural to conclude that the creative cutting movement had its roots in Germany. This is not correct! The father of the new cutting movement, who prefigured Munsteiner by more than fifty years, was not a German but an unassuming American pioneer by the name of Francis J. Sperisen.[39]

The connoisseurship of gem sculpture requires that the collector look beyond the traditional standards of *cut*. *Color, clarity,* and *crystal* are as important in gem sculpture as they are in any other gem, but the intention of the lapidary artist differs from the usual objective of simply maximizing brilliance. In some cases the artist is looking to create internal or holographic effects within the gemstone that are, in a sense, the opposite of the traditional objective, in that brilliance is not the primary intention. Fantasy cuts can be seen as a sort of half-breed: half faceted stone, half cabochon. When evaluating gem sculpture it is important to remember that they are works of art; as in the fine arts, balance, proportion, and the intention of the artist must also be considered. Thus the stone may be beautiful but the effect cannot be judged simply by measuring the total amount of brilliance. For example, a window may actually be part of the artist's intention. Body color may be as important as key color and *crystal,* which

39. Beginning in 1941, Sperisen, a self-taught lapidary working out of a studio in San Francisco, began a collaboration with Margaret DePatta, a metalsmith, who is today considered the doyenne of American art-jewelers. Sperisen worked with DePatta, cutting unusually shaped gemstones to complement her jewelry. DePatta was herself a student of the constructivist artist and founder of Chicago's Design Institute, Laszlo Moholy-Nagy. Moholy-Nagy, an important Hungarian-born artist trained at the Bauhaus, established a training curriculum for young artists that emphasized experimentation and the use of new materials such as thermoplastics. Moholy-Nagy had an abiding interest in motion and light. His objective was to create an abstract art that directly stimulated both the physical and psychic perception through the use of combinations of materials, shapes, color, and light. The artist created kinetic sculptures that juxtaposed transparent, translucent, and opaque materials designed to produce varying effects when exhibited in strong light. Many of DePatta's ideas

as we shall see, is of real import. The connoisseur must retain an open mind. The question is, has the artist been successful? Does it work? Beauty, however, remains the defining criterion.

Pendant in white gold and ebony by Margaret DePatta. The metalwork is designed to be seen as refracted through a double lens cut colorless quartz designed by Francis J. Sperison. This gemstone, which resembles the modern opposed bar cut, was deliberately cut as a lens (windowed). The effect is a realization of what art critic Norbert Lynton calls "the Constructivist ideal of massless sculpture inserted into space." As the viewer or the pendant moves, light, distorted as it passes through the stone, causes the metal mounted behind the stone to appear to move and change shape.

The cabochon: judging the cut

The word *cabochon* is derived from the French meaning "head." It is the oldest cut, being little more than a stream pebble flattened on one side and polished. Judging a cabochon requires a slightly different set of rules. Cabochons or "cabs" have no facets and are designed to transmit rather than reflect light. A fine cabochon does not sparkle, it glows. In modern times the cabochon has fallen into disfavor; for the most part, only opaque gem material, star and cat's-eye stones, and stones judged to have too many visible inclusions to be faceted are cut *en cabochon*. In a faceted stone, light is reflected internally. Multiple internal reflections will often cause visible inclusions to appear doubled or tripled like an image in a fun-house mirror. Because a cabochon transmits and does not reflect light, this sort of doubling does not occur. A cabochon ordinarily will be priced significantly lower than a faceted stone of the same gem variety.

A well-made cabochon that is not overly included can be a very beautiful gemstone. The fact that cabochons may be purchased at significantly lower prices than those asked for a faceted stone of the same gem variety should not be seen as a deterrent, but rather viewed as a buying opportunity. With part of his mind, the true aficionado approaches each gemstone as if through the eyes of a child, as if each were a thing entirely new.[40]

had their basis in the constructivist philosophy of Moholy-Nagy.

In what is DePatta's most famous piece, currently in the Oakland Museum of Art, she crafted a pendant in ebony and white gold in the shape of the inverted letter "Y"

mounted behind — and meant to be seen through — a Sperisen double lens cut quartz. This gemstone, which resembles the modern opposed bar cut, was deliberately cut as a lens (windowed) and exhibits no brilliance. The effect was a conceptual *tour de force*, a

realization of what art critic Norbert Lynton calls "the Constructivist ideal of massless sculpture inserted into space." As the viewer or the pendant moves, light, distorted as it passes through the stone, causes the metal mounted behind the stone to appear to move and change shape.

See Richard W. Wise, *A Cut Above: The New Cutters and The American Lapidary Renaissance*, National Jeweler Magazine, July 1996

40. I once employed a European-trained master goldsmith; he was an older man who, over the years,

CRYSTAL: THE DEFINING CRITERION

Cabochons may be cut in a variety of ways: high domed or low domed with flat, concave, or convex backs. None of that really matters very much — what matters is the result! A well-cut cab will glow with characteristics similar to a stone that has been faceted. The strength of the glow is substituted in the evaluation equation for the percentage of brilliance in a faceted stone. It is the degree of transparency, or what I have chosen to call *crystal* (see Chapter 5) that is the key issue here. If the stone has good *crystal* and is well cut, it will glow. Cabochons, particularly phenomenal stones such as stars and cat's-eyes, must be examined with the light perpendicular to the girdle of the gem; that is, directly overhead.

The two remaining Cs, clarity (visible inclusions) and color, are judged in the same way as faceted stones. However, in the case of the cabochon, the color evaluation is based on the body color: the hue, saturation, and tone of the light transmitted by the stone. There are no facets, therefore no key color to be evaluated.

CLARITY: BLEMISH OR BEAUTY MARK?

Clarity is a concept that is easily understood. No complex analysis is necessary, just the use of the eyes.

Inclusions and flaws

Rather than regarding inclusions in colored stones as harmful, in small sizes and numbers that do not in any way detract from their beauty, they should be regarded as adding to desirability, for they provide identifying characteristics.

GIA Colored
Stone Course, 1980

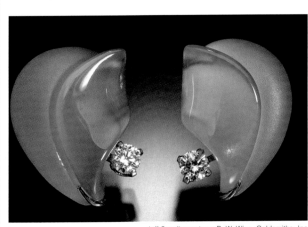

Jeff Scovil; courtesy: R. W. Wise, Goldsmiths, Inc.

These translucent paired blue agate gem sculptures, set as earrings, exhibit the characteristic grayish blue hue and show excellent crystal for gems of this species. Sculptures by Steve Walters; earrings by Douglas Canivet.

Gem formation is a dynamic series of processes that continue as the crystals form. Cracks, foreign bodies, minerals, even other crystals are normally *included* in this process. Hence the word *inclusion*, the technical term gemologists use to describe these tiny intruders. The world inside a gemstone is a complex and fascinating one, a miniature self-

had worked for some of the finest jewelers in the world, including Harry Winston. He knew a good stone when he saw one. He showed me some of his jewelry, which included stones that had numerous visible inclusions. "Why," I asked him, "do you use such flawed stones in your work?" "Ja, ja," he replied, "I know they are not so good but I like these stones because the inclusions are like internal facets, they make the stone more interesting and, I think, more beautiful. And, besides, they are much cheaper." Jurgen Sierau, personal communication, 1988.

contained universe. Inclusions tell the story of a gemstone's genesis and often provide clues to where it was formed. It is, in fact, inclusion study that allows gemologists to identify and separate rubies formed in Burma, for example, from rubies formed elsewhere.

The reader will note that the more common term, *flaws*, has not been used in this discussion. This is because *inclusions* become *flaws* only when their presence materially affects the beauty and/or the durability of a gemstone. This bears repeating: inclusions become flaws if their presence is substantially detrimental to the beauty and/or the durability of the gem.

The aficionado should understand that there is a real distinction to be made between inclusions and flaws. In fact, the use of the term flaw should be avoided. *Inclusion* describes the situation; *flaw* is pregnant with additional meaning. As has been said throughout this volume, a gem is all about beauty; it has that as its sole raison d'être. A small inclusion, or series of them inside a colored gemstone (invisible to the naked eye and not creating any sort of defect possibly leading to breakage), normally may be ignored in the value equation.

In some cases, inclusions make a major contribution to the beauty of a gemstone.

For example, the star in a star sapphire (see Chapter 5) is produced by inclusions of rutile crystals, long thin hairlike structures

Jeff Scovil; courtesy of R.W. Wise, Goldsmiths, Inc.

Inclusions play a central role in this contemporary pendant by Bruce Anderson. The right half of the piece is a gem sculpture in quartz. Here the lapidary artist selected a particularly interesting composition, a combination of hair-like rutile and grainy black graphite inclusions as the centerpiece of this flat asymmetrical gem. The goldsmith echoes the pattern in the plaque at left using white gold appliqued with yellow gold and oxidized palladium. A fancy cut yellow beryl (heliodor) serves to focus the eye and lends a visual balance to the overall composition. Quartz sculpture by Glenn Lehrer.

without which there could be no star. In other cases, myriads of microscopic inclusions produce the very desirable billowing moonglow effect in moonstone and the signature "sleepy" glow of Kashmir sapphire.

Inclusions are also very helpful in determining how, where, and when the gem material was formed. Important questions such as country of origin and natural versus synthetic formation may be answered by studying inclusions.

There are two standards for judging clarity: the visual, using the naked eye; and the microscopic, using ten power of magnification to examine the interior world of a gem. The microscopic standard is used for colorless diamonds; the visual standard for all other gems, including fancy color diamonds. Diamonds that are flawless under ten power are termed *loupe clean* or *flawless*. This leads to a question: if a diamond has a tiny inclusion barely visible under 10X, is the stone flawed? The answer is technically yes, even though the inclusion *does not materially affect the beauty or durability of the given gem*. (For a full discussion of diamond clarity grading, see Chapter 5.) With colored stones the issue is straightforward. Colored stones that have no visible inclusions when viewed by the naked eye are termed eye-clean or eye-flawless.[41] Visual inclusions will result in most cases in a discount from the price of an eye-clean gem. The amount of the discount depends on how much an inclusion disturbs the eye and affects the beauty of the stone. This judgment involves an individual decision that the aficionado must make when considering a purchase of a visibly included gem. From a connoisseur's perspective, no gem, with the possible exception of emerald, can be considered fine if it has visible inclusions.

It is a good idea for the budding aficionado to become proficient with the jeweler's loupe. This basic instrument is available in many shapes and sizes and strengths. The ten-power or 10X loupe is the most practical because it has enough depth of field to be able to keep the whole gemstone in focus while providing sufficient magnification to see inside it.

41. Current Federal Trade Commission guidelines make no distinction between grading clarity in colored stones and diamonds. Therefore, using the term *flawless* to describe an eye-clean sapphire that has visible inclusions under 10X magnification is technically a violation of federal law (FTC 23.26). In order to remain on the good side of the FTC, I will use the term *flawless* to describe gems that have no visible inclusions under 10X magnification and *eye-flawless* will be substituted for the term *flawless* to describe the clarity of colored gemstones.

Chapter 4

Connoisseurship: Secrets of the Trade

Nor trust o'ermuch the treacherous candleshine, Your eye for beauty's warped by night and wine. When Paris judged the three and gave the prize To Venus, there were clear and cloudless skies. Night hides each fault, each blemish will condone, The hour can make a beauty of a crone. To daylight pearls and purple gowns refer; Of face and limb let day be arbiter.

Ovid

Primary hues

Dividing color into its primary and secondary hues is very useful and good practice for the aficionado. In many, though not all cases, colored gemstones are evaluated by how closely the color of the stone approaches one of the eight spectral hues. This is particularly true, as will be discussed in the appropriate chapters, with ruby, emerald, tsavorite and spessartite garnet, tanzanite, and sapphire. These are referred to as *primary hue gemstones* in this volume. The very finest ruby is, in theory, one with a primary hue of one hundred percent red with no secondary modifying hue. In nature few stones even begin to approach this ideal. A gem with a primary hue of eighty-five percent or better will be a high scorer, provided that it has vivid saturation and proper tone for its type. A visually pure orange sapphire will be more desirable than a slightly yellowish orange sapphire. In short, a gem that exhibits a visually pure single hue is usually more desired that one which shows both a primary and secondary hue. This is a generalization with a number of exceptions, as will be discussed in the sections on padparadscha sapphire, malaya garnet, alexandrite, and topaz.

The visualization of beauty: light

Gemstones are creatures of the light. Not one of the qualities discussed thus far can even be seen, let alone appreciated, without light. Jewelry store shoppers can often be heard to say that such and such stone looks great in the store display, implying that the use of proper lighting is somehow misleading. No one would try to read this book in the dark, yet no one would suggest that the book's content, the ideas contained within these pages, cease to exist when the lights are turned off.

In preindustrial times the world was much simpler. There were only a few kinds of light: sunlight, moonlight, and firelight. Thanks to modern technology, we now can choose from many different types of lighting. Incandescent light is light produced by a flame (lamplight, candlelight, firelight). Daylight is light from the sun or from a fluorescent lamp expressly designed to reproduce it. Specialized types of incandescent and fluorescent lamps have been developed which emphasize specific portions of the visual spectrum, and each projects light of a different color temperature. Light no longer simply illuminates, it also creates. Lamps that are slightly yellowish are used in the home-furnishing industry to add a warm and fuzzy feeling to displays. Pinkish lighting in beauty parlors adds a healthy glow to the client's skin.

Historically, daylight — specific- ally north daylight or light coming through a north-facing window at noon — has been the standard for evaluating color in gemstones. This is because noon daylight is relatively white and therefore balanced. However, gem dealers have long recognized that the quality of daylight changes at different times of the day and in different parts of the world. North daylight in the Sonoran desert is qualitatively different from north daylight in Bangkok.

In fact, the quality of natural daylight is affected by several variables, including geographic latitude and air quality. In cities with high levels of air pollution, such as the gem capitals of Bangkok and New York, daylight is noticeably more yellowish. In addition, the relative strength and color composition of daylight changes as the day progresses. "Don't buy blue sapphire after two in the afternoon" is a bit of advice I heard on my first buying trip to Bangkok. This dealer's truism is based on the fact that as the day progresses the color composition of daylight also progresses, from red through yellow and into the blue range. The hue of a blue sapphire

viewed in natural light late in the afternoon will appear more highly saturated than the same stone viewed in the yellowish light of midmorning.[42]

The color temperature of light is measured in kelvin units. Daylight ranges

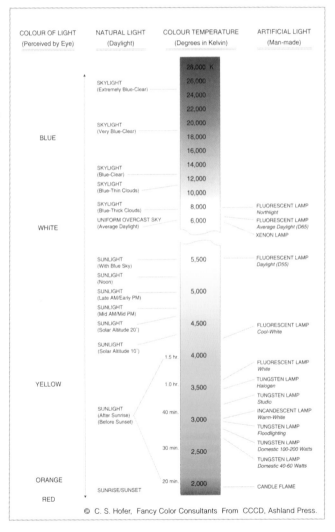

COLOUR OF LIGHT (Perceived by Eye)	NATURAL LIGHT (Daylight)	COLOUR TEMPERATURE (Degrees in Kelvin)	ARTIFICIAL LIGHT (Man-made)
		28,000 K	
	SKYLIGHT (Extremely Blue-Clear)	26,000	
		24,000	
		22,000	
	SKYLIGHT (Very Blue-Clear)	20,000	
BLUE		18,000	
		16,000	
	SKYLIGHT (Blue-Clear)	14,000	
	SKYLIGHT (Blue-Thin Clouds)	12,000	
		10,000	
	SKYLIGHT (Blue-Thick Clouds)	8,000	FLUORESCENT LAMP Northlight
	UNIFORM OVERCAST SKY (Average Daylight)	6,000	FLUORESCENT LAMP Average Daylight (D65)
WHITE			XENON LAMP
	SUNLIGHT (With Blue Sky)	5,500	FLUORESCENT LAMP Daylight (D55)
	SUNLIGHT (Noon)		
	SUNLIGHT (Late AM/Early PM)	5,000	
	SUNLIGHT (Mid AM/Mid PM)		
	SUNLIGHT (Solar Altitude 20°)	4,500	FLUORESCENT LAMP Cool-White
	SUNLIGHT (Solar Altitude 10°)		
	1.5 hr.	4,000	FLUORESCENT LAMP White
YELLOW	1.0 hr.	3,500	TUNGSTEN LAMP Halogen
			TUNGSTEN LAMP Studio
	SUNLIGHT (After Sunrise) (Before Sunset)	40 min.	INCANDESCENT LAMP Warm-White
		3,000	TUNGSTEN LAMP Floodlighting
	30 min.	2,500	TUNGSTEN LAMP Domestic 100-200 Watts
			TUNGSTEN LAMP Domestic 40-60 Watts
ORANGE	20 min.	2,000	CANDLE FLAME
RED	SUNRISE/SUNSET		

© C. S. Hofer, Fancy Color Consultants From CCCD, Ashland Press.

42. Viewed in daylight, red, orange, blue, and violet gemstones look best early in the morning and late afternoon. Yellow, green, and purple, as well as colorless gems look their best during the midmorning and midafternoon.

43. Facing north toward blue sky adds blue to the color of daylight.

44. Duratest Corporation markets a daylight equivalent called "vitalite" (5,500 kelvin) which is used by the American Gemological Lab. The MacBeth division of the Kollmorgen Corporation produces several

from 2,000 to 5,500 kelvin; that is, from red to orange to yellow then white at noon and following the reverse order back to red as the day comes to a close at sunset. Noon daylight is the most balanced. North daylight at noon falls between 5,500-6,500 units kelvin.[43]

A number of grading laboratories now use fluorescent lamps that emit light within the above parameters. Several companies produce daylight-equivalent fluorescent lamps used by gem professionals for grading and display purposes.[44] This type of lighting is available at relatively low cost and fits standard fluorescent fixtures. The availability of daylight-equivalent lighting creates the opportunity to control and stabilize the viewing environment. If gems are consistently viewed in a single lighting environment, one variable, at least, is removed.

Jewelers and gem dealers prefer an incandescent spotlight because spots, like the sun, throw a concentrated beam of light that maximizes the brilliance of a gem. Fluorescent lighting is diffused and produces a brilliance that is relatively subdued by comparison. Fluorescent light of sufficient power to show off a gem will light up a retail store like the inside of a fish market, but is not generally flattering to precious metals or to a woman's skin. Incandescent lighting is rated at around 3,200 kelvin; this means that incandescent light is distinctly yellowish. Fluorescent lighting, by contrast, can be adjusted to any kelvin temperature from a balanced white (5,500-6,500 kelvin) to distinctly bluish (7,000+ kelvin).

Although daylight — specifically north daylight between 5,500 and 6,500 kelvin — is the standard, colored gems must and should be viewed in incandescent light as well as in daylight or daylight-equivalent fluorescent lighting. When evaluating a gemstone, the aficionado should ask to see the gem in both types of lighting. This may be accomplished by taking the stone to a natural light source or, as is often the case, dealers will have daylight-equivalent lighting in their offices or, at gem shows, inside their booths.

Ideally a gemstone should be beautiful in all types of lighting. It is not necessary to remember all the technical aspects of lighting. However, it is important for the aficionado to understand that lighting quality may vary due to a number of factors, to be aware of these variables, and to observe the gem in all types of lighting as part of the evaluation process.

Diaphaneity or crystal: the fourth C

So long as the depth of its colour does not interfere with the transparency of a sapphire, the darker it is in colour the more highly is it prized.

Max Bauer, 1904

"Crystal" is probably the most misused word in the gemstone lexicon. Technically, a crystal is a substance with a definite atomic structure. Most gemstones are cut from

daylight-equivalent fluorescent lamps rated between 5,500-6,500 kelvin. The Gemological Institute of America uses 6,500-kelvin lighting manufactured by MacBeth in all its grading environments. The

American Gemological Lab uses Duratest vitalite for grading colored gemstones. Recently, System Eickhorst, a German firm, introduced the lighting system

Dialite Pro X, based on my recommendations. This system uses Solux 4,700-kelvin halogen lights coupled with 6,000-kelvin fluorescent tubes, making it possible to view a gem in a good

average daylight environment. See Richard W. Wise, "Light Up Your Life," in *Asia Precious Magazine, Guide to Industry Services*, 1998, pp. III-V.

crystals. Scientifically speaking, glass is the opposite, a substance without a definite crystal structure. Still, when the words "crystal clear" are used to describe certain types of glass which are by definition noncrystalline, the meaning is, well, clear! In gemstone connoisseurship, *crystal*, the common term for *diaphaneity*, refers to a limpid quality, an ultra-transparency that fine gemstones will exhibit.

A gem of the finest water

The idea that diaphaneity, transparency, or *crystal* is an important criterion in the evaluation of gemstones is not new. It is one, however, that has been largely ignored in the development of modern scientific gem grading systems. In earlier times, the combination of color and transparency was referred to as the gem's *water*. There was a hierarchy: a gem was classified as *first water* or *second* or *third water*. Gems that had both poor color and little transparency were referred to as *byewater*. The most exemplary stones were said to be "gems of the finest water."[45]

As early as the fourth century BC, Kautilya, the ancient Indian Machiavelli, lists among the qualities of a "good gem . . . [that it be] transparent and reflecting light from inside."[46] Sometime around 1433 the Chinese admiral Ying-yai Sheng-lan uses the term *water* to describe a particularly "clean, clear" quality of amber.[47] The famous Jean Baptiste Tavernier, seventeenth-century gem merchant, used the phrase "gem of the finest Water" to describe exceptional diamonds, gems, and pearls he encountered on his six voyages to India.[48]

Although *water* is an old and rather poetic term, it is not easily measurable. I think that our modern mania to reduce all terms to the scientific has cost us much in the way of romance and some in the way of accuracy as well. Another more modern synonym for *diaphaneity* is used to describe diamonds: the term is *super-d*. This designation, one that sounds about as romantic as a name-brand motor oil, refers to antique diamonds from India's legendary Golconda mines — stones that are reputed to exhibit an extraordinary transparency.

Gem expert Benjamin Zucker suggests, "Place a Golconda diamond alongside a modern, recently cut D-colour diamond and the purity of the Golconda stone will become evident."[49] Mary Murphy Hammid, in an essay on Golconda diamonds written for Christie's auction house, maintains: "Golconda diamonds have a degree of transparency rarely seen in stones from other localities . . . it is variously called soft, limpid, watery or clear. It is not to be confused with clarity. . . . It is not to be confused with color grade. Rather, it is a quality in which light appears to pass through the stone as if it were totally unimpeded, almost as if light were passing through a vacuum."[50] Fancy color diamond expert Stephen Hofer speculates that the quality of ultra-transparency may be the result of a quiescent geological environment on the Deccan Plateau that allowed for the development of a particularly well formed diamond crystal lattice.[51]

45. In the sixth edition of the *Dictionary of Gems and Gemology* published by GIA, Robert M. Shipley defines "water" as a term "occasionally used . . . as a comparative quality designation for color and transparency of diamonds, rubies and other stones. . . ." p. 243. Color and transparency together equal "water." Shipley goes on to mention a hierarchy — first water, second water, etc. Clearly even from earliest times, the quality of diaphaneity was recognized as an important and indispensable criterion in gemstone connoisseurship.

46. Rangarajan, *The Arthashastra*, pp. 777-778.

It is possible for a gemstone that is technically flawless to appear murky or sleepy. Sometimes, as with certain types of sapphire and spinel, this is a result of a large number of microscopic inclusions. In this sense, *crystal* might be regarded as a sort of subset of clarity, but visually, it is a distinct quality. A stone can be completely flawless and still have poor crystal. Regardless of cause, some gemstones are simply clearer or cleaner and crisper looking than others.

Perhaps the most famous example of this phenomenon is to be found in the legendary sapphires of Kashmir, the finest of which exhibit a *sleepy* or *fuzzy* appearance resulting from light refracting through and reflecting from myriad microscopic inclusions. Some Sri Lankan sapphire as well as Tanzanian pink spinel will exhibit similar phenomena. In these examples it is clear that inclusions are the culprit, and diaphaneity is really a distinct quality. When we say a stone is limpid, clear, or crystalline, we are talking about a quality quite distinct from clarity. Experts refer to such stones as "having good crystal."

From a strict grading perspective, the inclusions that create the *fuzzy* appearance in some gemstones are not visible (or at least not resolvable under 10X magnification) and have little effect on the clarity grade given a particular stone. In the case of Golconda or *super-d* diamonds, the presence or absence of ultra-transparency would have absolutely no impact on the clarity grade listed on a laboratory grading report.

Tiny inclusions are one, but only one, of the possible causes of poor crystal. Poor diaphaneity has several causes. Consider a strongly blue fluorescent diamond. Such stones are often described as visibly *oily* due to a loss of transparency when the diamond fluoresces in natural daylight. Fluorescence will be noted in a grading report, but its presence or absence cannot be said to affect the stone's clarity grade.

Many varieties of gemstones tend to lose something when viewed in certain lighting. Incandescent light is the usual culprit. Most varieties of tourmaline and garnet and some varieties of corundum "close up," "muddy," or "bleed color" when exposed to the light of an ordinary light bulb. The cause of these phenomena is not completely understood. The point is, the gem loses some transparency and some of its beauty. Therefore, another criterion is needed to describe this quality.

Crystal must be judged in various lighting environments. Different types of light have distinct color temperatures. As described above, north daylight at noon, the traditional gemstone-grading standard, is balanced between yellow and blue at 5,500 degrees kelvin. As kelvin temperature decreases, light becomes yellower; as the temperature increases, the light becomes bluer. Incandescent or light-bulb light at 2,800 kelvin is distinctly yellowish. The lighting temperature determines the color of the light, and that in turn impacts the visual appearance of the gem being viewed in that light.

47. Ying-yai Sheng-lan Ma Huan, *The Overall Survey of the Ocean's Shores, 1433* (Bangkok: White Lotus Press, 1970 reprint), p. 111.

48. Jean Baptiste Tavernier, *Travels*

In India, 1676, trans. V. Ball (New Delhi: Munshiram Manoharlal Publishers Pvt. Ltd., 1977), vol.II, p.98 .

49. Benjamin Zucker, *Gems and Jewels: A Connoisseur's Guide* (New York: Thames and Hudson, 1984), p. 86.

50. Mary Murphy Hammid, "Golconda Diamonds," *Christie's*

Magnificent Jewels (October 23, 1990, catalog), pp. 301-302.

51. Stephen Hofer, personal communication, October 2000.

Jeff Scovil; courtesy of Mountain Minerals

Three green tourmalines photographed in incandescent lighting. The two stones at either end maintain their transparency (crystal) while the center stone closes up and turns "sooty." Note the elongated bow tie–shaped black bands of extinction in the stones to the right and left.

The tendency of gems to change appearance, or to lose color, between natural daylight and incandescent light has traditionally been called *bleeding*. In blue sapphire, for example, one of the qualities that makes a Kashmir stone so desirable is that it doesn't bleed color. Due to an absence of chromium, the color of a fine Kashmir sapphire will remain unaltered as the lighting environment is changed. The color of blue sapphire from other sources may wash out; that is, lose color (hue, saturation, and tone) in bright sunlight.

The appearance of some gemstone varieties, including some ruby and sapphire and most varieties of garnet and tourmaline, will also change as the lighting environment changes. However, it is not quite accurate to use the term *bleeding* to describe the result. I doubt if any jewelry professional who regularly works with colored gemstones has failed to notice these changes. And although language lacks precision there is little choice but to use it to describe the visual effect. Tsavorite garnet seems to *close up* (lose transparency) in incandescent light while rhodolite turns *muddy* and brownish. Green and blue tourmaline pick up a gray mask and appear dull and *sooty* like the chimney of an oil lamp. Pink to red tourmaline acquires a *muddy* brownish mask that reduces transparency. Not all the effects are negative, aside from its loss of transparency: Thai ruby turns a purer red, losing its purplish secondary hue, when viewed in incandescent light.

These changes affect not only *color* (hue, saturation, and tone) but *crystal* as well. Such effects are general, but not universal. For example, ninety-eight percent of all rhodolite garnet will *muddy*, or turn brownish, losing both transparency and color saturation in incandescent light. This leaves only about two percent that retain both *color* and *crystal* under the light bulb. All other Cs being equal, if the stone is of high color, clean and well made, this two percent constitutes the crème de la crème of rhodolite garnet. The same may be said for pink tourmalines that do not *muddy*, green tourmaline that does not *gray out*, and tsavorite that retains its *open color* in incandescent light. *Crystal* becomes relatively more important in higher quality

52. George Frederick Kunz and Charles Hugh Stevenson, *The Book of The Pearl: The History, Art, Science and Industry of the Queen of Gems* (1908; reprint ed., New York: Dover Editions, 2003), pp. 370-371. Kunz suggests that the method to be used to "know good pearls" is to let a ray of sunlight fall on the pearl at an angle while the gem is held in a black velvet cloth. The light will penetrate into the skin and reveal if the pearl is speckled or has any defects.

53. Tavernier, *Travels*, vol. 2, p. 87. A pearl of this weight would probably be no more than 10mm in diameter. Most cultured pearls

gemstones; however, it is fair to say that the diaphaneity of diamond with a clarity grade of I3 is not particularly significant.

> No pearl is completely transparent, but among different specimens there are many degrees of translucency. Different qualities of pearls are described as in the case also of diamonds, as being of different "waters," and the differences between them depends upon the amount of light transmitted in each particular case.
>
> Max Bauer, 1904

Historically *crystal* has also played a part in the discrimination of the finest pearls. Before the introduction of cultured pearls, most of which are seeded with an opaque sphere ground from the shell of a freshwater mollusk, transparency, or at least translucency, was a characteristic very much valued in the finest pearls.[52] In his seventeenth-century *Travels to India,* gem merchant Tavernier describes the world's paramount pearl (circa 1670), a gem at that time in possession of a minor prince of Muscat. "This prince possesses the most beautiful pearl in the world, not by reason of its size, for it only weighs 12 1/16 carats, nor on account of its perfect roundness; but because it is so clear that you can almost see the light through it."[53] Tavernier also repeatedly uses the term *water* to describe the quality of pearls.[54]

As we have shown, diaphaneity, transparency, or *crystal* is a necessary grading criterion that deserves more than just a footnote in the discussion of quality in gemstones. Several factors including microscopic inclusions, ultraviolet fluorescence, and the color of the lighting environment may affect *crystal.*

The distinctions made here are real, in that they reflect observable phenomena that affect the beauty and desirability of gemstones. They are real also because they reflect demonstrable price differentials in the marketplace. From a grading perspective, *crystal* is a distinct and vitally important criterion; without this standard, it is impossible to describe the finest gemstones adequately. In short, crystal is the true fourth C of gemstone quality evaluation and connoisseurship.

The three Cs of gem grading; (*color, cut, and clarity)* are a good shorthand method to categorize the basic criteria used in the evaluation of beauty in gemstones. These three Cs are like the "three Rs" — they are the bedrock basics. The addition of the fourth C, *crystal*, both clarifies and completes the basic curriculum. In the next section the discussion turns to the more subtle nuances of connoisseurship.

The face-up mosaic: multicolor effect

On close examination, the face (key color) of a faceted gemstone is far from uniform. It is a complex mosaic, a shifting crazy quilt of color. Some facets are bright, others dull; some one color, some another. In the connoisseurship of gemstones, multicolor effect is simply the tendency of a gemstone

contain an opaque bead implant made from the shell of a Mississippi River clam. A relative lack of transparency (crystal) is probably the only visual qualitative difference that can be found between natural and cultured pearls.

54. Transparency in pearls can often be observed in antique jewelry. Pearls in jewelry made before 1930 will, in all probability, be natural. Often such pearls, particularly small ones, will show a distinct translucency; the Japanese use a term that translates as "wet" to describe this look. This is a phenomenon unknown in their cultured cousins except, as we shall see in Chapter 20, in tissue-nucleated Chinese freshwater pearls.

to show multiple hues or tonal variations of the same hue when viewed face up. [55]

As every gemologist knows, light behavior — refraction, reflection, and total internal reflection — is a function of proportion and cut. One light ray may enter the gem through the crown, bend and exit through the pavilion. Other rays will totally reflect inside the gem, bouncing like a pinball around the interior surfaces of the stone and eventually exiting through the crown. The behavior of each light ray, the length of its path, and its eventual exit point determines what we see in the face-up mosaic of the gem.[56]

The length of the path that light follows determines the saturation and the tone of the color we see. The longer the light path, the more color the ray picks up in its rapid passage through the interior of the gemstone. In addition, the ray also loses some color through selective absorption. In a singly refractive gem, this explains why some facets may exhibit differences in darkness or lightness (tone) or appear duller or brighter (saturation) than other portions of the stone. In a doubly refractive gem, the scene is made more complex by the splitting of each ray into two components, each containing a portion of the visible spectrum. In dichroic gems, additional hues may be added to tonal variations, further complicating the face-up mosaic.

Traditionally, gemstones such as ruby and sapphire have been judged in part by their reaction to two specific types of lighting, natural light and incandescent lighting, the modern equivalent of light from a candle. Stones that lose or *bleed* color when moved from natural to incandescent light are considered less desirable than those that hold their color in both types of light. In ruby and sapphire, multicolor effect takes the form of tonal variations of red and blue. In a visibly dichroic ruby, for example, some of the reflections will remain the same as when the stone was viewed in daylight while others will become a lighter red or pinkish. The stone appears to bleed or lose color as lighting environments are shifted. The lighter-toned reflections, the pinkish flashes, give the color a bleached-out appearance, like a curtain partly faded in the sun. This phenomenon is particularly prevalent in blue sapphire. Multicolor effect is classified as *weak*, *medium*, and *strong*.

Multicolor effect is sometimes a fault and sometimes is not. In some gemstone species it materially contributes to the stone's appeal. In primary color gems, such as ruby, sapphire, emerald, and tsavorite, where the ideal is a visually pure single hue — pure red or green, for example — the addition of any other hue or a change in saturation and tone is less than desirable. In such cases, the multicolor effect is a defect. In gems such as tourmaline and topaz multicolor effect can be and is a definite plus. The key issue is how it adds to or subtracts from the overall beauty of a given stone. In the case of topaz and tourmaline, the stone does not truly bleed color.[57] A little purple adds to rather than subtracts from the beauty of a red tourmaline. A bit of red at either end of the gem adds to the attractiveness of a

55. Multicolor effect is a new term chosen to replace the more common "dichroic effect" because that term is confusingly similar to the term *dichroism*. Dichroism describes a physical property of light. When light enters a dichroic substance it divides into two distinct rays, each containing a portion of the visible spectrum. Most gems other than diamond, spinel, and garnet are dichroic; a few, like tanzanite, are trichroic. Multicolor effect is a term that describes the tendency of a gem to show two or more hues or variations in saturation and tone of a single hue when viewed face up. Multicolor effect is a property that may or may not be caused by dichroism.

56. Thanks to Stephen Hofer for coining this evocative term.

57. The term "bleeding" describes a

peach-colored topaz. Multicolor effect and its impact on the beauty of specific gem varieties will be addressed in Part II.

Daystones, nightstones . . .

Some gem varieties look their best in direct sun or skylight.[58] Others look good in fluorescent light but fall apart when observed under the direct sun. Some individual gems will hold up well and may even appear more beautiful when viewed in subdued incandescent light. Opal is famous for this characteristic. The phenomenon is a product of a number of factors. The negative side, as discussed above, may manifest itself in several ways, including color bleeding, reduced transparency, and dulled saturation resulting from the addition or intensification of a gray or brown mask.

Some gemstone varieties are said to *prefer* or look their best in light of a certain kelvin temperature. Stones that look their best in daylight I term *daystones*; those that put their best foot forward in incandescent lighting are called *nightstones*. Topaz, aquamarine, and alexandrite are true ladies of the evening. Tourmaline and garnet are daystones. It is important to remember that individual members of a gem variety will act differently. The terms *daystone* and *nightstone* provide a convenient aid for the aficionado to mentally classify gems and to think about their behavior in different kinds of light. A good rule of thumb: check a daystone in incandescent. If you like the look of the gem under the light bulb, you will love it in daylight.

Buying gemstones: some strategic advice

It is difficult at best to advise anyone on the proper strategy for buying a gemstone. Each transaction invariably involves a relationship between two people, the buyer and the seller. However, some advice on what *not* to do may be useful.

Reinforcement:
developing color memory

The judgment of color in gemstones takes practice. Some experts maintain that the mind has no memory for color. Certainly it is true that this facility can be acquired only with training. Even experienced dealers will often carry comparison stones, gems of known quality, to compare with gems being offered for sale. Connoisseurship can be obtained and maintained only by constantly viewing and comparing gemstones. Comparison is the key. Experts achieve their mastery by constantly viewing and comparing one stone to another.

Dealers have a strategy of their own for taking advantage of the buyer's lack of color memory. The technique is simple. The dealer will begin by showing his lowest grade parcels, one after another. The objective is to "wash the eyes," to break the buyer down, frustrating him, by showing him so many poor quality stones that after a while even mediocre gems begin to look good.[59]

One method for remembering color was for centuries a closely held secret among the ethnic Chinese gem dealers of

situation where the stone loses color or becomes paler or lighter in tone and less saturated as the lighting environment shifts from daylight (or daylight-equivalent) to incandescent lighting.

58. To view a gem in skylight, turn your back on the sun to see the gemstone with the light diffused around your body. This viewing environment is superior to looking in direct sun, as it eliminates glare. Skylight is bluer than direct sunlight, particularly when you face north. Many gemstones *bleed* or lose some of their saturation and tone in direct sun. This is not a fault, but rather is to be expected. For

comparison purposes a gemstone should be observed in all possible environments: sunlight, skylight, shaded natural light, fluorescent light, and incandescent light.

Thailand.[60] We will call this memory aid *reinforcement*. As stated above, the mind has no innate color memory. How then does the aficionado develop this sense? The clue is to be found in the Thai word that denotes the finest ruby color: *kim-kim*, which translates as "salty." Saltiness is, as we know, an attribute of taste. In this situation, the dealer attempts to *reinforce* the sense of sight with that of taste. This reinforcement takes place on the most basic level. Primary color is identified with a primary taste. Thus, the dealer both sees and tastes the salty red color of the ruby.

Other well-known attempts at reinforcement try to back up sight with sight. This approach has caused much confusion through the centuries. In the East, the first three colors of fine ruby are called pigeon blood, chicken blood, and beef blood. Such terms are not easy to define nor are they of much practical use —try squeezing the first two drops of blood from a pigeon's nose, as the ancient Hindus advise, some afternoon while browsing among the rubies at Tiffany's![61] The problem, of course, is that a sense cannot reinforce itself. Other examples of this method, such as comparing the color of a gem to that of a specific flower, may have a strong poetic appeal but on a practical level would be fraught with difficulties. Flowers have been used as a comparison for centuries; little wonder, for like a beautiful gem they are a visual burst of pure color, a balm to the eye. Unfortunately each blossom may be a slightly different hue. Furthermore, the beauty of a flower is fleeting while the perfection of a gem is eternal.

The pick of the litter

Dealers love to sell parcels of gemstones. This is often because the dealer himself purchased the stones in a parcel and he would rather sell several stones than just one. If the aficionado develops his passion beyond the level of novice, he will often find himself looking at a number of stones contained in a paper envelope or parcel. Just as inevitably he or she will be offered entire parcels by dealers at what are said to be "bargain" prices. Such offers can be very tempting. The collector should resist such temptation with every fiber of his being.

The construction of parcels is a minor art form and is practiced with care by gem dealers. It is good to remember that gems always look better grouped together in a parcel. Every parcel can be divided into at least three portions. First there are the *eyes,* the finest stones in the parcel, so called because they flash their lovely lashes at us. They call to us because they are beautiful, but they are also like the sirens of Odysseus: they mean to tempt us, and they will play us false. The second portion consists of the mediocre stones that are usually the largest number in the parcel. They look pretty good when viewed together but, for the connoisseur, pretty good is not good at all. The savvy aficionado is aware of this and always isolates and views each stone singly. The third section of the parcel contains the *dogs*. This is a technical term and refers to the real bow-wows of the parcel. Usually there are at least as many *dogs* as there are

59. Richard W. Hughes, *Ruby & Sapphire* (Boulder, Colorado: RWH Publishing, 1998), p. 225. I had firsthand experience with this selling strategy. On my first trip to Bangkok I spent most of a week looking at one low-grade parcel after another. Luckily I split my time between two brokers, spending about three hours a day with each. (The exercise was not completely in vain; the broker who showed the low-quality stones also provided a free lunch.) Toward the end of the week I did manage to purchase a two-carat ruby at a bargain price.

60. Barry Hodgin, personal communication, 1986.

61. Souindro Mohun Tagore, *Mani Mala: A Treatise on Gems* (1879; reprint ed., Nairobi, Kenya: N.R. Barot, 1996), vol. 1, pp. 241-242.

Far from arbitrary, the construction of parcels is a minor art form. Gemstone parcels normally contain a range of qualities.

eyes.

Dealers will normally quote two prices, the parcel price and the pick price. The difference between the two prices should give the buyer some idea just how large the disparity is between the eyes and the dogs of the parcel. If there is no disparity there is no reason why the dealer should not allow selection at the parcel price. Selection from

a parcel is called *the pick*: always pick! The dealer can always sell the inferior stones at a reduced price; the collector's objective is to *pick the eyes* out of the parcel, preferably at the parcel price. Sometimes the dealer will ask the buyer to make a selection before he establishes the price. This puts the buyer at a distinct disadvantage. If selection is allowed, the price should be stated before the buyer does the work of picking.

Pairs and suites

A matched pair of stones is worth approximately fifteen percent more than two single stones. Three or more matched stones are called a suite. Add ten percent per carat for each stone added to the suite. Parcels sometimes give the aficionado the opportunity to pick a pair or a suite. Dealers, on the other hand, will usually charge less for a larger pick from a parcel. Tactically, the aficionado should first establish the pick price before making a selection, then select from the parcel. By long-established custom in the trade, once a price has been established, it cannot be withdrawn. The buyer will often have to remind the dealer of that fact, sometimes emphatically, once a particularly astute selection is made. Picking a pair or a suite may justify the higher selection price.

Investing in gemstones

Gemstones are hard assets. Historically they have been seen as a hedge against inflation and the breakdown of more abstract forms of investment such as stocks and bonds. Gems are a small portable concentration of wealth. Their size has made them an excellent choice for those who wish to hide assets and for refugees who have been forced, for political or religious reasons, to flee their homes. One somewhat tongue-in-cheek theory has it that gemstones are a permanent store of value. According to this theory, gems never increase or decrease in value but have remained stable for thousands of years while currencies have fluctuated wildly.

Investments such as stocks and bonds trade in an orderly market. The New York Stock Exchange, for example, guarantees that its members' stocks can be traded at any time the exchange is open. For this reason, investments of this kind are liquid. Stocks and bonds have an established value and exchanges operate on volume so the commission on any given transaction is very small.

Gemstones do not trade in an orderly market. This is something of an understatement. There are no exchanges to facilitate trading, though in recent years auction houses have fulfilled the role to some extent. Each gemstone is unique and so, therefore, is its price. Gems normally pass through many hands before they reach those of the collector. When the investor wishes to sell he must often resort to the wholesale market. The gap between retail and wholesale must be bridged if the gem investor is to make a profit. These are real problems and the collector should be aware of them before deciding to invest.

Auctions provide a potential though risky option for the collector-investor. Since the 1970s major auction houses have provided a venue for buying and selling of particularly fine and rare gemstones. Fancy color diamonds have benefited most from the publicity and excitement generated by the auction process. As of the end of the 1980s fancy color diamonds held nineteen of the twenty record per-carat prices paid for gemstones. Other gem varieties have benefited as well. Kashmir sapphires, Burmese rubies, and Paraiba tourmalines regularly achieve "retail" prices at auction. The reader should remember the words "particularly fine" and "rare" in this context. The collector wishing to build a portfolio should follow a very simple strategy — *buy only the best*. Gemstones of mediocre quality usually sell below "wholesale" at auction.

Gemstones do increase in value, sometimes dramatically. Witness, for example, price increases in Paraiba tourmaline, Kashmir sapphire, and fancy color diamonds since 1980. Gemstones are a long-term investment. Gemstone prices seesaw, like most other investments, but over the long term values have risen significantly.

The certificate game

The past two decades have seen a proliferation of independent gemological laboratories. Gem labs issue grading reports which are often referred to as "certificates" in the gem trade. These reports may cover a number of grading issues including country of origin, the presence or absence of color and clarity treatments, and actual quality grading of a given gem. Certificates can be a useful tool for the collector. They are not, however, the be all and end all. Yes, they look impressive, but it is also too easy for the timid or inexperienced aficionado to become dependent on them. This tendency is what experts call "buying the cert." Laboratories certify gemstones but unfortunately no one certifies laboratories.

There are a number of highly qualified gemological laboratories: the Gemological Institute of America, American Gemological Laboratories, American Gem Trade Laboratory, the European Gemological Laboratory, and the American Gem Society, to name just the more important American labs. However, each of these laboratories has its own methodology and often these methods do not overlap. There are no uniform requirements, no universally accepted methods. Grading expertise is another variable. Depending on what sort of service is required — country of origin determination, presence of treatments, gem grading — each lab approaches these issues in its own way. Thus, it is possible for one lab to issue a report concluding that a gem is untreated while another determines that the stone has been heat enhanced. One lab may call a sapphire "pink" while another calls it "padparadscha" simply because of a disagreement over definitions. Dealers are very aware of these differences and will try to use a lab that will provide the most useful certificate.

The serious collector will find it advisable to become conversant with the reports issued by the major gemological laboratories as well as with their reputed strengths and weaknesses. Better still, look at the gem; look at a lot of gems. There is no real shortcut to connoisseurship.

Connoisseurship: Grading Special Cases

Good gems are hexagonal, rectangular or circular in shape, pure in colour, easily settable in jewellery, unblemished, smooth, heavy, lustrous, transparent and reflecting light from inside. Any gem of faint colour, lacking lustre, grainy, blemished, with holes in it, cut badly or scratched is bad.

Kautilya, 400 BC

CONNOISSEURSHIP IN PHENOMENAL GEMSTONES: STARS AND CAT'S-EYES

A cat's-eye is an optical effect that can be produced in a number of different gemstones by the way the inclusions are oriented in the cutting of the finished stone. The inclusion responsible is normally rutile, a mineral that crystallizes in long hair- or needlelike structures. Rutile hairs often occur in dense parallel masses like broomstraw along a specific crystal direction. The cutter fashions the stone *en cabochon* so that it includes rutile needles going in only one direction. When light shines directly on the stone, a band of light is produced that runs perpendicular to the direction of the needles. The phenomenon can also be observed in a spool of thread. In a gem, its translucency and the dome of the cabochon, cut convex to concentrate the reflection, can produce a sharp line that resembles the iris in a cat's eye. This same phenomenon is the cause of the star in star sapphire.

Jeff Scovil; courtesy of Mine Design

A 14.40-carat blue star sapphire of unexceptional color with a well-formed star.

Sapphire crystals are six-sided. As sapphire crystals grow, the rutile inclusions growing inside the crystal align themselves along the six directions of crystal growth. If the cabochon is oriented and cut properly, it produces three crossing bands of light, each ray at a sixty-degree angle and perpendicular to each of the six concentrations of rutile needles, forming a six-sided star.

Phenomenal stones such as stars and cat's-eyes have special grading criteria in addition to the four Cs. *Color, clarity, crystal* and *cut* are still part of the equation, but of equal importance is the phenomenon itself. Ideally, in star stones the star should be distinct, perfectly centered, and have all six rays or legs straight and of equal length and strength. The star is tested by positioning the stone directly beneath a single ordinary incandescent light source or by placing the stone in direct sunlight. Ordinary light and a single light source are key. Two light bulbs will produce twin stars. Stones that require the concentrated beam of a flashlight or maglight to bring out a distinct star are much less desirable. The stone must be viewed directly under the light source to check the centering of the star or eye.

The more distinct, centered, and perfectly formed the star or eye, the finer the stone. A strong punchy phenomenal effect is a necessary condition for a stone to be considered fine, but it is not, by itself, sufficient to make a determination.

Hue, saturation, tone

The judgment of color of star and cat's-eye gems follows the same rules as faceted stones of the same variety. Thus the finest color (hue, saturation, and tone) of a star sapphire mirrors that of faceted blue sapphire; the same applies to ruby. However, the color seen in phenomenal stones is the body or transmitted color, not the *key* (reflected) color used in defining quality in faceted gemstones.

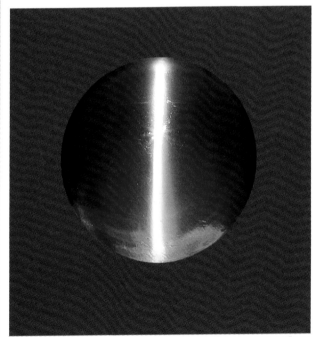

Harold and Erica Van Pelt; courtesy of Kalil Elawar

Exceptional alexandrite showing a bright, straight, well-formed cat's-eye running directly down the center of the cabochon.

Translucency and crystal

The fourth C plays a defining role in the evaluation of cat's-eyes and star stones. Phenomenal stones are often dark toned and only semi-translucent. Stones of this description often will have a very distinct star or eye. Once that is established, the more translucent and limpid the stone, the more visually pleasing it will be. All other factors being equal — hue, saturation, tone, the definition of the star or eye — the more transparent the stone, the finer the stone. A high degree of translucency is the demarcation between the very good and the very finest qualities in the connoisseurship of phenomenal gemstones. The finest star or cat's-eye stone is one that has a clean, limpid, beautiful body color that also shows a bright well formed star or eye.

Cat's-eye stones can be thought of as one-legged stars, except that in the evaluation of a cat's-eye, the stone is rotated three hundred sixty degrees under the light source. In the finest cat's-eyes, the eye will appear to expand and contract, open and close, like the iris of a cat's eye. As with star stones, the eye should be distinct, centered, and straight as an arrow.

Cut

Star and cat's-eye stones must be cut *en cabochon* and are normally cut either oval or round. If the shape is oval, the eye and the star follow the long axis of the stone.

Rarity

Star stones, ruby and sapphire, are considered less valuable than faceted stones in the marketplace. Heating technology makes it possible to "burn out" the rutile inclusions responsible for the star phenomenon, clarifying the crystal and improving the color so that a more valuable faceted gem can be cut from the resulting rough. For this reason, there are very few high quality star sapphires and rubies, and most of what is available will be somewhat deficient in color.

CONNOISSEURSHIP IN COLORLESS DIAMONDS

Cut: the first C

The form, the outward shape of a diamond, has from earliest times been an important factor influencing the desirability of a diamond. The *Ratnapariksa,* a Sanskrit text written sometime before the fourth century BC, sets forth the standards for evaluating a diamond. According to the text the most important thing is that the diamond have the ideal bipyramidal crystal form — "the six sharp points, the eight identical plane facets, the twelve narrow, straight edges are the basis of the natural qualities of the diamond."[62] Of course in those days the technology necessary to cut a diamond did not exist and gems of perfect crystal form were also the most brilliant and dispersive. Since the invention of faceting, man has worked to perfect the form of the diamond to maximize the optical qualities of brilliance,

62. Lenzen, *History of Diamond Production*, p. 16.

dispersion, and scintillation for which the gem is so highly valued.

Before proceeding further it is necessary to define our terms. *Brilliance*, as discussed earlier, is the total quantity of light reflected by the gemstone back to the eye of the viewer. *Dispersion* is the property of breaking white light up into its component colors; this is the property observed as a rainbow when light is passed through a prism. *Dispersion* is a property of all transparent gemstones but it is usually masked by the color in colored gems. Dispersion is a defining criterion in diamond.

Scintillation describes the breakup of light into individual points or flashes. A given gem's scintillation is directly related to the number of facets cut into it. *Scintillation* is to be distinguished from *brilliance*, which is the amount or quantity of light reflected. The more facets a gem has, the more scintillation. Scintillation doesn't produce more light (brilliance), it simply breaks the refracted color into segments. This would seem to lead logically to the conclusion that the more facets a gem has the better. However, this is not the case. The more facets cut, the smaller each must be. Eventually a point is reached where too many very small facets produce tiny little points of light creating a visual fuzziness that begins to obscure

the beauty of the stone. In short, too much scintillation can be too much of a good thing!

In recent years, diamond-cutting standards have reached a level of precision rarely approached in colored gemstones. Diamond is singly refractive and is generally not color zoned. As we know, color is the prime criterion in judging the beauty of colored stones. Diamond, because it has no

EightStar Diamond

American Star, a 13.42 carat ideal cut (D-Flawless) round brilliant cut diamond.

color, is appreciated chiefly for its brilliance, dispersion, and scintillation. These qualities are a function of cut. Cut is the critical issue and without question the most important of the four Cs in the evaluation of colorless diamond. Good cutting is responsible for the brilliance, dispersion, and scintillation—in short, the beauty —and is, therefore, the most important criterion in evaluating a diamond.

In a search for the cutting style that would yield the best combination of dispersion and brilliance, a master cutter by the name of Marcel Tolkowsky developed a set of proportions and angles which maximized the brilliance of a *round* diamond. In 1919 Tolkowsky observed and measured a large number of diamonds. He then reduced the proportions of those with the greatest brilliance and dispersion to a mathematical formula that has come to be known as the "ideal cut." Over the years there have been many subtle changes to Tolkowsky's notion, depending on who was calling the diamond "ideal."[63]

Although Tolkowsky reduced his standard to a mathematical model, his method was empirical: he arrived at his conclusions by comparing actual diamonds. The collector buying a Tolkowsky "ideal" cut diamond was buying the eye of a great diamondtaire. Actual measurements of brilliance and dispersion by sophisticated modern instruments prove that his model is indeed one excellent way of proportioning a diamond.

However, the ideal cut is of limited value, since Tolkowsky confined his investigation to the round diamond. The collector will find much greater confusion where other shapes are concerned — there are no generally accepted ideal proportions for any other shape.

From the beginning, some experts have argued that establishing one set of proportions as ideal and labeling all others as less desirable is wrong. For years a debate over the concept of "ideal" proportions has been raging inside the diamond trade. Just as the space between any two existing points on a line is infinitely divisible, it is possible to proportionally alter the ideal measurements in an infinite number of ways to produce an infinite number of formulae that will maximize the brilliance of a diamond. Thus, by using computer modeling, it is at least theoretically possible to define an infinite number of ideal cuts. This, at least, was this author's argument in early 1998.[64]

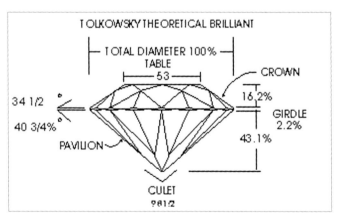

63. Tolkowsky's 1919 model diamond was an old European cut, the precursor to the modern brilliant. 64. Richard W. Wise, "Diamond Cutting: New Concepts, New Millennium," *The Guide, Gem Market News*, March-April 1998, p. 7.

For many years diamond pricing also has been based on the Tolkowsky model. Gemologists were taught that there were four classes of cut. At the top of the heap sat the Tolkowsky ideal. As stones varied from these proportions they were discounted. As of this writing, it is still possible to have as much as a seventy percent price differential between round diamonds carrying identical color and clarity grades solely on the basis of the stone's proportions. This has been the jeweler's fudge factor. So long as cut grades were kept off grading certificates, sellers could meet and beat competitor's prices simply by offering the same color and clarity and a poorer cut.

Toward the end of the 1990s, under increasing consumer pressure, laboratories began issuing cut grades on their diamond grading reports. These grades were loosely based on traditional Tolkowsky proportions. Diamond dealers who fiercely resisted this trend feared that once the buyer was able to obtain a certificate that graded all four Cs, the diamond would be reduced to the status of a commodity. Their fears were well founded but, as it turns out, their worries may be over.

Multiply tiny variations in proportions by a factor of ten thousand and you have a general idea of the method used in a landmark study of diamond cut and brilliance by the Gemological Institute of America. The GIA computer modeled ten thousand variations in an attempt to determine, once and for all, what are the best proportions for a round brilliant cut diamond.

What the GIA researchers discovered is that there are several sets of proportions that will maximize brilliance. Further, they discovered that dispersion parameters are similarly dispersed. All sorts of odd proportions will work, and the best proportions for dispersion do not overlap with the best sets of proportions for brilliance.[65] In short, according to GIA, there is no ideal cut. Stones that deliver maximum brilliance are deficient in dispersion and vice versa. There are hundreds of subtle variations. Science has at last discovered its own limitations. The subtlety of the human faculty of judgment and the old wisdom has been vindicated. Science, it seems, cannot reduce the delectation of gemstones to a series of formulas and angles.

As of this writing, some labs are beginning to use instruments specifically designed to measure the actual brilliance of a diamond.[66] The king may be dead, but the throne remains empty. This means short-term anarchy while the members of the trade pick their teeth and wonder what all this means. The market is not likely to wait and will, as usual, have the final say, at least where price is concerned. Scientific measurement is the wave of the future. Given GIA findings, this seems the most obvious course. Though most laboratories still issue cut grades based on the mathematical model developed by Tolkowsky, that standard is clearly the wave of the past. Grading laboratories were about to enthrone a specific set of cutting proportions just as those proportions were becoming obsolete.

65. Hemphill et al., "Modeling the Appearance of the Round Brilliant Cut Diamond: An Analysis of Brilliance," *Gems & Gemology*, Winter 1998, pp. 158-183; Reinitz et al., "Modeling the Appearance of the Round Brilliant Cut Diamond: An Analysis of Fire, and More About Brilliance," *Gems & Gemology*, Fall 2001, pp. 174-197.

66. One laboratory, Diamond Profile, evaluates cut by measuring light return using a digital imaging spectrophotometer.

The GIA study appears to have changed everything. It seems that grading based on an optical model, using instruments measuring the actual brilliance and dispersion of a diamond, is inevitable. It really seems to make the most sense. In the brave new world of laboratory grading, we will see grading reports issued with actual measurements of brilliance and dispersion. The old standard of four classes of cut, based on a mathematical model that once ruled the market, eventually will be consigned to the dustbin of history. Few will continue using an abstract mathematical model that is just one among many.

For the aficionado collector this creates a dilemma and an opportunity. Good cutting is of primary importance. As instrumentation gains wider currency, many diamonds previously discounted because they differed from Tolkowsky's model will become more valuable simply because they deliver the goods.

In theory diamond cut can be graded much as cut is graded in colored stones; i.e., by visually measuring light return to the eye (see Chapter 3, "Performing the test"). However, there are a couple of problems. Diamonds are relatively well cut when compared to colored stones. A ruby with eighty percent brilliance is considered a very well cut stone. A diamond with eighty percent brilliance is a poorly cut stone. An exceptionally well cut diamond can be as much as ninety-nine percent brilliant.[67] Detecting the difference between ninety-five and ninety-nine percent light return is very difficult, if not impossible, for any but the

most experienced. The ability to do so creates some real opportunities for the diamond connoisseur. It may also mean that, freed from the tyranny of the *ideal cut*, lapidaries may achieve a certain degree of freedom similar to that of colored stone cutters (Chapter 3). The future is difficult to predict.[68]

Buying for beauty: a contrarian approach to round diamonds

I believe that in the near future the old mathematical standard will be replaced by an objective scientific standard that uses modern instruments to measure the actual brilliance and dispersion in individual diamonds. A given diamond cut will be graded by actually measuring its brilliance and dispersion without reference to any sort of mathematical standard. The technology is in place to make such measurements. In fact, a few gem laboratories have begun to use these instruments.

A window of opportunity has opened for the savvy connoisseur. It is possible for the collector to purchase a diamond subject to laboratory analysis and to submit said diamond to a lab that uses actual light measurement to grade diamonds. The aficionado can then use the lab report to test his own judgment. This assumes that the aficionado has spent a good deal of time comparing diamonds. Comparison is, as always, the key. The eye must be developed and this can be done only by constantly comparing one stone to another. This is definitely not a route to be taken by the consumer interested in saving money on a

67. Wise, "Diamond Cutting," p. 7.

68. Ibid., p. 9.

one-time purchase of his fiancée's engagement ring. The serious aficionado should start with certified ideal cuts to establish a point of departure; the dilettante should stick with certified ideals.

Color in diamond

Diamond is a special case! Diamond is colorless so there is no need to discuss either hue or saturation. Color in diamond is normally limited to tints, tonal variations of yellow and less frequently gray or brown. The word tint is used to discuss hues that are so light in tone that a stone would be termed yellowish or brownish rather than yellow or brown; the darker the tint the less desirable the stone. If the diamond does have a well-defined hue then it is a fancy color diamond, and therefore in an entirely different category and evaluated like any other colored stone.[69]

Color in colored gemstones is judged face up, color in colorless diamond is judged face down.[70] Body color, not key color, is the criterion. This technique makes sense for two reasons. First, diamond is singly refractive; the color is the same regardless from which crystal axis the stone is viewed. Second, turning the stone face down eliminates the distraction of brilliance and allows the grader to observe the minute tints (tonal variations) of yellow, which define relative colorlessness. The objective is the total elimination of color. Diamond colors are graded on an alphabetical scale from D to Z; there are no A, B, or C grades. D is totally colorless. Z is discernibly yellowish.

The letter grades indicating the tonal variations in a face-up stone are first grouped in threes. D through F are called *colorless*. That is, there is no discernable tint of yellow when the gem is viewed face up. G through I are termed *near colorless*. J through L show a *faint yellow* when viewed face up. From N to Z the groups get larger; N through R are termed *very light yellow*, S through Z are called *light yellow*.[71]

This grading method sometimes can lead to seeming contradictions. Dealers are sometimes heard to say that the stone is slightly yellowish, e.g. J color, but it faces up white, which translated means that the stone's key color appears colorless when the diamond is viewed face up. The dealer's point here is that the stone appears whiter (less yellow) and is therefore worth more than its color grade would indicate. This visual discrepancy may be a function of cut or a byproduct of ultraviolet fluorescence.

D   G   I   L   Z

Courtesy of J. Landau, Inc.

Diamonds face down in grading tray with tonal variations of yellow body color illustrating the range of GIA diamond grades D-Z.

69. A tint can be thought of as a discoloration of the stone that interferes with its crystalline colorlessness.

70. Actually the diamond is placed table down at a forty-five degree angle in a white grading tray under a specially designed fluorescent light source (GIA Gemolite). The point here is to judge the amount of yellow in the transmitted color as seen through the pavilion of the stone.

71. Despite terms such as *light yellow,* diamonds graded S-Z are not considered yellow diamonds. According to the GIA standard, to be called yellow, a diamond must have a more saturated yellow hue than the Z master stone viewed face up. Fancy color diamonds are graded face up, as are all colored gemstones.

72. The Gemological Institute of America stipulates the use of a

Diamonds are color graded in a special lighting environment. Given the variability of natural daylight, experienced graders prefer diffused fluorescent lighting with a kelvin temperature rating of 6,500.[72] This type of lighting is difficult to find in a normal jewelry store or at a gem show. Jewelers prefer to show stones under incandescent spotlights because they maximize the diamond's brilliance. This is perfectly legitimate; remember, gems are creatures of the light. However, jewelers specializing in gems will often have special grading lamps in their offices or at gem shows.

Fluorescence

About one third of all diamonds will fluoresce blue in ultraviolet light. The strength of this phenomenon will vary from weak to strong. Although fluorescence is not visible to the human eye, its effect is. Blue is the color complement of yellow. If it is strong enough, blue ultraviolet fluorescence will nullify to some degree the yellow in a diamond's body color, resulting in a stone that appears "whiter" (colorless) than it would appear if fluorescence were not present. In earlier times these colorless blue fluorescent diamonds were referred to as "blue-whites."

In the past twenty years, "blue-white" diamonds have gone out of favor mainly because of the problems they created for the professional grader.[73] This situation had nothing to do with the visual appearance of the stone. During the hard asset investment craze of the late 1970s, thousands of

dollars, sometimes tens of thousands, rode on the color grade given a diamond on a laboratory report. A strongly fluorescent stone was usually downgraded.[74] For this reason, blue-white fluorescent diamonds have been available more recently at something of a discount.

Recently, the Gemological Institute of America conducted a color preference test comparing fluorescent blue diamonds against diamonds of comparable color that were inert under ultraviolet light.[75] In this test, professional graders expressed a clear preference for the appearance of blue fluorescent stones. Surprise, surprise! In the world of colorless diamonds, blue fluorescence will improve the look of a diamond. Not only will the blue nullify some of the yellow in the body color, but also the fluorescence often will lap over into the visible spectrum, actually punching up the saturation of the stone and giving it a whiter-brighter appearance. Given the Gemological Institute's standing in the industry, this test and its results should have a real effect on future diamond prices; it should certainly be noted by the connoisseur.

In the connoisseurship of colorless diamonds, fluorescence can be very positive. A yellowish diamond may appear a good deal whiter due to blue fluorescence. And, to paraphrase the late jazz great Duke Ellington, if it looks good, it is good!

Fluorescence does have a single downside. If it is very strong, the diamond will appear fuzzy or "oily" when the stone is viewed face up in the rich ultraviolet of

6,500-kelvin Gemolite bulb, available through GIA's Gem Instruments division (see Chapter 4).

73. Under FTC guidelines, the use of the term "blue-white" is considered an unfair trade practice if the stone

"shows any color or any trace of any color other than blue or bluish" under north daylight lighting (23.14). Thus it would seem that any diamond graded below F on the GIA-GTL colorless scale legally cannot be termed a *blue white*.

74. Verilux, the light tube used since the 1950s for diamond grading by GIA, was designed to have low ultraviolet emissions to avoid stimulating fluorescent stones. However, due to a change in manufacturers, bulbs made since

the early 1990s actually emit a good deal of ultraviolet light. Fluorescent diamonds graded in the last decade are likely to have received a higher color grade than the same stone graded a decade earlier. Grading experiments using filters to

direct sunlight. This effect reduces the transparency of the stone and is detrimental to the beauty of the diamond. Gemologists grade fluorescence in a special ultraviolet light box; grading reports usually designate fluorescence on a scale from faint to strong. Diamonds should always be examined in natural daylight to check the visual effect of fluorescence.

Clarity grading diamond

Diamonds are graded for clarity using the loupe standard; this means the stone is examined using 10X magnification. As stated earlier, this method is distinctly different from the standard for colored stones; in that case the naked eye is used as the standard for judging clarity. The dual standard exists for a number of reasons. A fine diamond is relatively colorless and has exceptional diaphaneity; that is, it is normally crystal clear. The existence of visual inclusions, therefore, becomes relatively more important. Even microscopic inclusions can affect crystal (diaphaneity).

The adoption of a microscopic standard (or what dealers call a loupe-clean standard) for diamonds also had something to do with the *appearance* of rarity. Before the invention of the magnifying lens, visual appearance was, by default, the only standard for judgment. As diamond supplies increased in the twentieth century, it was necessary to create a means whereby apparent rarity was increased. What better way than to introduce an absurdly stringent standard of judgment? Why "absurdly"

stringent? Because, by definition, the first five categories of diamond clarity — *internally flawless* (IF), *very very slightly included* (VVS1 and VVS2), *very slightly included* (VS1 and VS2), and *slightly included* (SI1) — are visually identical. By definition, the inclusions in the first six clarity

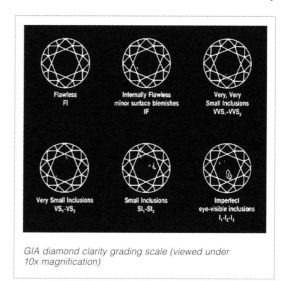

GIA diamond clarity grading scale (viewed under 10x magnification)

grades, *internally flawless* through SI1, do not materially affect the beauty or durability of the stone. Only in gems graded SI2 and *imperfect* I1, 2, and 3 do the inclusions become flaws. The first six clarity grades are visually identical. Why pay the thirty to forty percent premium demanded in the marketplace for VVS or even VS gems? [76] Clarity grading in colorless diamond has more to do with the politics of beauty than with beauty itself. This fact is not completely lost on the market!

screen out ultraviolet produced by Verilux bulbs have resulted in downgrading of color on an average of between one half and one and one half color grades. See Thomas E. Tashey, "The Effect of Fluorescence

on the Color Grading & Appearance of White and Off White Diamonds," *The Professional Gemologist*, vol. 3, no. 1, Spring/Summer 2000, p. 5.

75. Thomas M. Moses et al., "A Contribution to Understanding the

Effect of Blue Fluorescence," *Gems & Gemology*, Winter 1997, pp. 244-259.

76. At what clarity is a diamond eye-clean? I was taught that any gem from SI1 up (SI1, VS, VVS grades and of course I-Flawless) were by definition

eye-clean (no inclusions visible to the naked eye). It seems, though, that inclusions are allowed to be larger in larger gems. A five-carat diamond might very well have eye-visible inclusions and have a

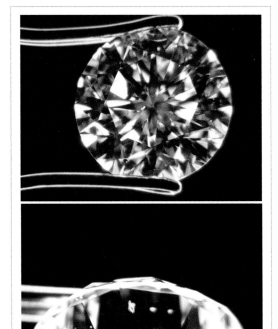

A 2.24-carat round brilliant-cut diamond with a GIA-GTL clarity grade of SI1 viewed under magnification. (top): Invisible to the eye, grade-making inclusions are barely visible under 10X magnification. (bottom): Side view magnified to 20X. Inclusions of this size have no appreciable effect on either the beauty or the durability of the gem, but will substantially lower the price.

An examination of the very accurate wholesale diamond price list issued by *The Guide* shows that the visual standard of clarity matters most in the market. Except for the highest grade, the legendary *D-Flawless*, diamond prices in all color grades increase in proportionate increments from SI1 to IF. The largest percentage jump, seventy-three percent, is between the grade

SI1, which is the lowest eye-clean grade, and *imperfect* (I1), the first grade in which inclusions are visible in the face-up position.

What then is the difference between a D-color diamond graded flawless and a D-color diamond with a clarity grade of SI1? The answer, other than a forty percent higher price tag for the flawless stone, is very little. From the perspective of beauty, assuming that both gems are eye-flawless, there is no difference at all.

CONNOISSEURSHIP IN NATURAL FANCY COLOR DIAMONDS

Unlike colorless diamonds, which are evaluated face down by analyzing the stone's body color, fancy color diamonds, like all gems of color, are evaluated face up by analyzing the stone's key color. Key color is the refracted color, the color of the brilliance as distinguished from the body color, the color transmitted through the body of the gem.

As a class, fancy color diamonds are so rare, and the prices they command are so high, that rarity, not beauty, is the engine that drives this market. The fancy color diamond market can also be said to be certificate driven. Fancy color diamonds are usually sold with a written color description and guarantee of natural origin issued by a gemological laboratory. These reports are known as "certificates" in the gem trade. By far the most influential certificates are those issued by the Gemological Institute of America's Gem Trade Laboratory (GIA-GTL). [77] It is fair

laboratory grade of VS2. I am referring to the eye-clean boundary, no matter at what letter grade. Cf.

Gary Roskin, *Photo Masters for Diamond Grading* (Chicago: Gemworld International, Inc., 1994).

77. John M. King et al., "Color Grading of Fancy Color Diamonds *Gems & Gemology*, Winter 1994, p. 222.

to say that virtually all important fancy color diamonds are accompanied by a grading report issued by GIA-GTL.

In 1994 GIA-GTL completely revamped its grading criteria for fancy color diamonds. The new grading standards essentially

© The Gemological Institute of America

Which is more desirable, Fancy Intense or Fancy Deep? The language on the certificate isn't much help. The question should be, which is more beautiful? — but it's a difficult call. The 2.18-carat emerald cut on the left was graded Fancy Intense Blue by GIA-GTL. The 2.47-carat gem at right carries a grade of Fancy Deep (the same grade as the Hope Diamond).

raised the bar for certain rare colors of diamond to receive one of GIA-GTL's coveted fancy color labels. Fancy color is a name traditionally applied to all hues of colored diamonds. In the new standards the GIA linked the color grade to the rarity of the hue! This will require a bit of explanation.

GIA-GTL uses twenty-seven hue names but only nine grades for classifying fancy color diamonds. The nine grades are based on the saturation and tone of the hue. Moving from pale to vivid and light to dark the nine designations are *faint*, *very light*, *light*, *fancy light*, *fancy*, *fancy intense*, *fancy vivid*, *fancy deep*, and *fancy dark*. *Fancy deep* and *fancy vivid* were designations

added in 1994.[78] These categories have become the industry standard for describing color in diamonds. The nine grades are not applicable to all colors. The first three grading levels, *faint*, *very light*, and *light*, do not carry the prefix "fancy" and are used on GIA-GTL grading reports to describe stones of hues other than yellow, and brown of very low saturation and tone. Brown and yellow diamonds of similar saturation and tone would receive a letter grade on GIA's colorless diamond scale.

A diamond with the faintest trace of bluish hue will be graded "light blue" on the GTL fancy grading scale. A yellow, gray, or brown stone of identical saturation and tone will be classified somewhere between S and Z on the GIA colorless diamond scale.[79] The latter grade classifies the stone as an off-color colorless diamond. Yet the yellow or brown stone has at least as much color saturation as the blue stone. However, though neither stone has much face-up color at all, rarity dictates that the yellowish or brownish stone receive a low letter grade on the colorless scale and the bluish stone receive the very desirable accolade *fancy light blue*.

The author examined a diamond accompanied by a GIA-GTL grading report that designated the stone as *fancy blue*. The stone appeared to have a primary gray hue of twenty percent tone, with a five percent blue secondary hue. In short, the diamond

78. King, "Color Grading," p. 222. *Fancy vivid* refers to medium-toned gems (forty to sixty percent) with vivid saturation. *Fancy deep* refers to colors of medium to dark tones with vivid saturation. For a full

discussion of the relationship between hue, saturation, and tone see Chapter 3.

79. S-Z are called "very light yellow" on the GIA colorless diamond grading scale. Stones graded at this

level will show very little color face up because the hue lacks sufficient saturation and tone to be considered more than yellowish. Blue diamonds of a similar tonal level face up would be graded as blue. King, "Color Grading," p. 237, states: "Because

yellow is by far the most common, a greater depth of this color is required for a stone to receive a "fancy" grade. In contrast, colors such as pink and blue are both relatively rare and occur in much

Fancy color diamonds are graded using a de facto two-step scale. As with other colored stones, the first and most important step is at the point where the gem is eye-clean or eye-flawless (GIA grade SI1-SI2). A stone that shows no visible inclusions in the face-up position will command a substantial premium over a stone that is visibly included (GIA grade I1-I3). A small premium will be charged for a stone that is loupe clean; that is, flawless under 10X magnification (GIA grade IF).[86] Fancy color diamonds are rare; therefore, there is no need to adhere to the overly stringent standard used for colorless diamonds. There is no need to create an impression of rarity where none exists.[87]

Grading under magnification is the second step in the two-step scale. According to dealers I interviewed, stones with grades above SI2 using the colorless clarity grading scale would carry some dollar premium over the stone that is visibly eye-clean. As to how high the premium, there was no consensus. Some dealers maintained that there were only two grades: eye-clean and imperfect (eye-visible inclusions). One thing is clear: the higher the degree of rarity of a particular color the less important clarity becomes. It is fair to say that in what might be called the "connoisseur categories" — *fancy intense*, *fancy vivid*, *fancy dark*, and *fancy deep* — fancy color diamonds are so rare that those graded VS2 and above carry only the smallest dollar premiums over eye-clean stones.

Treatments

Given the prices asked for fancy color diamonds, it is not surprising that methods have been found to induce or enhance diamond color artificially. Treated stones sell at dramatically lower prices than those of natural color. The two most common types of treatment are irradiation and high pressure/high temperature (HPHT). Diagnosing the origin of color often requires the use of sophisticated instruments and techniques not available to the jeweler-gemologist. The aficionado is well advised to consider only fancy color diamonds evaluated by GIA-GTL or other competent independent laboratories and that have "natural color" clearly stated on the grading report.

CONNOISSEURSHIP IN PEARLS

It is amazing, after a day's buying is done, to see how the value of the pearls increased once we had bought them. Sheikh Mohamed would bring them out, gloat over them, weigh and grade them properly instead of haphazard as he did when buying. . . .

Alan Villiers, 1940

To begin to understand pearls you first must bracket much of what you already know in general about the qualities of gemstones. It takes some people a long time to warm up to pearls. Pearls, it seems, lack that old flash and dazzle. Faceted gems trumpet their charms in a burst of visual pyrotechnics. Diamond dazzles us with brilliance; ruby

86. Stephen Hofer, personal communication, 2002.

87. One prominent industry pricing publication, *The Guide*, has developed standardized pricing grids for the more common fancy color diamonds at FL-VVS, VS, SI, and I1 graded under 10X magnification. These categories show percentage increases as high as fifty percent between FL-VVS and SI grades for certain colors (blue and pink). Are such percentages justified by the realities of the market? I believe they are not.

Tibor Ardai; courtesy of Assael International,Inc.
A fine white Australian South Sea pearl.

subtleties of the gem. John Singer Sargent, that famous painter of wealthy Belle Époque beauties, required seven separate brushstrokes, each stroke using pigment of a different hue, to create a realistic picture of a single round white pearl. No, the pearl is not simple, but to appreciate its beauty requires close attention and serious effort.

In modern times we like to use scientific rather than poetic language when we talk about gems. This sort of language is comforting, since it sounds so precise. Thus we talk about the pearl's *surface* rather than its *skin*. However, the older term is more accurate because it is more evocative and more precisely connotes the feeling one gets looking at a beautiful pearl. Like the skin of a beautiful woman, the *skin* of a pearl can be silky smooth or blemished, translucent, luminous and alive, or opaque, chalky, and lifeless.

Pearl grading uses a specific set of terms that are different from, though somewhat analogous to, those used to grade colored gemstones. Once again, beauty is the bottom line. The criteria used to grade pearls are *body color*, *luster*, *orient/overtone*, *translucency*, *nacre thickness*, *symmetry*, and *texture*.

Body color

Pearls today come in many colors. Saltwater akoya pearls may be gray, yellow, or white. South Sea pearls may be white, cream, golden, or steel gray to black. Chinese freshwater pearls come in plum, bronze, peach, and champagne. In pearls, the

drenches us in color. Not so the pearl. No, pearl is quieter and far subtler. Which leaves us precisely where? Well, setting poetry aside, the point is that grading pearl is a different sort of experience.

A pearl's chief asset is its skin. Faceted gemstones have no skin. They have a cold surface polished to a hard luster and rows of precisely arranged facets. The skin of a pearl, by contrast, glows rather than gleams.

The uncritical dismissal of the pearl is really due to lack of attention to the chromatic colors — red, orange, yellow, green, blue, and violet — as well as the nonchromatic hues of white, black, and even brown and gray are included as possible body colors. Pearls, like faceted gems, can be said to have hues made up of primary and secondary components; thus, plum may be more precisely described as violetish red.

The actual body color or hue is not part of the connoisseurship equation; no particular hue is more beautiful than another. As discussed a bit further on, compatibility with the skin of the wearer, or what I call *simpatico,* is more important. In South Sea and akoya white pearls, a green tint in the body color is considered a fault. With gray it is a bit more complex: Is it grayish and dull or silvery and bright? With gray it's really a question of whether the gray acts as a mask. A grayish pearl with a dull luster is less than desirable; a grayish pearl with good luster appears more silver than gray and is much sought after.

The pearl's body color by itself is insufficient to define the beauty of the gem. It is the combination of *body color, luster, translucency,* and *orient* that characterizes a fine pearl. Think of the beautiful glowing skin of a healthy baby or the dewy complexion of a beautiful young woman. These are excellent analogies because healthy skin has qualities similar to the skin of a pearl, and these are the qualities that give a pearl its sense of life.

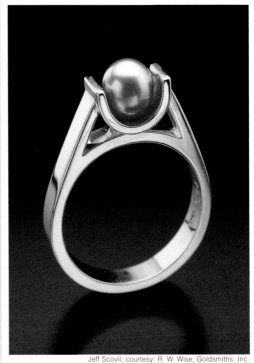

Jeff Scovil; courtesy: R. W. Wise, Goldsmiths, Inc.

Ring featuring a Chinese freshwater pearl with an almost metallic luster and a distinct pinkish orient/overtone.

Orient and overtone

A fine pearl must have that subtle misty iridescence that connoisseurs call *orient,* a glow that seems to emanate from inside the pearl and cling to its skin, like sunlight through an early morning fog, a quality that led the English Renaissance poet Thomas Campion to enthuse: "looked like rosebuds fill'd with snow."[88]

Orient is derived from the Latin word *oriens,* meaning "the rising of the sun."

88. Richard W. Wise, "A Meditation on Pearls," *Pearl World,* vol. 9, no. 3, July-September 2001, pp 10-11.

Luster is caused by light reflection; *orient* is the result of light diffraction. Nacre or pearl essence is composed of translucent layers of aragonite, a type of calcium carbonate made up of tiny polygonal crystals mortared together by conchiolin, a protein that acts as a binder. In some types of mollusk the structure of nacre includes a series of tiny grooves, as many as three hundred to the millimeter, that acts as a reflection (diffraction) gradient, breaking light up into its constituent colors and creating iridescence or the rainbow effect. The more grooves the more distinct the orient.[89] The number of grooves and the spacing determine the colors we see. Some species and varieties of mollusks have this groove structure; some do not.

Orient is not found in all species of pearls. Of the Australian South Sea pearls, only the very finest exhibit orient, and it can rarely be called distinct, yet for South Sea black pearls it is the defining characteristic. Orient is sometimes found in Burmese pearls and in freshwater pearls from China. Orient may occur naturally in Japanese akoya pearls, but it is more often a faux-orient resulting from pink dye. Orient, or overtone, is the quality that gives the pearl its air of mystery and its life; it characterizes the finest of pearls.[90]

Orient may occur in any spectral hue or mixture of hues. For instance, the finer examples of black pearl will normally appear greenish, bluish, pinkish, or, in rare cases, purplish (or some combination) against a tonal continuum (body color) of gray through black. The *apparent* color of the pearl, the color we see, is a combination of the gray-black body color and green, pink, or purplish orient. White South Sea pearls may appear pinkish.

Orient will appear in cultured pearls only with relatively thick nacre coating. Akoya pearls are rarely left in the shell long enough to build up sufficiently thick layers of nacre to exhibit true orient.

Body color and *orient* can be separated by a fairly simple procedure. Place the pearl under the light of an incandescent bulb. The portion of the surface that directly reflects the bulb's image will have the *orient* color. In a round pearl that will be the center of the orb. The area outside and surrounding the reflection will exhibit the *body color*. This procedure works particularly well with black pearls. With Chinese freshwater pearls, however, this method may yield exactly the opposite result. Concentrated incandescent light will often bleach out the color toward the center of a round pearl turning it brownish or grayish leaving the orient color in the surrounding halo. Chinese freshwater pearls look their best in natural light.

Luster

Luster is the reflection of light off a surface. Luster in a pearl is analogous to brilliance in a transparent gemstone. In a fine pearl, the reflection off the pearl's surface is crisp, sharp, and well defined. As quality decreases, the reflection becomes fuzzy and dull. The proper way to evaluate a pearl's luster is to position a pearl under an

89. Yan Liu, J.E. Shigley, and K.N. Hurwit, "What Causes Nacre Iridescence?" *Pearl World*, vol. 7, no. 1, December 1999, pp. 1, 4.

90. Some evaluation systems separate overtone and orient. In its new pearl course, for example, the Gemological Institute of America (GIA) distinguishes between *overtone* (additional chromatic colors that overlay the body color) and *orient* (iridescence that seems to emanate from just below the surface of the pearl). In my view this approach is needlessly complex. The body color is the body color; pink, white, etc. When is an overtone not iridescent and how does one distinguish between secondary hues that originate on the surface and those from within the pearl? A distinction should, however, be made between iridescence (rainbow effect) and

incandescent light bulb. If the pearl is particularly lustrous you will be able to see the shape of the light bulb clearly mirrored in the reflection off the pearl's surface. The more clearly defined the image, the higher the luster of the pearl. If the bulb is clearly visible and well defined, the pearl is of the highest possible luster. If you can read the trademark on the bulb you really do have a gem!

Nacre thickness

Pearls with distinct orient will naturally have thick skins.[91] Experienced dealers will often examine the nacre thickness by shining a light through the drill hole and peering through the hole using a 10X loupe. A simple method to check the thickness of the nacre in a strand is to roll the pearls on a white surface under strong lighting. Thin-skinned pearls will wink; that is, they will appear brighter and darker as the pearl is rotated. This winking effect is simply the mother-of-pearl bead showing through the nacre.

Another method is called candling. The pearl is held over a concentrated light source or placed on the lens of a flashlight. The concentrated beam of a maglight is perfect for performing this test. Since nacre is semi-translucent, this will often allow the bead to be visible. In thick-skinned pearls the bead will appear as a roundish dark smudge. In thin-skinned pearls the bead will exhibit a series of parallel stripes. These stripes are the growth layers of the bead insert itself, which is normally cut from a clam or oyster shell. Pearls that show these

striations have very thin nacre coatings and should be avoided. Black pearl, because of the color and opacity of the nacre, will not show through. Thin-skinned black pearls will often exhibit a brownish secondary hue or mask.

Simpatico

Artists have a great appreciation of pearls. Iowa artist Sara Bell professes an ongoing love affair with the pearl. Bell devoted a year of study prior to executing her recent oil painting aptly titled *Pearl.* "My mother wore a natural pearl engagement ring that contained all the colors of the rainbow," she said. "I was frustrated trying to find pearls in jewelry stores. The ones I saw were mostly plain opaque white. They didn't look at all like my mother's."[92]

The precise realism of a painting entitled *Girl with a Pearl Earring* by the seventeenth-century Dutch master Vermeer fascinated Bell. Vermeer's technique of painting a pearl closely mirrors the process by which nature itself creates the pearl. The paint is built up in thin layers using multiple colors. This is the same technique painters use to give a quality of aliveness to a subject's skin. In her own work Bell found she needed mixtures containing the entire range of primary and secondary colors to make a realistic rendering of the simple white orb. Her finished painting bears an uncanny resemblance to the real thing.

Water is an ancient term that has fallen into disfavor, but that aptly connotes the

true orient. The former is a result of light interference; the latter is caused by refraction.

91. One exception to this is the so-called late harvest pearl. Akoya pearls are often harvested in November when the waters off Japan are at their most frigid. The nacre of late harvest pearls is dense and closely grained. After processing (bleaching and dyeing) the surface will appear opaque despite the fact that the nacre is quite thin. This technique has been known to fool experts. Sydney Soriano, personal communication, 1999.

92. The artist is simply reacting to the look of the newer thin-skinned akoya pearls. Two decades ago pearls were left in the oyster for longer periods, normally exceeding two years. Thicker-skin akoya pearls will exhibit the attributes the artist describes.

beautiful combination of luster, translucency, body color, and overtone which characterizes the finest of pearls. Real translucency, the ability to see through a pearl, is rare in cultured pearls because most pearls are seeded with a machined bead cut from the opaque shell of a freshwater mussel. However, the nacreous layers are themselves translucent. Also, Chinese freshwater pearls, at least those that are tissue nucleated, have no solid nucleus and may exhibit translucency to a certain degree.

The pearl has another quality, unique among gems: its beauty can be enlivened or subdued by placing it in contact with a woman's skin. The Italian word *simpatico* is a term I have chosen to describe this somewhat mysterious quality. A pearl, no matter how beautiful in itself, will seem to come alive if it is placed next to skin of a certain color, texture, and tone with which it is *simpatico*.

Pearls' *simpatico* can be determined with a simple test. The pearl or pearl strand should be placed against the inside wrist of the intended wearer. The inside wrist is a protected area of the skin which rarely tans and is the same color and texture as the area around the throat and ears, the likely area where the pearl will be worn. The *simpatico* between the skin and the pearl becomes readily apparent when several pearls of different hues are compared in this way. Simpatico is a test of compatibility, not quality.

Symmetry

Other factors are also necessary qualifi-

Jeff Scovil; courtesy of Pacific Pearls

The range of natural shapes and colors available in Chinese freshwater pearls.

cations for a fine pearl. Symmetry historically has been of great importance. A perfectly round pearl was the most desired of all. However, since the introduction of the cultured pearl in the late 1920s, round pearls are no longer the great rarity they once were. The thin-skinned akoya pearl has accustomed consumers to expect a spherical perfection of form. Who can resist the perfection of an oval or egg-shaped pearl or the sensuous curves of a pear shape? Ah, but still, there is something so elegant about a round!

In the marketplace, the closer the pearl comes to achieving perfect symmetry, the greater its value. In the marketplace, round is the most desired shape, followed by pear, oval, and button. All other shapes are classified as *baroque*. Prices of baroque pearls can vary widely. The nuclei implanted in cultured pearls are perfectly round and blemish-free; however, nature has no commitment to symmetry and can play many little tricks during the pearl's growth. As a result, the average harvest yields only a very small percentage of perfectly round pearls.

Designers often find inspiration in off-shaped pearls or baroques. Several historically important jewels such as the Canning Brooch were crafted from freeform pearls whose shape suggested a sculptural form.[93]

Size

Other factors being equal, the larger the pearl the more valuable it will be. Pearl prices increase in an arithmetic progression up to seven and one half millimeters. From eight millimeters the price increases become larger. South Sea pearls, both black and white, are seldom seen under eight millimeters. This is because the mollusk itself is larger than the oyster that produces the akoya and freshwater pearl and is capable of accepting implants of up to ten millimeters. In the warm waters of the South Pacific, nacre will accumulate at roughly five times the rate that it accumulates in the relatively cool waters off the coast of Japan. The physical and economic conditions in the

South Seas are right for the production of larger pearls. For this reason akoya pearls above 8mm will increase dramatically in price whereas South Sea pearls will not. Above 12mm, pearl prices take another giant leap. At 16mm a cultured pearl is considered to be quite rare; a fine round pearl over 20mm is a museum piece.

Texture

A pearl's surface may be bumpy or smooth or textured. Texture on the skin may be interpreted as coarse and, if it detracts from the pearl's beauty, a distinct negative. But many bumpy baroque pearls, particularly freshwater pearls from China, exhibit excellent luster coupled with rainbow-like iridescence caused by light rays refracting and colliding with each other as they bounce from the pearl's surface. Perhaps this is a visual *mea culpa* to make up for the baroque's lack of formal perfection. This phenomenon is distinct from orient, which is normally monochromatic and is caused by light entering the translucent crystalline layers of nacre. Technically described as light interference, this rainbow iridescence is never found in a smooth symmetrical pearl.

Bumps, blemishes, tiny pits, or anything intruding on a perfectly flawless skin is considered something of a negative. The skin should be smooth and silky. Most pearls will have slight imperfections visible somewhere on the skin or surface of the pearl; the issue is how much they disturb the eye. In the case of symmetrical pearls, connoisseurs are most concerned with how

93. The Canning Brooch depicts a merman whose upper torso is composed of a single baroque pearl. Baroque pearls were often used in this way, particularly during the Renaissance. Made in Italy around 1580, the Canning Jewel was named after Lord Canning, the British Empire's first viceroy to India. Collection of the Victoria & Albert Museum, London.

the pearl will "face up," that is, if imperfections will still be visible when the pearl is set. The best face-up position is found by rotating the pearl. In baroque and button shapes imperfections visible on the backside are of much less of a concern. However, pearls with surface cracks anywhere on the skin are considered almost worthless.

It may be that we are entering another golden age of pearls. In Roman times, pearls were ounce for ounce the most valuable things on earth. The fashion for pearls has waxed and waned over the centuries, at times eclipsing the value of diamonds and other crystal gems. In the twentieth century, pearl production and demand reached its height in the 1920s, only to plummet in the early 1930s under the twin pressures of the stock market crash and the uncertainty generated by the introduction of the cultured pearl.

Today there are greater quantities of more varieties of pearl than at any time in history. The American freshwater pearl, the Chinese freshwater pearl, and the black South Sea pearl are available in quantity. South Sea pearls from the Philippines and Indonesia are new to the market. Burmese and Baja California pearls are reentering the market. Pearl sales have increased dramatically in this decade and the consumer has become more accepting of variations in shape, size, and color.

The pearl horizon seems sunnier than at any time in the past sixty years. However, a few dark, dirty little clouds lurk just at the edge. Pearl treatments have also multiplied. In addition to bleaching, a venerable treatment stretching back into history, dyeing, irradiation, waxing, coating, heating, and other treatments are proliferating as the demand for the pearl increases. Although treated pearls are of little interest to the connoisseur, treatments are acceptable so long as they are disclosed to the buyer. But, in many cases, these treatments are not disclosed.

Hints on the appreciation of pearls

As one well-known dealer who grew up in the Japanese pearl business once pointed out, perfectly round pearls are either an extreme rarity or a highly processed fraud.[94] The point is that most pearls are not round, not white, nor are they perfectly matched. Pearls, even the cultured variety, are a natural product. We have become so enamored of the highly processed, thin-skinned Japanese akoya pearls that we are unable to appreciate the true virtues of real pearls.

Baroque pearls are not to be disparaged. Symmetry is only one part of the value equation. As with all gemstones, beauty is a balance of factors. In the case of pearls these factors include *hue*, *orient* (translucency), *luster*, *texture*, and *shape*.

94. Fuji Voll, personal communication, 1988.

Chapter 6

Caveats

In buying Precious Stones much precaution is required. Few wares are liable to more faults and imitations than these.

E. W. Streeter, 1879

emstone enhancement

The treatment of gemstones to enhance their visual appearance has a history of at least three thousand years.[95] Some of these ancient treatments are still in use today. Advances in technology have added a number of new tricks to the repertoire. Dyeing, oiling, heating, irradiation, and lasering are some of the better-known treatments.

Traditionally, a distinction has been made between treatments: those which should be disclosed to the buyer and those that need not be. Treatments which are not permanent, such as dyeing, were to be disclosed. Permanent treatments, such as the heat treatment of ruby and sapphire, and those done ubiquitously — that is, to all gems of a particular type (such as oiling of emerald) — need not be disclosed. The rationale for this is difficult to justify or understand.

Terminology is important. Some organizations such as the American Gem Trade Association, an organization of gemstone wholesalers, make a distinction between *treatment* and *enhancement*. AGTA prefers the latter term because it sounds better. From the perspective of the aficionado the terms are interchangeable.

Something has been done, other than cutting and polishing, to change the look of the gem. That something should be disclosed in writing on the sales document.

Recent revisions of guidelines published by the Federal Trade Commission in the United States have begun to clarify this issue. According to the new guidelines, disclosure of a treatment is required if it has "a significant effect on the stone's value."[96] Given that all treatments are done to increase the attractiveness of a gemstone, all treatments really do have a "significant" effect on the stone's value and should be disclosed.

The issue is somewhat muddied by the fact that some types of treatments have a real effect on the value and price of a gemstone in the marketplace and others do not. One example is lasering, the use of a laser to drill a tiny channel into a diamond so that acid may be introduced through the hole to bleach dark inclusions and thus improve the diamond's apparent clarity. Under previous guidelines, only nonpermanent treatments were to be disclosed to the buyer. Lasering is permanent and does affect price so under the new guidelines must be disclosed to the buyer.

95. Kurt Nassau, *Gemstone Enhancement* (London: Butterworth, 1984), p. 7.

96. Chapter I of Title 16 of the Code of Federal Regulations Part 23: Guides for Jewelry, Precious Metals, and Pewter Industries. The legal requirement to disclose a treatment turns on the definition of "significant." The FTC guidelines do not require full disclosure. The FTC decided that there should be a practical, commonsense limitation on when disclosures should be made. The federal register's notice, which goes along with the regulation and further defines how it is to be interpreted, stated: "Disclosure of permanent treatments is necessary only where the treatment's effect on the value is likely to affect a consumer's purchasing decision." Thus, if the treatment has no monetary effect on value it would seem that no disclosure is necessary.

Other types of enhancement, such as heat treating of aquamarine and tourmaline, are both impossible to detect and have little or no effect on the value of these gemstones. Heat treating of ruby and sapphire is detectable and will have some effect on price, particularly on larger, finer stones. In certain cases it's the treatment that makes the gem. Tanzanite, for example, in its natural state, is an unattractive dark gray to rootbeer brown. Heat treatment, baking the stone in an oven at approximately twelve hundred degrees Fahrenheit, drives off the brown, leaving behind a lovely violet to violetish blue. The types of treatments used on specific gem varieties and their effects on that gemstone's value will be discussed later in this book in the chapters dealing with the specific gem.

In the detection of treatments, gemologists are constantly playing catch-up. Treatments often are created initially to fool the prospective buyer. It is up to the gemologist to figure out first that something has been done, and second, how to detect it. With advances in treatment technology it has become almost impossible for the average jewelry store gemologist to keep up. This situation has led to the rise of the gem laboratory. These labs are staffed by specialists and have the advanced equipment necessary to detect gemstone treatments. The aficionado would be wise to insist that any and all treatments be disclosed in writing on the sales document. In cases where the purchase is significant, the buyer should insist on a certificate from a recognized gemological laboratory with a specific statement regarding the presence or absence of any treatments or enhancements.

Chapter 7

New Sources

The list of precious and semi-precious stones must be kept open sine die, like the lists of the heavenly bodies, of the elements, the planets, the species of insects. New discoveries are constantly being added.

Louis Kornitzer, 1930

Africa: cradle of new gemstones

In the 1960s one completely unknown gemstone, and a host of new varieties of known gemstones, were discovered in East Africa. Tanzanite, a normally blue but sometimes green variety of the mineral zoisite, was discovered near Merelani in Tanzania. Tsavorite, a rich green variety of grossular garnet, was also first found in Tanzania near the village of Komolo, not far from the Kenya border.

Since that time various unusual garnets as well as sapphire, ruby, spinel, and alexandrite have been unearthed in East Africa, all within a geological formation known as the Mozambique belt. Consisting of high-grade metamorphic rocks, this geological formation stretches three thousand miles up the east coast of Africa: from Mozambique in the south-southeast through the countries of Tanzania, Kenya, Ethiopia, and Somalia and extending into the Red Sea. The rocks of the Mozambique belt are a diverse mix of volcanic rocks, ancient sediments, and intrusions that have endured several metamorphic phases, entirely altering the original character of the rocks.[97] In most cases, gemstones from these new locations have visual characteristics which are different from the same gemstone types found at traditional sources.

© R.W. Wise

Masai warrior takes a break along the road to Tsavo National Park, Voi, Kenya.

97. N.R. Barot, personal communication, 1998.

Other parts of Africa have also yielded new finds of known gemstones. Zambia produces fine amethyst, and along with Zimbabwe, is producing emerald with visual characteristics that differ from those found at traditional locations in Colombia. Recently, demantoid, green tourmaline and mandarin garnet have been found in Namibia; red and green tourmaline and spessartite garnet strikes have been made in northwestern Nigeria. Ethiopia is producing opal with a distinctive chocolate brown body color.

One of the most exciting new areas is Madagascar. In recent years a huge variety of gemstones has been found on the spice island. Sapphire, ruby, emerald, alexandrite, tourmaline, and an array of interesting new varieties of garnet, all with unique visual characteristics, are currently being mined.

Brazil: gem paradise

Since 1554 when the Portuguese explorer Francisco Spinoza first discovered green tourmaline in the foothills of the Brazilian state of Minas Gerais, Brazil has consistently yielded new surprises to titillate and amaze the gem world. Tourmaline, along with spinel, is the most consistently underappreciated gem of all time. Originally termed "Brazilian emerald," it took two hundred years and the birth of modern gemology before tourmaline was recognized as a distinct gem species.

In addition to tourmaline, Brazil is a major producer of an abundance of gems, including aquamarine, amethyst, citrine,

© R.W. Wise

Eighty-five years old, this venerable garimpeiro is still working the mines; Minas Gerais, Brazil.

emerald, garnet, opal, and diamond. A twenty square-mile area surrounding the town of Ouro Preto, in the state of Minas Gerais, is the sole major producer of commercial quantities of topaz. Two hundred miles north, near Hematita, lies the site of the single major find of gem-quality alexandrite.

In the early 1980s a new source of emerald was located in the state of Goiás at Santa Terezinha. Perhaps the most exciting discovery of all was near the border of the western state of Rio Grande do Norte, just outside the village of Paraiba. A new variety of tourmaline was found which derived its incredibly saturated color from trace elements of copper and gold. Named Paraiba tourmaline (see Chapter 27), this discovery set the gem world on its ear as the price of this gemstone escalated to heights previously unheard of for the lowly tourmaline.

North America

While certainly no gem paradise, North America, or more specifically, the United States, produces its share of beautiful gemstones. America's oldest gem mine is located in the state of Maine. Tourmaline deposits were first discovered at Mount Mica, outside Paris, Maine, in 1820. This deposit, despite several interruptions, is currently in production.[98] In 1972 a huge pocket of gem quality tourmaline was located thirty miles away at Plumbago Mountain, in Newry, Maine. These two mines are part of a single geological formation called a pegmatite that runs in a straight line from Brunswick on the Atlantic coast through Paris and Newry to the New Hampshire border. Approximately seventy-five percent of the gemstones mined at Plumbago are pastel pink to violetish red gems. The remainders, along with the majority of production from Mount Mica, are the lovely mint green stones for which Maine is justly famous.

California is also known for its tourmaline. The major tourmaline producing area is found at the Pala and Mesa Grande districts in San Diego County. These areas were major producers of tourmalines in the late nineteenth and early twentieth centuries. In the mid-1990s several of these historic sites — the Tourmaline Queen, Pala Chief, and Elizabeth R. mines — closed for decades, were reopened and are currently producing small amounts of gem tourmaline. The Old Himalaya Mine in nearby Mesa Grande is still worked sporadically.

In ancient times, certain agates, specifically carnelian, were ranked among the precious gemstones. If beauty is any criterion, history is about to repeat itself. Along with carnelian, which is found in Washington State, gem chrysocolla, found mainly in Arizona, deserves a place among the new precious stones.

Australia: new wins from Down Under

While no entirely new species of gemstone has been found in Australia, a number of new varieties of known gems have been located in the land Down Under. Perhaps the most famous of these is opal.

Generally speaking, Australia produces the finest opal in the world. In fact, just about all the opal in the world market comes from Australia. Before the Australian discoveries, the only known source of gem opal were the diggings southwest of the northern end of the Carpathian Mountains, in what is now Slovakia. This source of opal was known in Roman times, and produced opal with a milky white body color.

98. Richard W. Wise, "Oldest Mine in the U.S. Reopens," *Colored Stone* *Magazine*, July/August 1992, cover, p. 8. See also John Sinkankas, *Gemstones of North America*, vol. 3 (Tucson, Arizona: Geoscience Press, 1997), pp. 468-470.

Opal was first discovered in the Australian state of Queensland at Springshure in 1872. Opal types are classified by body color, into six basic types: black, white, gray or semi-black, boulder, crystal, and fire opal. Five of the six basic opal types, excluding the orange-based fire opal, are found in Australia. Two other precious stones, sapphire and diamond, are found in Australia.

Chrysoprase, the apple green variety of chalcedony, has been discovered at two locations in Australia. One deposit was found at Marlborough Creek in Queensland and another near Yerilla in Australia's Northern Territory.

PROBES: A NEW LIST OF

The new precious gems: one man's opinion

The charge legitimately can be made that the selection of stones I have designated as precious and included in Part II simply represents the author's opinion and is entirely subjective. As for the opinions asserted in Part II, the same charge can be made. In reply to the first charge, I plead guilty. The term "precious" is a qualitative designation and, as has been demonstrated earlier in this volume, is a somewhat arbitrary label. Simply put, the gems selected are, in my opinion, the most beautiful and the most important gemstones available today.

As for the aesthetic judgments: these should be seen as what the late philosopher Marshall McLuhan called probes. They are attempts to clarify; they represent the author's best shot at the truth. If the reader simply accepts uncritically the author's conclusions, this book will have failed in its primary objective to aid the reader in developing true connoisseurship. A fine gemstone is like a fine wine. It must be held up to the light, tasted, rolled around on the tongue, savored, and finally judged. Not all wines appeal to all palates — so too gemstones. An honest disagreement based on reasoned contemplation is the beginning of true discrimination. The author welcomes such disagreements.

Many of the essays in Part II, particularly those on gemstones discovered in the last fifty years, contain the first critical discussions of the aesthetics of these gem species and varieties written for public consumption. They are, therefore, a jumping-off place, a beginning, a point of departure. Other opinions will certainly follow, some of which will challenge the author's conclusions. So be it! Or, as the Roman emperors are reputed to have said when they entered the Coliseum: "Let the games begin!"

In my opinion, the finest — the most beautiful — examples of each gem variety may be termed precious. As a practical matter, it is not possible to discuss in detail every variety of every gemstone. Naturally, essays on traditional gemstones are included here, but an equal emphasis is placed on the newer precious stones. Some of these new precious gems are recent discoveries, some are simply newer sources of traditional favorites, and some are gem species such as tourmaline that have been kicked around for centuries and are just now beginning to be appreciated. The primary criterion I have chosen is beauty, not tradition.

In one case, akoya pearl, the ubiquitous white Japanese saltwater pearl that is part of every woman's wardrobe, has been excluded from the list. This is because the culturing process is so short and the pearl has such thin skin and is so highly processed (bleached and dyed) that it no longer possesses the quality characteristics that make for a true natural product.[99]

Preciousness is an evolving concept, as discussed here earlier. Thus this book's list of precious stones specifically includes, for the first time in two thousand years, four varieties of chalcedony: Holley/Mojave blue agate, gem chrysocolla, carnelian, and chrysoprase. These varieties were selected because of their breathtaking beauty. No one who looks at these four gems with an unbiased eye could possibly call them semi-anything.

Durability and rarity, as limiting factors, have also played a part in the selection. A gemstone should be durable enough to be set in jewelry. In fact, it was partly the amazing durability of gemstones that first brought them to man's attention. Therefore faceted gemstones with a hardness less than six and one half on the Mohs scale, stones that are softer than steel, have been excluded from the list of the precious stones included here. Although advances in lapidary technique have made it possible to fashion many exotic materials, this does not automatically make them precious gemstones.

Extremely rare materials, those not available in sufficient quantity to make a market, have also been excluded. Gemstones such as red beryl, which is every bit as beautiful as its two siblings, emerald and aquamarine, is not covered simply because there is too little of the material around, and space dictates that a line be drawn somewhere.

99. "When Mikimoto first cultured his pearls, he left his oysters in the water for four to six years, a time span that produced a luxurious nacre coating that would last for generations. During every decade since 1960, most Japanese pearl farmers clipped another year off culturing times. In the 1990s we first saw pearls that had been in the water six months or less. The nacre was so thin you could flick it off with a fingernail." Fred Ward, "The Wisdom of Pearls," Pearl World, The International Pearling Journal, vol. 11, no. 2, July August/September 2002, p. 11.

Due to their extreme rarity, fancy color diamonds exist in a world of their own. They are without question one of the rarest, most costly substances on earth. They are, in fact, the only diamonds that are truly rare. Connoisseurship, or at least the current value of fancy color diamonds, is based on the rarity of a given hue. Beauty is, at best, a secondary consideration. Despite this fact, fancy color diamonds are of great interest to collectors, and for that reason have been included in this volume.

In one case, at least, the limitation is the author's. Jade is certainly a precious gemstone. Unfortunately, I feel that I have insufficient knowledge and expertise to do an authoritative analysis of this gemstone. Perhaps this deficiency can, with careful study, be recouped in a subsequent edition of this book.

Part II addresses the thirty-five or so gem varieties that I believe should be included in any contemporary list of precious gemstones. In this section the principles discussed in Part I are applied to these specific gem varieties. The reader should note that the essays in Part II assume that the reader has studied and understands these principles.

Chapter 8

Alexandrite

Ceylonese alexandrites are, on the whole, finer than the Uralian, the columbine red colour seen in artificial light being especially beautiful. . . Its colour by daylight was a fine sap-green with a trace of red, while in candle-light it appeared a full columbine-red, scarcely distinguishable from a purplish-red Siamese Spinel.

Max Bauer, 1909

Ask the mirror on the wall, which is the rarest gemstone of them all? If the answer is not alexandrite, trade in the mirror. With the exception of some varieties of fancy color diamonds, alexandrite is indeed the rarest gemstone. Alexandrite is a variety of chrysoberyl that changes color when exposed to different light sources. Daylight and incandescent are the traditional light sources for testing a gemstone for color change.

Alexandrite was discovered in 1830 in the gravel of the Sanarka River in the southern part of Russia's Ural Mountains. The stone was named in honor of Alexander Nicolajevitch, heir to the Russian throne, soon to become the ill-starred czar Alexander II. Later, small deposits of alexandrite were located on the island of Ceylon. For the next ninety-some years these were the only known sources of this rare gemstone.

What is truly remarkable about alexandrite is not that it changes color; several gemstone varieties, including sapphire and some types of garnet, will shift color when exposed to different light sources. Most other gemstones that exhibit color change will change only to the next one on the color wheel; e.g., from red to violet or blue to purple. Alexandrite fairly leaps across the color wheel, shifting from hues of green to blue green in daylight to red purple in incandescent light.

In the mid-1980s the first and thus far only major new strike of alexandrite was made in the Brazilian state of Minas Gerais at Hematita. In this case the term "major" should be put in perspective. Once news of the find leaked out, three thousand garimpeiros, the Brazilian term for independent prospectors, descended on a small valley, five hundred feet wide by six hundred fifty feet long, and began digging.

The run lasted approximately twelve weeks, April to June of 1987, with an average of one death by gunshot per week until the bloodshed caused a government order to shut down. By this time the area was essentially mined out. The estimated production from this strike was two hundred fifty thousand gem carats in the rough.[100] Figuring a weight loss of forty percent in cutting the stones, this translates into 150,000 carats of cut gemstones. A very small amount when compared, for example, to diamond, with a production of over one hundred million carats per year. Alexandrite is a very rare gem.

100. Keith Proctor, "Chrysoberyl and Districts of Minas Gerais," *Gems & Gemology*, Spring 1988, pp. 26-28.

Alexandrite from the Pegmatite

Before this strike, small amounts of alexandrite had been found a bit further north in Minas Gerais at Malacacheta. Since the big strike ended in June 1987, production from Hematita has been sporadic. Small amounts of alexandrite have come from Tanzania and Madagascar; very limited amounts have begun coming out of Russia since the fall of the Soviet system.

Color shift: the key factor

Alexandrite is defined by its color change. If it doesn't change color, it's not alexandrite; it is simply chrysoberyl. The traditional view is that the best alexandrite shifts from an emerald green to a ruby red. This is a bit wide of the mark. A majority of gems from Hematita show a teal or greenish blue to a slightly yellowish green in daylight, turning a violetish red to purple in evening light. The strength of the color change is the key element in the judgment equation. To be considered a fine stone, the color shift must be distinct and dramatic with little of the former color left after the shift. Generally speaking, tones with a ninety percent shift should be considered fine. For example, a stone that is teal green in daylight should become purplish red under the light bulb, with no more than a tiny bit of green left over after the lighting environment has been changed.

Harold and Erica Van Pelt; courtesy of Kalil Elawar

Brazilian alexandrite from Hematita showing exceptional color change and a remarkably pure green hue in daylight.

Judging the shift

Although gems should always be looked at in a variety of lighting environments, when

101. In the mid–nineteenth century, candlelight actually established the standard for comparison. At 1,500 kelvin, candlelight enters the red range of color as perceived by the eye. The color temperature of the average light bulb, by contrast, is 2,700 kelvin, distinctly into the yellow range. This is, no doubt, part of the reason why alexandrite that turns the mythic true red at night is almost impossible to find.

well as other cat's-eye gems. The finest cat's-eye stone is first of all a fine cabochon, one that glows, has a limpid, transparent body color, and, in addition, shows good color change and a bright well-formed eye.

As with alexandrite generally, cat's-eye alexandrite is usually either very light or very dark in tone. Darker stones in this case are more desirable because they will exhibit a much stronger eye. Though much rarer than faceted alexandrite, the cat's-eye type does not command nearly as high a price. Rough stones with a high de- gree of clarity, crystal, and color change are almost always faceted to bring the highest price. Therefore the most available cat's-eyes are stones with tonal values of at least eighty-five percent. In daylight these stones will appear almost black, and it is neces-sary to shine a strong light directly into the stone to observe the color change.

pleasant chat, the gentleman brought out a large box containing a dozen matched cat's-eyes. The suite was magnificent! The dealer was disappointed because after a brief examination it was clear that the fifty-carat gem I had brought was just too small to complete the suite. Does this mean that large alexandrite cat's-eyes are not rare? No, but it does point out the sort of temporary glut that can occur when a large pocket of even a very rare stone is found. Fine alexandrite is rare in any size. Rarity increases at three carats and dramatically

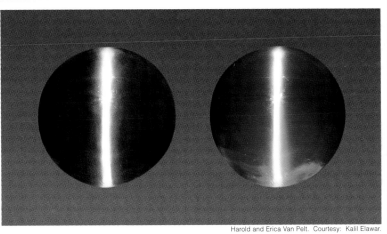

Harold and Erica Van Pelt. Courtesy: Kalil Elawar.

Exceptional cat's-eye alexandrite showing both the green daylight and the purplish red incandescent colors.

The rarity factor

In 1990, shortly after the big strike at Hematita, I transported a large fine alexandrite cat's-eye about the size of a small walnut to a local dealer in the Brazilian town of Teofilo Otoni. The dealer was seeking a single stone to complete a matched necklace suite. After coffee and a

over five carats; the next jump in rarity is at ten carats. Large fine alexandrites are true museum pieces.

Chapter 9

Amethyst

The Mursinsk (Siberian) amethyst at times is very dark violet blue, surpassing that from Ceylon, but mostly it is pale violet-blue or spotted and striped violet-blue and colorless.

Gustav Rose, 1837

Quartz is earth's most plentiful mineral; it is the primary component of dust, making up twelve percent of the earth's crust. It is surprising, therefore, that the finest examples of amethyst, the purple variety of quartz, are so rare and difficult to find.

Hue and tone

Amethyst occurs in a continuum of primary hues from a light-toned slightly pinkish violet to a deep Concord grape purple. Amethyst is expected to be eye-clean and, given its relatively low cost, should always be finely cut.

Jeff Scovil; courtesy of Commercial Mineral

A 6.00-carat amethyst from the Four Peaks Mine, Arizona, showing a slightly reddish purple key color; a fine example of "Siberian" color.

Amethyst may exhibit one or both of two possible secondary hues, red and/or blue. A light rosy red, what we think of as pink, is the usual secondary hue found in lighter-toned stones. The ideal tone for amethyst is between seventy-five and eighty percent; at this tonal level the secondary hue, if there is one, will be blue. The color in amethyst may occur in overlapping zones of purple and blue. When the stone is viewed face up, the color will be a slightly (ten to fifteen percent) bluish purple. The blue adds a velvety richness to the purple hue.

Multicolor effect

Multicolor effect is a key element in the connoisseurship of amethyst. The finest gems show a rich grape juice–purple body color with deep red flashes in incandescent lighting. As shown on the color wheel, mixing red and blue make purple. Amethyst is a nightstone. When the stone is faceted, the relatively yellowish light of the incandescent bulb draws deep red flashes of brilliance from the center of the stone. This describes the finest color in amethyst and is called *deep Siberian* color. The red flash is the chief difference between deep Siberian and *Siberian,* the number two color. Under the light bulb, Siberian stones will show a deep purple but no red in its key color. This difference is visible only in incandescent light.

Saturation

The usual saturation or intensity modifier in amethyst is gray although occasionally brown is also seen. In darker-toned stones the mask may be very hard to see, but pure chromatic hues are always vivid. Dark purple is normally a rich warm hue. Gray will dull the hue and give it a cool aspect. Brownish stones appear muddy and overdark. The finest stones will show little or no gray or brown mask.

The finest

To reiterate, the finest amethyst can be described as an eye-clean stone with a primary purple hue between seventy-five

Jeff Scovil; courtesy of R.W. Wise, Goldsmiths, Inc.

A 48.85-carat amethyst gem sculpture by Michael M. Dyber. The stone is a visually pure purple (Siberian color) of about eighty percent tone coupled with excellent crystal.

and eighty percent tone with perhaps fifteen to twenty percent blue and (depending upon light source) red secondary hues— the *deep Siberian* quality.[106] Following this is the second quality, or *Siberian*, which has a slightly bluish purple key color. *Deep Siberian* color is exceptionally rare. I have

106. As indicated by the quotation at the beginning of this chapter, the term *deep Siberian* is more than a bit of a misnomer. Very little amethyst from the Siberian source ever achieved the finest quality. If there is a best source for amethyst it is — or rather, was — the West African country of Zambia. Gems from this strike were prevalent in the market in the late 1980s and early 1990s. I bought several kilos of rough Zambian amethyst in Nairobi in 1990. This material contained beautiful dark blue zones that, when faceted, added a bluish secondary hue to the purple. This mixing of purple with a bit of blue lent the Zambian amethyst a lovely rich hue. Very little material has been available from this source since the mid-1990s.

spent weeks searching for this quality in Brazil and in Africa and often returned home empty-handed.

Commercial grade amethyst occurs in tonal variations of violet, from ten to sixty percent tone. Lighter-toned gems (thirty to forty percent tone) with a pinkish violet hue are called *rose de France*. Gems of this type with a high degree of transparency (good crystal) are quite inexpensive and quite beautiful.

Beware of synthetics

The collector must beware of synthetic amethyst. Synthetic amethyst, like most synthetics, is made to imitate the the use of sophisticated gemological instruments normally unavailable to the jeweler-gemologist.[107] Testing services are available, but given the relatively modest prices of even very fine smaller stones, the cost of testing may exceed the cost of the gem. The collector should buy only from dealers willing to certify natural origin on sales slips. An independent gem lab should test larger stones.

The rarity factor

Fine amethyst is rare in any size. Amethyst can be found in extremely large sizes. Stones tend to decrease in value on a per carat basis over twenty-five carats.

107. A competent gemologist can perform a fairly simple test based on what is called "Brazil law twinning." This test is not one hundred percent certain, because it is theoretically possible to produce synthetic amethyst that would react like natural amethyst when using this test. However, this type of synthetic is not currently available in any quantity in the market. David Stanley Epstein, personal communication, 2000.

THE BERYL FAMILY

Our *pousada*, or guest house, sits with its with its backside hanging over a cliff overlooking the Brazilian town of Nova Era. Puffy white cumulus clouds glide across an aquamarine sky. The rainy season has just ended. The foothills are clad in a coat of green velvet, the grass cropped close by the broad flat teeth of grazing cattle. Hill follows hill, rolling toward the horizon like a sea of verdant waves. In the valley that contains the town, a winding river sambas along the valley floor, the water, like the clay tiles on the village roofs, stained a deep, reddish brown. Just above the river a dirt road carves a livid ruddy scar, paralleling both the river's color and course.

The color of the iron-rich lateritic soil here is characteristic of the entire northeastern portion of the Brazilian state of Minas Gerais, and is similar to other gem-rich areas throughout the world, including central Thailand, upper Burma, and the opal mining areas of western Queensland.

Five hundred million years ago super hot liquid magma injected itself into gaps or cracks in the pre-existing country rock. As these intrusions cooled, rare minerals such as lithium, boron, beryllium, and manganese concentrated in pockets, aiding and abetting the formation of gem crystals such as tourmaline, emerald, and aquamarine.

Our jeep bounces along a one-lane dirt track, following the course of the Piracicaba River as it works its way westward off the main highway. Our destination is the *Posso Grande* aquamarine mine. Brazilians are optimistic by nature. In Portuguese *posso grande* means "it can be big." And it still could be!

The Posso Grande Aquamarine Mine outside the town of Nova Era, Minas Gerais, Brazil.

Our guide, Emilio Castillo, a jolly, rotund *pedraista* (gem dealer) who has lived for twenty-eight years in Nova Era, tells us that Philippe, the mine's owner, has hit pay dirt no less than four separate times in this area. Philippe is a seasoned *garimpeiro*, or independent miner, and, like many of his brothers, has a sort of Zen attitude toward fortune. In short, he lives for the day. With each strike he has made a fortune, and each time he has watched that fortune slip through his fingers.

Unfortunately for Philippe, his much-touted luck appears to have deserted him. Just as he hit a pocket deep in the hill, disaster struck —a mudslide has buried his tunnel. We arrive at the mine to find Philippe and his five-man crew at loose ends. The mine is several hundred yards up a steep hillside above the river. Two previous tunnels had proved unproductive, and it will take backbreaking weeks of labor to dig away the slide by hand. Still, Philippe is philosophical. He is cutting green bamboo with his machete, the heart of which will be sliced and fried up for lunch. Money is tight, food is scarce, and there is no capital available to purchase heavy equipment that could considerably speed up the excavation.

Back at his home, Emilio pours several kilos of previously won Posso Grande aquamarine rough onto a table. Most pieces weigh less than three grams, all a limpid blue crystal without a trace of green. Aquamarine rough

R. W. Wise

Rebekah Wise sorting aquamarine rough from the Posso Grande Mine. Note the pure blue hue. This aquamarine has not been heat-treated.

is normally greenish. Both the green and the blue color are derived from iron —the blue from ferrous iron and the green from the yellow of ferric iron. Gentle heating will drive off the ferric iron, leaving just the blue, but in this case, heating will not be necessary. With Emilio's permission, we select several pieces that we will cut into one- to three- carat gems.

After a country lunch at Emilio's home, and a detour so that he can present us a gift of a bottle of *cacháca*, the fiery Brazilian cane liquor, we continue our journey. The sky is cloudless and the afternoon turns sultry. We find ourselves bouncing our way up yet another dirt road, this time on the north side of the mountain from Posso Grande toward Capueirana, a village in the Nova Era region.

Nova Era first drew the attention of the gem world because of its emerald, a light- to medium-toned slightly yellowish to grass green limpid stone that was discovered in the 1980s. Many of the mines that produced Nova Era emerald are clustered around this small village.

"This is also the back road to Hematita," Paulo Zonari, our host and driver, remarks. "Ten years ago this was one of the busiest roads in Brazil." Busy indeed! For three months, thousands of *garimpeiros* worked a small valley east of Nova Era. This was the first and only major strike of alexandrite anywhere. After three months, and an average of one death by gunshot per week, the valley was mostly mined out. Fortunes were made and fortunes were lost—often in a hail of bullets.

This afternoon we are to visit an emerald mine, one of the few still working in the area. We pass through the small village. The tiny whitewashed houses and tin-roofed shacks flank both sides of the narrow dirt track. A group of men are gathered on the verandah of a local bar to exchange the day's gossip. Glasses and beer bottles sit on narrow homemade wooden tables. The men are dressed like miners, in shirts and dirt-soiled pants; some are shoeless. Their swarthy faces are burned even darker by the tropical sun. They gaze, eyes narrowed, in our direction — some curiously, others with suspicion. We pull up to a gate. A small concrete house sits several yards up a hillside. It looks more like a small *fazenda*, or farm, but we have arrived at our destination — the mine owned by Sergio Martinez.

About twenty-five yards above the house a square hole leads to a round shaft — similar to the *lebin*, the square reinforced vertical shafts dug for millennia in the ruby-bearing soils of the Mogok Valley of upper Burma. This one is a bit more up to date. A tin roof covers the

Richard Wise prepares to descend a vertical shaft leading to an emerald mine, Nova Era, Minas Gerais, Brazil.

shaft and a motorized pulley system has replaced the simple hand crank used to lower the miners and retrieve the gem gravel. I am strapped into a leather harness rigged to a tripod above the shaft. Below us a gaping black hole, perhaps six feet in diameter, drops three hundred feet straight into hell. Paulo introduces us to the mine manager; he will be my guide into the depths of the mine.

Suddenly we are at the bottom of the shaft. It is quiet. The single sound is an echoing drip of water coming from below us. We rappel off the shaft wall into a horizontal tunnel. There is no reinforcing structure, no supports of any kind. The cavernous shaft that has been carved out of coal-black schist reaches back into the darkness like the view into the belly of a whale. Am I apprehensive, perhaps a bit scared? Hell, no — I love this stuff! A look back into the shaft, and I see the hanging harness, swaying limply. I was the only volunteer!

Tiny flakes of mica twinkle like stars as the manager's flashlight plays across the sides and roof of the tunnel. The floor is wet and slippery and slopes upward. The air is cool and damp as we work our way deeper into the shaft. Behind us the steady dripping of water seems impossibly loud. We are, it seems, at the very roots of the mountain. At *Posso Grande* we found large "books" of mica, as much as twelve inches in diameter; here tiny flakes mix into the crumbling black schist.

My guide takes me down several tunnels, pointing out areas where emerald was found. The work here was done mostly by hand, dug out with pick and shovel and transported by wheelbarrow to the tunnel's mouth, then raised the three hundred feet to the surface. There is no one working underground today, but in the unnatural quiet it seems that I can still hear the faint echo of rock against steel.

I am not sorry to find myself back at the surface. The sky is somehow bluer and the air seems sweeter. Three men are at work on a huge pile of schist, two breaking up the larger chunks and one washing the gravel on a large corrugated steel table — all looking for the telltale green flash of emerald.

Later in the trip, Haissam Elawar tells me the real story of the Martinez mine. "About one year ago," Haissam begins, holding up his index finger to emphasize his point, "about thirty people invaded this mine." Haissam is Brazilian, born of Lebanese parents. He is a strongly built fellow with a broad face and an infectious laugh. To make a long story short: the owner of the mine was naturally upset having these squatters setting up in his mine and refusing to leave. He called the police. The police, including a high-ranking colonel-of-police, entered the mine. A gunfight ensued and the colonel, along with several others *garimpeiros* and police, was carried out on a slab.

The beryl family consists of four varieties: aquamarine, emerald, morganite, and red beryl.

Chapter 10

Aquamarine

An aquamarine, particularly of good deep blue-green colour, is a stone of great beauty, and it possesses the merit of preserving its purity of tint in artificial light.

G-F Herbert Smith, 1910

Aquamarine is one of the few gemstones that sometimes require the hand of man to give nature a bit of a nudge to produce the most beautiful gems.

Although the English word *aquamarine* comes from the Latin for "sea water" which denotes a greenish blue hue, the gem aquamarine is valued chiefly for the purity of its blue hue, a condition normally achieved by gently heat treating the gem to drive off the green.[108] Aquamarine contains two types of iron, ferris and ferric. The former is responsible for the blue, the latter the green. Low temperature heating drives off the ferric iron, leaving behind the blue. Far from having a negative effect on the value of this gemstone, heat enhancement puts the finishing touches on nature's efforts.

Heat treatment is not always necessary. Some aquamarine rough occurs naturally in a pure blue color. However, it is safe to say that a majority of aquamarine is heat treated. This type of treatment actually increases the value of aquamarine.

Jeff Scovil; courtesy of Mine

A 9.39-carat Mozambique aquamarine showing a visually pure blue primary hue with no secondary green; tone is sixty percent. .

Hue, saturation, tone

In judging the desirability of aquamarine, the marketplace considers tone, not saturation

108. Some connoisseurs prefer the greenish blue of natural untreated aquamarine.

or hue, to be of primary importance. In simplest terms, this means that the darker the stone, the more it will be valued. Unfortunately, darker-toned stones are almost always grayish. The reader will recall that color in gemstones breaks down into three components: *hue*, *saturation*, and *tone* (see Chapter 3). In evaluating most gemstones, hue is far and away the most important of the three components. In aquamarine, this situation is altered: the darker the blue the better the stone. Thus, *tone* is primary. The hue should be, of course, a visually pure blue.

In practice, even gems that have been heat treated will normally show a bit of green, usually between five and twenty percent. Although some connoisseurs prefer a greenish stone, a greenish secondary, what might be called a true *aquamarine* hue, is generally considered a negative. A pure blue hue is the most desirable. The greater the percentage of green secondary hue, the less desirable the gem.

Aquamarine tends to be pale (ten to thirty percent tone) and stones of this description will have a washed-out look. The ideal tone is between fifty and sixty percent. Aquamarine is never too dark; all other factors being equal, the darker the tone the better the stone.[109]

The collector should take care not to be seduced by the gem's body color. Aquamarine is normally light in tone and quite transparent and it is easy to be drawn in by the stone's lovely internal glow. This can be a costly mistake unless the gem in question is cut *en cabochon*. The key color of aquamarine is often quite a bit paler of hue and lighter in tone than its body color, so much so that a delicate light to medium blue body color will often translate into a light-toned pallid key color.

Although a slight brown mask may be found in unheated stones, gray is the normal saturation modifier or mask found in aquamarine. Darker-toned stones will often be distinctly grayish and have a somewhat dull appearance. A bit of gray (five to ten percent), according to some experts, is said to enhance or to darken the blue. But, while a bit of gray can enhance, a bit more makes for a stone that is distinctly grayish and therefore dull. As in most gemstones discussed in this volume, a pure hue is still the most desirable. Therefore, in darker-toned gems, the smaller the percentages of gray the finer the stone.[110]

Despite current market opinion, the author prefers a stone that is perhaps a little lighter in tone (fifty percent) but has a visually pure robin's egg, medium blue hue with no visible green secondary hue or gray mask. This hue coupled with fine crystal is extraordinarily beautiful, particularly when compared to darker (grayer and duller) examples.

Nightstone

Aquamarine is a true lady of the evening, a nightstone. The aficionado is advised therefore to pay particular attention to the gem in daylight. As a rule of thumb, if it looks good by day it will only improve under the light of the bulb.

109. C.R. Beesley, *Colorscan Training Manual* (New York: American Gemological Laboratories, Inc., 1984), part 2, p. 1.

110. Ibid.

Crystal

Historically dealers used the term "gem of the finest water" to describe stones that combined exceptional color with a high degree of transparency. Crystal or what gemologists term *diaphaneity* is the true fourth "C" of quality in colored gemstones. One rarely thinks of "crystal" in connection with aquamarine because it always seems so transparent. However, super-diaphanous aquamarine does exist. Some of the finest is found in the northern part of the Brazilian state of Minas Gerais near the town of Padre Paraiso and also further north and east near Medina. Exceptional crystal punches up sthe luster, brilliance, and saturation of the gem. Gems of this description are best described as "icy" blue and even lighter-toned gems with fine crystal can be strikingly beautiful.[111]

In the early 1980s a process was developed to artificially enhance colorless topaz to create a pure medium-toned blue that looked almost identical to the finest aquamarine. The market was then flooded with inexpensive blue topaz, causing a precipitous drop in the price of aquamarine. It took almost a decade for aquamarine to recover, but recover it did and today fine aquamarine sells for yet higher prices.

Much of the finest aquamarine comes from Brazil, specifically from the state of Minas Gerais. Although in recent years Africa has eclipsed Brazil as a source for aquamarine, the standard is still Brazilian. In 1954 a particularly fine crystal weighing thirty-four kilograms was found on a fazenda north of the town of Teofilo Otoni. The crystal was named Marta Rocha after the Miss Brazil of that year. Her eyes were reputed to match the color of the crystal perfectly. Experts at the time pronounced gems cut from the Marta Rocha to be the finest quality aquamarine ever found. The sultry Miss Rocha is no longer with us but gems cut from the Marta Rocha crystal can be found at the Hans Stern Museum in Rio de Janeiro.

Treatments

As mentioned above, aquamarine is normally heat treated to drive off the yellow component of its hue in order to enhance the blue. This treatment is applied at relatively low temperature and is not detectable by gemological testing. Heat treatment actually adds to the value of aquamarine. Some aquamarine gems are left in the natural color, however.

The rarity factor

Fine aquamarine is rare in any size. This gem is often available in very large sizes and prices tend to decrease on a per carat basis above twenty-five carats.

111. Richard W. Wise, "Garimpeiro   June 2000, p. 42.
Dreams," *Gemkey Magazine*, May/

Chapter 11

Emerald

*The second-finest shade of green emerald is to be found in stones from the original
Chivor mine. This shade tends to have more blue than the Muzo shade. To some
neophytes the Chivor blue-green stones appear, at first sight, to have more warmth
and fire. The Muzo stones often appear to be over-dark or to have a hint of
yellow in them.*

Benjamin Zucker, 1984

Though emerald is undoubtedly precious, it is certainly not among the new precious stones. Before the discovery of emerald in Colombia in the sixteenth century, the green variety of corundum was called *oriental emerald*. The only source of true emerald known to early Mediterranean cultures was the fabled Cleopatra's mines in the Desert northeast of Aswan [112].

Two mines, both discovered — or rather stolen from their Native American owners by Spanish conquistadors — in the sixteenth century, have set the standard for evaluating fine emerald. Separated by less than one hundred miles, these two mines, Muzo and Chivor, produce emerald that is superior in all respects to the pale, highly included stones from the mines of ancient Egypt.[113]

Chivor was in production first, sometime before 1555. Muzo, a source of larger and even finer crystals, was located five years later. The chief difference between emeralds found at Muzo and Chivor lies in the secondary hue. Geologically, the Chivor deposit is

older; these stones tend to have a slightly bluish secondary hue, while those from Muzo tend slightly toward the yellow.

Although some connoisseurs maintain that stones mined in the sixteenth and seventeenth centuries, called "old mine" emerald, were the finest of the fine, Colombia is still a major source of fine

Fine Colombian emerald.

Tino Hammid.

112 Actually located in Egypt's eastern desert region southwest of Marsa 'Alam. One European site, Habachtal, Austria, State of

Salzburg, was reportedly worked during the Middle Ages. However, provable finds date back only to 1797. See Extra Lapis, English No. 2,

Emeralds of the World, Lapis International L.L.C. East Hampton, Ct. p.30.

113. John Sinkankas, *Emerald and Other Beryls* (Radnor, Pennsylvania: Chilton Book Company, 1981) p. 29.

emerald.[114] About three years ago a new source was discovered in an area near Muzo called La Pita. Stones from this source are almost impossible to separate from Muzo stones.[115] Other recent discoveries in Pakistan, Afghanistan, the Brazilian states of Bahia and Goiás and lately in Hiddenite, North Carolina, [116] now produce stones that rival some of the best that Colombia has to offer.

Hue

Emerald, like ruby, blue sapphire, and tsavorite garnet, is one of the primary-color gemstones. That is, the most desirable color is the purist green possible. Although it is true that a small percentage of yellow (ten to fifteen percent) will enhance or frame the dominant green hue, the purer the green the finer the stone. Emerald personifies the pure idea of green. Close your eyes and picture the richest, purist green you can imagine: rich meadow grass growing by a shaded pool in high summer — that is the finest color in emerald![117]

Emerald is usually either a bit yellowish or a bit bluish; in practice, it may have a bit of both as secondary hues. A slightly bluish secondary hue (ten to fifteen percent) adds a richness and warmth to the overall appearance of the gem. For this reason it is a more desirable secondary hue than yellow. As always, the gem should be examined in all light sources. Incandescent light will bring out the blue. This is the primary reason why some connoisseurs prefer an emerald that is slightly yellowish in daylight. They feel that a bit of yellow balances against the

tendency toward blue under the light bulb.[118] If the stone shows more than a fifteen percent blue secondary hue in incandescent lighting it is overblue. African emerald from Zambia often suffers this fault.

Saturation and tone

The color green achieves its optimum saturation, its gamut limit, at about seventy-five percent tone. Thus, emerald achieves its most vivid saturation at this tone. Gray is the normal saturation modifier in emerald. Gray will reduce or dull the hue. Gems with visible gray should be avoided. Sometimes the gray component will be very difficult to discern. Aside from a sense of dullness, the hue of a grayish emerald will appear distinctly *cool* in incandescent light.

Clarity and crystal

Emerald is most often found with some visible inclusions. It is rarely eye-clean in sizes above one carat. Because of this, a greater degree of tolerance should be exercised when judging the clarity of emerald. More attention should be paid to diaphaneity than to strict flawlessness. The finest emeralds exhibit a wonderful clear crystal that gives the stone a marvelous inner glow. If the stone has this trait, a few visible inclusions — what experts call "jardin" (garden) — are easily forgiven. Such stones are more highly valued than those which are strictly flawless but lack the limpid quality of good crystal.

Most aficionados prefer emeralds cut in the traditional step or emerald cut. This cut

114. Zucker, *Gems and Jewels,* pp. 54-55. Zucker's excellent essay on emerald was written before stones from the Pakistan and the newer Brazilian deposits became available, in the market, and is therefore a bit dated.

115. Ray Zaicek, personal communication, 2003.

116. Discovered in 1875, *The North American Gem Mine* has produced over 3,000 carats of gem quality emerald since it opened in 1998, including a number of fine gems such as the 8.85 carat Carolina Duchess.

117. The Arab scholar Ahmad ibn Yusuf al Tifaschi, writing in the thirteenth century, described this color as *zhubabi,* defined as "a very deep green without any other shade of color." He further described it as similar to the iridescent color of the back of a spring fly (not a house fly, mind you, rather the big juicy

Jeff Scovil. Courtesy: Gonzalo
*Fine natural emerald crystal from the Muzo-La Pita
mining area.*

only rival for the title of "greatest of the green." This is partly a function of emerald's relatively low (1.57-1.58) refractive index and partly a result of cutting style.[119] A slightly bluish green emerald with excellent crystal appears to glow with an appealing richness and warmth that is alien to tsavorite. Emerald is soft where tsavorite is hard. To fully understand this quality the budding connoisseur must educate his eye by comparing a large number of emeralds. Stone to stone comparisons between emerald and tsavorite can also be useful.

Treatments

Emerald is a gemstone which the collector must approach with fear and trembling. A majority of the emerald available on the world market is treated with a variety of substances to enhance the color and clarity of the stone. Rough emerald is often highly fractured. Since earliest times, various oils have been used to hide cracks to improve the clarity of the gem. This practice has been going on for so long that it has become accepted and is rarely disclosed to the buyer.

In recent years, polymer plastics have begun to replace the traditional oiling. Opticon is the brand name of a popular polymer with a refractive index that virtually matches the refractive index of emerald, making it impossible to detect without sophisticated testing. In addition, green dye may be introduced into the polymer filling, which can improve the apparent color of the stone dramatically.

has seventeen long, narrow, steplike facets. A majority of emeralds are cut in this style, both because it accentuates the warm satiny hue of the gem and, by happy coincidence, it is usually the most efficient use of the rough material.

Like satin

Experts describe emerald's brilliance as "satiny," like the luster of a satin ribbon. Emerald has a softness which contrasts with the "crisp" brilliance of tsavorite garnet, its

outdoor type). Multicolor effect, the tendency for a gem to show tonal variations of green in the face-up position (see Part I), along with any defect in the transparency (crystal) of the gem, were considered the

other major faults in emerald. See Huda, *Arab Roots of Gemology*, p. 104

118. C.R. Beesley, personal communication, 2000.

119. Refractive index measures the degree to which light is bent as it enters a substance. Emerald is a beryl colored green by a combination of chromium and vanadium. Tsavorite is a garnet

colored green by chromium and vanadium. Tsavorite garnet has a refractive index of 1.74 against emerald's of 1.56-1.58. Tsavorite is also much more dispersive (see Chapter 12, tsavorite).

Jeff Scovil. Courtesy: Paul Tucker Collection

Emerald crystal with cut stone from Hiddenite, North Carolina. The stone is lighter than optimal tone and shows some gray mask that gives the hue a cool dull look, effectively reducing the color saturation.

Recently many labs around the world have adopted a uniform seven-step classification to describe emeralds that have been treated with colorless oils or polymers. The classifications are as follows: *none*, *no significant*, *faint*, *faint to moderate*, *moderate to strong*, *strong to prominent*, and *prominent*. Stones that fall into the first four classifications, *none* to *faint to moderate*, are rare and worthy of consideration. Regardless of appearance, stones that fall into the last two classifications, *strong and strong to prominent,* are best avoided.

The aficionado should bear in mind that these are grade levels of treatment, not clarity. That is to say, an emerald graded *none* is not necessarily a flawless stone, it is simply a stone that has not been oiled or treated with polymers. An untreated emerald can still look like a piece of a broken Coke bottle. A stone may appear flawless to the eye and still be found to have a *prominent* level of treatment. This means that the treatment has effectively covered up many sins.

Beware synthetics

Synthetic emerald can also be a problem. There are a number of types of synthetics currently available in the market. The aficionado's best defense against both treated and synthetic emerald is a certificate from a recognized independent gemological laboratory.

The rarity factor

As with all rare gemstones, fine emerald is rare in any size.

Current industry opinion is that oiling, and to a lesser extent the use of unhardened polymers, is acceptable, though dyeing is not. However, in practice, many dealers turn a blind eye to both types of enhancement. Given the high prices of fine emerald, collectors are advised to insist on full written disclosure backed up by an expert laboratory analysis before finalizing the purchase of an emerald.

CHALCEDONY:
ARISTOCRATIC AGATES

Chalcedony has been an important gem material since the very earliest times. It may be the oldest mineral used as a gemstone. Chalcedony was often used to make pointed and cutting weapons and tools. Therefore it is not surprising that our ancient ancestors, while looking for material for crafting these items, would chance upon beautiful examples of chalcedony that eventually found uses other than as arrowheads.

Fine quality agates have been found at a number of archaeological sites throughout the Mediterranean world. Agate beads dated to 7000 BC have been discovered at Catal Huyuk in Anatolia. The bead cloak of Queen Pu-abi, found in the royal tombs of Ur in Mesopotamia and dating from 2500 BC, contains hundreds of carnelian and agate beads. At Aidonia on the Greek mainland, agate seal stones of exceptional quality and workmanship have been unearthed from Mycenaean shaft graves dated back to 1500 BC. Carnelian, the orange variety of chalcedony, as well as other agates, were much sought after and were surely among the precious gems of antiquity.

In recent times the trend towards all things faceted has relegated chalcedony to the semi-precious backwaters. For most of the twentieth century, agates have been seen as a curiosity and not taken seriously as a gem material of rarity and value.

Thus far the terms chalcedony and agate have been used interchangeably. Chalcedony is the gemological term used to describe a type of quartz with a micro or cryptocrystalline structure, as opposed to single crystal quartzes such as amethyst and citrine. Agate is a nontechnical term used as a common name for chalcedony, but is more often used to describe chalcedony gems with visible bands of color. However, jasper, carnelian, and sardonyx are varietal names also used to describe specific types of banded chalcedony. Here the term agate is used in the more universal sense as a common name for all varieties of chalcedony.

Unlike crystalline quartz materials such as amethyst, which is a single crystal, this species of quartz is composed of tiny interlocking microscopic fibers. For this reason it is also called cryptocrystalline (hidden crystal) quartz.

Even though most chalcedonies have been ignored for most of the past century, several varieties of this gemstone have become more and more popular over the last two decades. Gem chrysocolla, Holley and Mojave blue agate, carnelian, and chrysoprase are increasingly in demand for jewelry. There is a very good reason for this upward spike. New sources of these agates have produced gems of such surpassing beauty that they have simply become impossible to ignore. American and European lapidary artists have made extensive use of these materials in gem carvings. A few years ago Town & Country magazine featured an article on blue agate attesting to the fact that chalcedony is enjoying a new surge in popularity.

The best examples of the first three types mentioned are found in the United States. The last two are found in Africa and Australia. All are from sources that have been discovered in the last twenty years.

Treatments

Since at least 2000 BC, chalcedony has been subjected to heat treatment to create carnelian. Heat treated agates were among the treasures unearthed from the tomb of King Tutankhamen (1300 BC).[120] Most of the carnelian currently on the market has been heat treated. Agate is quite porous and can be soaked in acid to create a dark outer layer in preparation for carving *en cameo*. Porosity also makes chalcedony a good candidate for dyeing. Dyeing will sometimes produce a very highly saturated unnatural-looking hue. For example, "green onyx" is colorless chalcedony that has been dyed rich dark green; it looks simply too green to be true and it is! Black onyx is also universally dyed. The blue varieties of chalcedony are also subject to dyeing. Under magnification, natural color agate will usually show evidence of thin color bands. Specialists call these bands *fortifications* of color. Heat treatment will burn out the bands. Acid treatment produces a dark, dense, "burnt" look in carnelian. Many first- to third-century Roman intaglios, engraved seal stones, fit this description perfectly. Because agates are relatively reasonable in cost, treatments are almost never disclosed to the buyer.

This section will consider the five most beautiful and commercially important varieties of chalcedony: gem chrysocolla, Holley blue and Mojave blue agate, carnelian, and chrysoprase.

120. Nassau, *Gemstone Enhancement*, p. 25.

Chapter 12

Gem Chrysocolla

Gem Chrysocolla is in high demand in the Fareast. In Taiwan they call it "blue jade" but to my eye it has a far more vivid hue

Michael Randall, 1992

The rare rich sky-blue variety of chalcedony has been referred to variously as *silicated chrysocolla*, *gem silica*, *agated-chrysocolla*, and *gem chrysocolla*. The issue lies with the term chrysocolla. True chrysocolla is a soft, noncrystalline mineral that owes its vivid color, ranging from turquoise to sky blue, to the staining effect of copper oxides. Gem chrysocolla, by contrast, is a relatively hard cryptocrystalline silicate that has been stained blue by the same copper oxides.[121]

Given the vast difference in hardness, the aficionado should have little difficulty in separating the two materials by appearance alone. True chrysocolla is opaque, with subvitreous luster, and has a hardness of two to four on the Mohs scale. Materials of this hardness normally can be scratched with a copper penny. Gem chrysocolla may be opaque to translucent and have a vitreous, or glassy, surface luster and, with a hardness of seven, it is harder than steel. Standard gemological tests can easily separate the two materials. True chrysocolla may have all the beauty of gem chrysocolla, except the luster, but it lacks the requisite hardness and durability necessary to qualify it as a gemstone.

Much of the finest gem chrysocolla is found in the copper mines of Pinel County, Arizona. In the 1960s a deposit of the gem was found on the island of Taiwan. In the East, gem chrysocolla is sometimes referred to as "blue jade," an unfortunate term that further adds to the linguistic confusion.

Hue, saturation, tone

Vividness of hue is the quality that assures gem chrysocolla a place among the precious gemstones. The hue varies from a slightly greenish medium dark-toned (fifty to seventy percent) turquoise blue to a similarly toned visually pure sky blue. The green secondary hue rarely exceeds ten percent. As with all blue gems, the smaller the percentage of secondary green, the more desirable the gem. Gem chrysocolla rarely shows any evidence of either a gray or brown mask. Thus, it has a consistently vivid hue. The tonal range of gem chrysocolla is also remarkably consistent.

Color fading

It is estimated that over eighty percent of gem chrysocolla is subject to a degree of color fading when exposed to a dry environment. This is particularly true of the Mexican material. As the stone dries out, the

121. Glenn Lehrer, personal communication, 1998.

translucency and the color saturation of the gem are both diminished. According to Chris Boyd, a dealer who spends summers in upstate New York and winters in Arizona, and who has worked with gem chrysocolla for many years, fading is an issue in areas with an average relative humidity below fifty-five percent. His stones look much better in New York than in the Arizona desert. Fading can be reversed when the gem is rehydrated by directly exposing it to moisture or to a moist environment for a short period of time.

Crystal

Given the consistency of hue, saturation, and tone, it is the degree of transparency that defines the various grades of gem chrysocolla. This gem is never completely transparent; it is translucent. It is the degree of translucency that is the defining factor. The greater the translucency the more the gem will be seen to glow in the light. It can be said that *crystal* is really the first C of connoisseurship in gem chrysocolla, as well as in the other agate varieties to be discussed in this section. Visually pure blues with a high degree of translucency are the most prized. A greenish blue gem with a high degree of translucency is more desirable than an opaque pure blue.

Cut

Gem chrysocolla is often cut in freeform (nonsymmetrical) shapes. Shape has little effect on value except that the more interesting freeforms may command a premium. Particularly translucent gems will some-times be faceted.

Clarity

Malachite and drusy quartz are the usual inclusions found in gem chrysocolla. Though technically inclu-sions, either can add to the beauty of a cut gemstone.

Inclusions and value

Drusy, tiny colorless quartz crystals growing on the gem, are the most sought after inclusions in gem chrysocolla. Although perfection in all characteristics tends to be the way the finest gems are

Glenn Lehrer

Gem carving (36.62 carats) in exceptionally fine translucent gem chrysocolla. The gem exhibits a highly saturated blue primary hue of sixty percent tone. Carving by award-winning gem sculptor Glenn Lehrer.

defined, the aficionado should be alert to pleasing compositions of gem chrysocolla juxtaposed with inclusions of drusy quartz. Malachite, since it is green, is a less desirable inclusion, though it can show a pleasing juxtaposition of color and pattern in a vivid blue gem. It is the skill and sensitivity of the cutter that makes all the difference is such cases.

The rarity factor

Gem chrysocolla with the qualities discussed above is extremely rare. I might find one fine piece every few years. If a fine piece is on offer, the aficionado must be prepared to accept the price, or not have a second opportunity for many years.

Chapter 13

Chrysoprase

Of all the so-called jaspers none were so highly valued (in ancient times) as those of a green color . . . but there is every reason to suppose that the true jade was always more highly prized than its jasper substitute for it was easily distinguishable, by its translucency, from jasper of a similar color.

G. F. Kunz, 1904

Chrysoprase is a green chalcedony that owes its "apple green" color to the presence of trace amounts of pimelite, a type of nickel. Chrysoprase is very close-grained microcrystalline quartz.

Two sources of chrysoprase were discovered recently in Australia, each producing, in substantial quantities, most of the material available in the market today. The first and most important source was a vast deposit found in 1965 at Marlborough Creek, Queensland. The second was unearthed in Western Australia in the Yerilla District in 1992. Material from Marlborough Creek shows the purest green hue and is the finer of the two. Other sources include Brazil, and Kazakhstan in Central Asia, a legendary find, much of which later was determined to be green opal. Opal of a similar color is often associated with chrysoprase. In earlier times it was referred to as *chrysopal*.

Hue, saturation, tone

The finest chrysoprase is usually described as apple green. It is sometimes called *imperial* chrysoprase, an obvious attempt at a comparison to jadeite. It is a vivid visually pure green between sixty-five and seventy percent tone. The material from Marlborough Creek normally ranges from a visually pure green to a slightly bluish green. Gems from Yerilla may show a yellowish secondary hue. This yellowish secondary hue is considered a fault. Gems with even the slightest trace of a visible yellow secondary hue are far less desirable.

Gray is the normal mask or saturation modifier in chrysoprase. The best of the Australian material shows no gray at all and can be best described as a vivid apple green. The general run of chrysoprase from these two sources is remarkably consistent in hue, saturation, and tone.

Another variety called lemon chrysoprase is found in Western Australia. It is a pale opaque lime green color and is actually not a chalcedony at all but a nickeloan magnesite.

Crystal

Given a consistent hue, saturation, and tone, the relative degree of translucency defines the quality grades in chrysoprase — the more translucent the material the higher the price. In fact it can be said that *crystal* is really the first C of connoisseurship in grading not only chrysoprase but also the other varieties of agate discussed in this section. Translucency tends to decrease

Steve Walters

Chrysoprase sculpture by gem sculptor Steve Walters. Note the milky-translucent quality of the body color.

abundance of material, chrysoprase is normally cut flawless. Stones from Western Australia will sometimes show small black dendritic inclusions. Any visible inclusions disqualify the stone from being considered top quality.

Color fading

Chrysoprase, like gem chrysocolla, has a reputation for drying out and fading when exposed to heat or a dry environment. This is certainly true for material from older European sources, chiefly Silesia. This seems not to be the case with material found in Australia; gems from New Marlborough and Yerilla are stable. However, it is still advisable to keep chrysoprase away from long-term exposure to direct sunlight and other forms of extreme heat.

The rarity factor

Since the start of the new millennium, high quality chrysoprase has been available in quantity and at very low prices. I learned long ago that abundance in gemstones is will-o'-the-wisp — here today, gone tomorrow! Whenever a large deposit of any gemstone is found, the material floods the market, temporarily reducing prices. The operative word here is temporarily! Deposits, even large ones, are quickly depleted. A successful collector is an accomplished opportunist and should not be put off by a relatively low price. A fine example of chrysoprase is well worth collecting.

with size. The finest qualities of chrysoprase are often compared to jadeite. Chrysoprase, however, never achieves the transparency of jadeite. Chrysoprase possesses a milky crystal, a characteristic of even the most translucent specimens. The finest jadeite exhibits a crisp, clean, limpid green hue.

Clarity

Ironstone is the normal inclusion found in chrysoprase. However, with the relative

Chapter 14

Carnelian

Fine dark stones of uniform colour and free from faults are described as "carnelian de la vielle roche," or as masculine carnelian. By transmitted light they appear a deep-red colour, and in reflected light a blackish red shade . . . all carnelians, whatever be their color, are strongly translucent.

Max Bauer, 1907

Carnelian was one of the most sought after gems of antiquity. The Egyptians, Sumerians, Hittites, Babylonians, and Mycenaeans adored this gemstone. The Roman historian Pliny said that "among the ancients there was no precious stone in more common use." A majority of classical Greek and Roman seal stones were carved in carnelian or in sard, which is another name for the brownish-orange darker-toned material. Sardonyx refers to chalcedony with alternating bands or *reinforcements* of white and orange that was favored for the making of beads.

The ancients differentiated between five types of *sardion*. Of first importance was the translucent male "blood red" stone; second came the paler yellowish orange, which was considered female. Third was the darker-toned brownish orange that we call sard. The fourth classification included agate with alternating layers or stripes of brownish orange and white, and fifth was blood-red stripes alternating with white. The first three types were found in all the best tombs.

Hue, saturation, tone

Regarding the components of color — *hue*, *saturation*, and *tone* — the modern value system almost mirrors the ancient. The dark red hue is still the most desired, although it is difficult to find a true blood red. Almost all carnelians will show some evidence of an orange secondary hue. Most of the fine carnelian beads unearthed from the royal tombs at Ur are actually a medium to dark orange to reddish orange. Thus, the finest quality might be described as a medium to dark tone (seventy to eighty percent) red primary hue (eighty to ninety percent) with an orange secondary hue (ten to twenty percent). Carnelian can also occur in a medium-toned (fifty-five to sixty-five percent) highly saturated visually pure orange hue. Highly saturated stones of this hue are at least as desirable as the so-called blood reds.

Crystal

As with all chalcedony, diaphaneity plays a defining role in the quality equation. An orange stone with good crystal is more desirable than a red stone that is opaque. *Crystal* is the first C of connoisseurship in the evaluation of carnelian. Recently some medium-toned (sixty percent) highly translucent orange carnelian has come on the market. This material, reportedly from southern Africa, has been nicknamed "citrus agate" due to its pure orange primary hue and its high degree of translucency. Stones of this description will command the highest prices, despite the fact they are not red or even reddish.

Jeff Scovil; courtesy of R.W. Wise, Goldsmiths, Inc.

Although not the legendary blood red, this natural carnelian cabochon is a fine example of the translucent visually pure orange "citrus agate" found in Namibia.

Treatments

Most of the carnelian currently on the market has been heat treated. Since ancient times, chalcedony has been subjected to heat treatment in order to create carnelian. Under magnification, natural color carnelian will usually show evidence of the thin bands called fortifications, even in stones that seem uniformly colored to the naked eye; heat treatment will burn out the bands. Acid treatment produces a dark, dense, "burnt" look in carnelian. Treated stones are less translucent than natural gems.

Most of the gems currently available are heat treated or enhanced in some fashion. Much of the material available at low cost, in calibrated sizes, is undoubtedly treated. Calibrated stones are cut to precise proportions, e.g., round stones are precisely 5mm, 6mm; ovals, cushions, emerald cuts, and pear shapes will be exactly 7x5, 8x6mm, etc. The aficionado should always be suspicious of calibrated stones.

The rarity factor

The real challenge may be in finding natural stones. The same problem is encountered with turquoise. Fine natural carnelian is available; however, it's much easier to treat low-grade material than to bother with the natural. This reflects one of the ruling dynamics of the mass market: that which can be reduced to a commodity will be reduced to a commodity. Natural gemstones are inconvenient because they don't occur in precisely uniform colors, shapes, and sizes. This unfortunate tendency can only be accelerated by the coming of the computer age.

Distortions in the market can work for the connoisseur. Noncalibrated stones, those without precise measurements in millimeters, may be available at reduced prices. Natural carnelian can often be bought at a better price in carvings. If the collector is attentive, a gem of exceptional quality often can be picked from mixed lots of uncalibrated gems at a lower price than those found in calibrated parcels.

Chapter 15

Blue Agate

*Think of quartz and words like "commonplace" and "abundant" come to mind. That
any member of this broad gem and mineral family could be a rarity of keen interest to
connoisseurs and collectors (not to mention designers and manufacturers) seems
incongruous and far-fetched.*

David Federman, 1992

Like many another gemstone,
blue agate is marketed under a
variety of aliases: damsonite,
Mojave blue, and Holley blue agate
are the most common. All are
chalcedony from a variety of locales,
with some small differences based on
color and transparency.

Mojave blue is a trade name
describing a slightly grayish blue
opaque to semi-translucent stone
found in the Mojave Desert, about a
hundred miles south of Los Angeles. A
similar quality material is found in
Namibia. Damsonite is an opaque
violetish material found in central
Arizona. Holley blue is an opaque to
translucent, purplish or amethystine-
hued variety that has been found in
and around Sweet Home, Oregon, and
was named, apparently, for the Holley
School near one of the sites. Another
variation, Ellensburg blue, is found as
glacial till scattered about the
Washington state township from which
it draws its name. Ellensburg blue
agate often has a purer blue hue.

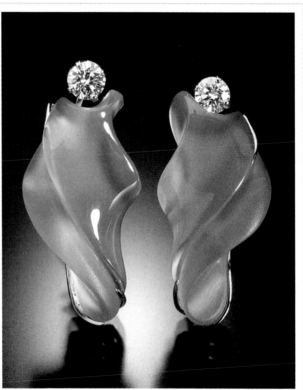

Jeff Scovil; courtesy of R.W. Wise, Goldsmiths,

*Earrings by Douglas Canivet featuring slightly grayish "Mojave"
blue agate show exceptional crystal for this gem variety (blue agate
is never more than translucent). Carvings are by Steve Walters;
the agate sculptures are accented with a pair of D-color
ideal-cut diamonds.*

Hue, saturation, tone

Regardless of source, blue agate is chiefly valued for its translucency and purity of hue. The general mine run of stones from California and Namibia tend toward a slightly gray, medium-toned blue hue, sort of a stormy-sky blue. In this system of evaluation, gray, along with brown, are not regarded as hues but are treated as saturation modifiers which, when present, dull or muddy the saturation or mask the intensity of the hue. A gray mask is nearly always present in blue agate. Like a dirty film on a window, gray dulls the hue, reducing the saturation or brightness of the color. The gray may be difficult to detect but pure hues are always vivid, so the presence of gray may be inferred from a cool dullish blue. Obviously, the brighter the blue the better the stone.

Purple is the normal secondary hue, and when it is present, adds dramatically to the beauty and price of the stone. Holley blue is famous for its amethystine secondary hue, but a hint of purple can also be found in damsonite and even in stones from other locations. Occasionally a stone will be found that has a purple primary hue, but these are exceedingly rare. Stones of this color will have a blue secondary hue; that is, they will be bluish purple rather than purplish blue. The market prefers bluish purple, purplish blue, and grayish blue, in that order. The greater the percentage of purple and the smaller the percentage of gray the better the stone. I have seen only three examples of a pure blue hue without measurable gray.

Crystal

As with all varieties of agate, it is diaphaneity or what is called "good crystal" that is a primary determinant of value in blue agate. This gem is normally found with a milky or cloudy body color. Translucent stones are rare and expensive. Although agates are normally cut *en cabochon*, especially transparent or limpid examples will occasionally be faceted.

Clarity

Blue agate is almost always cut flawless. Stones with inclusions other than drusy, a carpet of tiny quartz crystals growing on the surface, are almost without value as gemstones. Drusy is quite desirable, particularly when the cabochon is cut in a freeform shape. In this case it is a question of what artists call composition, a pleasing proportion of drusy balanced against the size and shape of the stone. Designer goldsmiths particularly seek stones of this sort.

Gems with banding can be quite pleasing, but will not command the price that a cabochon of uniform color will fetch.

Treatments

Both irradiation and heat can alter the color of blue chalcedony. As with amethyst, prolonged exposure to high heat will turn some stones an orangy yellow. Irradiation can be used to enhance the purple secondary hue. Prolonged exposure to the sun or dry environments may also bleach some of the color out of the stone. Soaking the gem in water can restore the color.

The rarity factor

As we step into the new millennium, blue chalcedony is only getting rarer as it becomes more desirable in the marketplace. The popularity of the gemstone has increased markedly in the past few years. Increasing market rarity coupled with actual rarity means that prices of the finest material are destined to rise. Blue chalcedony is normally sold by the piece rather than by the carat. Pieces too large to be used in jewelry are not usually found.

THE GARNET GROUP

Picture a remote valley sandwiched within a range of humpbacked hills in northern Tanzania in the long shadow of Mount Kilimanjaro. The month is February, the end of the blistering African summer. A lone figure struggles through a copse of sansevieria, the wild African sisal, whose sword-spike leaves can cut a man's skin to ribbons. This is the domain of the tsetse fly, of Kifaru the rhino, and of Simba the hunting lion.

The man lifts his head and stares across the wide savanna; the dry, windblown brown landscape is dotted with the spindly umbrella-shaped acacia trees. He begins walking slowly in a grid pattern, head down, carefully scanning the parched earth. Then, he pauses mid-step like a thoroughbred hunting dog on point, removes his bush hat, squints and wipes the sweat from his eyes with the back of his hand. Looking down, his trained eye detects the slightest hint of green twinkling in the equatorial sun. His breath catches in his throat; barely daring to hope, he squats down to get a better look. "Yes! here they are, crystal shards, brilliant as tiny green diamonds!" The search is over, but the real work has just begun.

R.W. Wise

Mining tsavorite garnet on the East African savannah; Scorpion Mine, Tsavo National Park, Voi, Kenya.

The garnet family is scientifically classified as a group. This means that although all garnets share the same atomic or crystal structure, they differ in chemical makeup. For this reason the properties of garnet, specifically hardness and refractive index, will vary greatly. Most people are familiar with almandine (also almandite), the brownish red iron-aluminum garnet, and with pyrope, the deep red magnesium-aluminum garnet. These are only two of the seven varieties classed by chemical composition, which include pyrope, almandite, grossularite, andradite, spessartite, and pyrope-almandite.

To further muddy the waters, recent discoveries in Africa have turned up garnets such as malaya and tsavorite with chemical compositions that fall between the traditional classifications, rendering these classifications unwieldy and all but obsolete.[122]

From the connoisseur's perspective, all this doesn't matter a great deal provided the stone can be identified. And in all cases positive identification is possible using the basic instruments and the services of a trained gemologist. It is only necessary to be aware that hardness and refractive index, and also rarity, differ markedly among the members of the garnet group.

In this volume the focus is on the three most distinguished members of the garnet group: malaya, spessartite, and tsavorite. Although two of these garnets, malaya and tsavorite, are among the latest discoveries, their outstanding visual characteristics make them irresistible candidates, demanding their presence among the new precious gems.

Treatments

Garnet is rarely subjected to any form of treatment. Heat treatment has thus far proved ineffective, and irradiation has little effect on the gem. However, the science of gemology is always engaged in a game of catch-up. When the guys in the black hats discover a method of enchancing the look of a gem material, gemologists are left with the task of, first, figuring out that something is being done, and second, determining what is being done. As garnet prices rise, sooner or later someone will figure out an effective way to make an inferior stone seem superior.

122. Carol Stockton and Vincent Manson, "A Proposed New Classification for Gem-Quality Garnets," *Gems & Gemology,* Winter 1985, p. 205. The authors suggest a new system of classifying garnet consisting of eight types: grossular (which includes tsavorite), andradite, pyrope, pyrope-almandine, almandine, almandine-spessartine, spessartine, and pyrope-spessartine (which includes malaya).

Chapter 16

Tsavorite Garnet

Tsavorite has a reputation of showing green at its best. So although it is nowhere near as expensive as comparable-grade emerald, it costs enough for purchasers to insist that it posses fine color.

David Federman, 1992

Tsavorite was discovered in 1967[123]; it is one of the newest of the precious gemstones. Technically a calcium aluminum silicate that crystallizes in the cubic system, it is a green grossular garnet. Grossular is one of seven members of the garnet family. Tsavorite is not the only member of the grossular species; grossulars can occur in a range of colors including yellow, orange, pink, and brown. Grossularite, a yellowish orange garnet, was named for the gooseberry, *grossularia* in Latin. Green grossular garnet occurs in a geological formation known as the Mozambique belt.

Tsavorite versus emerald

Tsavorite garnet is often compared to emerald. Given their similar appearance, comparisons are both inevitable and understandable. Emerald, like tsavorite, is a silicate, containing beryllium rather than calcium. Both are colored green by trace amounts of chromium and vanadium. Here, scientifically, is where the similarity ends. Emerald crystallizes in the hexagonal crystal system. It is doubly refractive: light that enters the gem is divided into two rays. Tsavorite, however, like all garnets, is singly refractive.

The key difference between emerald and tsavorite is refraction and dispersion. The refractive index of emerald is 1.57-1.59; the refractive index of tsavorite is significantly higher at 1.74. This means that light penetrating green garnet is bent at a greater angle than light entering emerald. Even more significant is the difference in dispersion, the way the two gems break up white light into its constituent rainbow colors. The dispersion of tsavorite is 0.28, twice that of emerald at 0.14. This, coupled with the higher refractive index, will "disperse" the light, adding to the life of the gem. The lower refractive index imparts to emerald what connoisseurs refer to as a sleepy or "satiny" appearance. Tsavorite will have a "crisper" appearance when fashioned in most cutting styles. However, when faceted in the traditional step or emerald cut, or when cut *en cabochon*, the visual similarity between the two gems, particularly in their finest qualities, can be uncanny.

Emerald at 7.5 on the Mohs scale is slightly harder than tsavorite, which is about 7.25. Hardness, however, is something of a misnomer when used as a measure of durability. The Mohs scale is really only a

127

123 Campbell Bridges states that he found the first traces of green garnet, either tsavorite or demantoid, in the African country of Zimbabwe in 1961.

measure of scratch-ability. A stone that is harder is simply one that will scratch one that is softer.

A more important measure of durability is toughness; in practical terms, how well the stone will stand up to setting and the abuse of day-to-day wear. Emerald has a well-deserved reputation for brittleness; it is easily chipped and is problematic, particularly as a ring stone, if worn every day. Tsavorite garnet, on the other hand, is not brittle, is tough enough even for invisible setting, and stands up well to daily wear.

Hue

Tsavorite miner Campbell Bridges has identified three mixtures of hue which, in his opinion, describe the finest colors in tsavorite garnet: forest, water, and grass green. Forest green is visually bluish, eighty-five to ninety percent green, ten to fifteen percent blue. Water green appears a bit yellowish: seventy-five percent green, fifteen percent yellow, and ten percent blue. Standing between the two is grass or leaf green, a visually pure green which contains eighty percent green hue with approximately equal amounts of yellow and blue.[124]

In fact, the market tends to favor bluish green stones and I agree. A visually pure green with perhaps fifteen percent secondary blue hue and between seventy-five and eighty percent tone is probably ideal. Unlike African emerald, tsavorite is rarely

overblue. Stones with twenty percent blue secondary, though rare, are extremely beautiful. The most beautiful tsavorite I have ever seen was a "Kentucky bluegrass green" from the Scorpion Mine near Voi, Kenya, in Tsavo National Park. The stone had a highly saturated eighty percent green primary hue and a twenty percent secondary blue hue; the tone was eighty percent.

Until recently garnet has been found in every color except blue. Thus any garnet with the slightest pretension toward a blue or bluish hue is regarded with a high degree of reverence.[125] Like emerald, yellow is the

Robert Weldon. Courtesy: Tsavorite U. S. A.

A paradigm example of tsavorite garnet from Kenya's Scorpion Mine, with a rich dark-toned (95%) green primary hue and perhaps five percent blue secondary hue.

124. Campbell Bridges, personal communication, 1995.

bane of this green grossular garnet. A bit of yellow may punch up the saturation, but ten percent or more of it —because of its lighter, brighter tone — begins to dilute the green visually. As a rule of thumb, gems that are visually yellowish should not be considered top color.

Saturation and crystal

Tsavorite, like many East African stones, is a daystone; that is, it looks its best in natural light. And, although incandescent may actually improve the color, some darker stones of optimum tone will pick up a "sooty" dark gray to black mask in incandescent light. The stone appears to close up, dramatically reducing transparency and beauty. The darker the tone, the more pronounced the effect. Lighter-toned gems hardly seem affected. In this respect tsavorite differs markedly from emerald, which does not display this tendency at all. As with all gemstones, the aficionado is advised to study carefully the effect of shifting light sources, particularly from daylight to incandescent.

Tone

To be considered tsavorite, a gem must have at least medium or sixty percent tone. Stones with tonal values below sixty percent have a watery or pastel appearance and are called green grossular garnet. Seventy-five to eighty percent tone is optimal. Stones with tonal values above eighty percent appear overdark.

The division of color in gemstones into hue, saturation, and tone is useful in discussion. In practice, beauty is a balance between these abstractions in which clarity and cut also play a part. In tsavorite, for example, the addition of yellow to green yields a lighter tone and a more vibrant color. The addition of blue yields a richer hue that is also darker in tone.

Clarity

The market is much more tolerant of inclusions in emerald than in any other gemstone. Tsavorite prices, on the other hand, are markedly affected by the presence of any inclusions which are eye visible. Tsavorite is normally sold flawless; gems with visible inclusions are marked down twenty percent and more, depending on the size and placement of the inclusions. A majority of included stones are cut *en cabochon*. Fine (eye-cleanish) cabochon tsavorite sells for approximately twenty-five percent of the price asked for a faceted stone of the same color. Visible inclusions in a faceted tsavorite garnet can lower the price as much as forty percent.

Cut

Those who persist in comparing tsavorite to emerald will always favor the classic emerald cut. As mentioned earlier, tsavorite has a higher refractive index and double the dispersion of emerald, giving it potentially much greater brilliance. The emerald cut's fifteen to seventeen relatively large facets restrain the natural sparkle of the garnet,

125. In the early 1990s a blue/red color-change garnet was discovered in Tanzania and more recently in Madagascar. Most of this variety exhibits a strong gray mask. However, at their best, these garnets look very much like the finest Brazilian alexandrite and have a very similar color change.

giving it an appearance that bears an uncanny resemblance to the satiny brilliance of emerald. However, the fifty-plus facets of the brilliant style release the garnet's full potential, allowing it to stand toe to toe when set with diamond.

The rarity factor

Traditionally, tsavorite mining has been clustered in an area approximately one hundred miles northwest of Mombasa, within a forty-mile radius of the Kenya-Tanzania border. In 1990 another source of tsavorite was located in Turkana, in northwestern Kenya near the Uganda border. Mining commenced in this area in 1994. Gems mined at Turkana are generally larger and darker in tone, perhaps due to a relatively higher content of chromium and vanadium oxide[126], than those found in the south. Towards the end of 1991 a deposit of vanadium-rich tsavorite was discovered in the Gogogogo area of southwestern Madagascar, about forty kilometers north of Ampanihy. More recently tsavorite has been found at several other locations in Tanzania, including Tunduru and Ruangwa near the Mozambique border. At the turn of the century (2000) a new mining locality was found south of the Taita Hills at Choki Ranch. This site has produced a significant number of larger stones. Given the extent of the Mozambique belt, other deposits of this type of garnet undoubtedly exist.

Tsavorite is decidedly rare in sizes above three carats, and generally unavailable in the market in sizes above five carats. According to Campbell Bridges, who has devoted the past thirty-five years to mining the stone, approximately eighty-five percent of material mined yields stones under one carat, ten percent yields stones above one carat, two and a half percent over two, and one percent between three and five carats. Stones over ten carats are about one tenth of one percent of total production.[127]

Tsavorite's extreme rarity means prices for larger sizes increase geometrically in price. In the early 1970s Tiffany & Co. was offered an exclusive marketing arrangement. Henry Platt, Tiffany's president and the man who gave the new green garnet its name, demurred, because quantities of larger stones sufficient to launch a profitable marketing campaign could not be guaranteed. Prices for fine tsavorite garnet will increase somewhat with size. With new strikes in Kenya yielding larger sizes, prices have moderated. As of this writing prices are at an all time low. Expect a price increase at one carat, two carats, four carats, and at six carats. In the 1990s five-carat stones cost roughly six times the price of a comparable one-carat stone. This is no longer the case. Stones over twenty carats are priced individually and are true museum pieces.

126 Campbell Bridges, personal communication, 2003.

127. Campbell Bridges, personal communication, 1998.

Chapter 17

Malaya Garnet

If malaya is the outcast of the garnet family, it is a splendid outcast indeed.

R. W. Wise, 1989

The course of the Umba River undulates like an uncoiling snake as it slithers through the parched East African savanna. It was at the river, about four miles west of the Tanzanian town of Mwakaijembe, about a hundred meters out from one of those bends, where the first signs of malaya garnet were found. The time was somewhere in the mid-1960s. Malaya, sometimes spelled malaia, is a Swahili word meaning outcast. When the rough stones were first found they were sometimes discarded simply because the miners, looking for sapphire, assumed they were worthless.

"You ask about size and rarity!" Dealer Roland Naftule pauses thoughtfully before responding to the question. "Nowadays anything over five carats is rare. All garnet except rhodolite is generally rare above four to five carats. At six or seven you have another jump. Above twenty, very scarce! Over one hundred carats — it's a museum piece."

"But, in the early days of the strike, there were rough pieces—water-worn pebbles the size of golf balls" That's how Naftule remembers it. "They cut huge pieces, over a hundred carats; one hundred eighty — that was probably the biggest." Campbell Bridges recalls the early days of the strike: "an abundance" of high-quality rough up to ten grams (fifty carats). Figuring in a thirty percent loss in cutting, rough of that size yields cut stones of almost thirty carats.

The country rock in this area, just south of the Kenya border, is biotite, quartz, and feldspar gneiss. The deposit was alluvial. Stones were found to a depth of about four feet along a long-dead river channel. Traces of malaya garnet have been found elsewhere, in Kenya at Lunga Lunga, and at points along the plain that stretches from the Kenya-Tanzania border to Mgama Ridge in the Taita Hills. More recently this garnet has also been reported in Tanzania at Tunduru, and also in Madagascar near the village of Bekily; as of this writing there is some small-scale production there. Most of this production is of stones under one carat, and consists of small parcels brought to local dealers by independent miners.

Hue

The color range of malaya is broader than spessartite and the orange hue rarely as crisp and pure as the finest of that species. Malaya ranges from a yellowish brown and brownish pink through a cinnamon to a crisp honey brown and reddish brown to a brick or

Jeff Scovil; courtesy of R.W. Wise, Goldsmiths, Inc.

A fine slightly pinkish orange honey color 2.77-carat malaya garnet of sixty-five to seventy percent tone exhibits the lovely mixture of hues that characterize the finest examples of this gem variety.

brighter (more saturated) and darker in tone. Thus a stone that is pinkish orange in daylight will often appear reddish under the light bulb.

Saturation

Because of the prevalence of a brown component, malaya rarely exhibits a fabulously vivid hue. Soft, rich, and velvety is probably a better description. However, due to its high refractive index, what the stone lacks in saturation of hue it will often make up for in brilliance. In our system of evaluation, both gray and brown are thought of as saturation modifiers or masks, as if the stone was being viewed at the bottom of a mud puddle. At times, however, if the brown is itself highly saturated, it becomes a hue, as in beautiful examples of chocolate brown diamonds, tourmalines, and garnets. The hues between orange and brown are a dominant part of the East African color palette. The total visual effect is what is important. Though orange is preferable, brown-hued stones are not to be dismissed out of hand.

Tone

Tonally, malaya can run the gamut from forty percent to eighty-five or higher. Darker brick orange stones are the norm; a sixty percent tone is probably ideal. In this tonal range the key color can be compared to honey, although stones with a purer orange primary hue can be described as

brown orange. The rarest and most beautiful are the honey peach, cinnamon, tangerine, and pinkish orange hues. Malaya is one of the few gem varieties where the most beautiful stones are not those of one pure spectral hue. Pinkish orange — seventy percent orange with thirty percent pink secondary hue — may be the paradigm. In the very finest stones there is a complete absence of the brown; such stones are very rare. Even pinkish orange stones with a distinct brownish component are desirable.

Some malaya, specifically stones from the newer source in Madagascar, are classified as color-change garnets. As the stone is moved from natural to incandescent lighting, the hue will not so much change as intensify, becoming tangerine. Malaya garnets with tonal values under sixty percent begin to appear washed out. Eighty-five percent is overly dark brown and definitely overcolor.

Given its tendency to shift color, malaya garnet should be carefully examined in a variety of lighting environments. This garnet usually darkens appreciably in tone when exposed to incandescent light. In fact, since the hue we call brown is actually a dark-toned orange, darker-toned orange stones will sometimes turn an unattractive brick orange brown when the lighting environment is changed from daylight to incandescent.

No longer an outcast, malaya garnet is a modern gemstone success story. Since its introduction in the United States in the mid-1980s malaya has not only knocked the accepted garnet classifications into a cocked hat, it has also established itself surprisingly well among consumers. Given malaya garnet's increasing popularity and continued lack of production, can upward pressure on prices be far behind?

Chapter 18

Spessartite Garnet

Everyone knows that yellow, orange, and red inspire and represent ideas of joy, of riches, of glory, and of love.

Paul Signac, 1905

Spessartite, also called spessartine, is the true orange garnet of the purist hue. The garnet family is scientifically termed a group because its members are related more like cousins than siblings. Members of the garnet group all have an identical atomic structure and crystallize in the cubic system, but have different chemical compositions. Three garnets can occur in a primary orange hue: spessartite, malaya, and hessonite, a type of grossular garnet.

Spessartite has the highest refractive index of the three orange garnets and when well cut has more potential brilliance and is "crisper" in appearance than either hessonite or malaya. Due to the variation in refractive index, spessartite measures between 1.78<1.81, malaya 1.765 but less than 1.81, and hessonite between 1.74-1.75. Separation of the three varieties is fairly straightforward and easily determined by a qualified gemologist. Spessartite at 7.25 on the Mohs scale is also among the hardest members of the garnet group.

Though rare, spessartite has been found in many places, including Sri Lanka, Madagascar, and Brazil; however, tradition-ally the finest stones come from a single source, the Little Three Mine in Ramona, California. A new source was discovered in the early 1990s in Namibia near the Angolan border. The newer Namibian material was originally marketed under the name "hollandine" but the name that seems to have stuck is "mandarin." Thus, orange garnet labeled mandarin is likely to be Namibian spessartite. Gems from this source tend to have a distinctive "juicyfruit" orange key color. Kashmirene is yet another trade name for spessartite from Pakistan. Another new find of spessartite from western Nigeria entered the pipeline in 1999. This new material reportedly was found near the village of Iseyin, about three hours northwest of Ibadan. The best of this new Nigerian spessartite strongly resembles the best from Little Three.

Origin is mentioned as part of the discussion and as a general guide. To paraphrase the late great gemologist, G.F. Kunz: gems have no pedigree. Exceptional stones may come from any source, and poor examples can be found at the most celebrated locales. Another early source of very fine spessartite was Amelia

Courthouse, Virginia. Unfortunately this area now sits beneath a housing project.

Hue

Spessartite can occur in a range of hues from distinctly yellowish orange through orange to a distinctly brownish orange, orange brown, or reddish brown to brownish red. The primary hue may be orange, brown, or red with any of the others playing the part of a secondary hue. Red spessartite is probably the rarest but the most distinctive stone; those that command the highest prices are a visually pure (ninety percent) primary orange hue with no more than ten percent of brown or yellow as a secondary hue. Dark-toned gems with a fifteen to twenty percent brown secondary hue are called "burnt orange" and place second in desirability and price. Yellowish orange stones, seventy percent orange with no more than thirty percent yellow secondary hue, can also be strikingly beautiful and place third in both beauty and price. Reddish orange spessartite, which resembles dark-toned rhodolite garnet, comes in last in overall desirability.

Saturation

The finest more or less pure orange spessartite will be exceptionally crisp and brilliant. Stones with a yellowish secondary

Jeff Scovil; courtesy of R.W. Wise, Goldsmiths, Inc.

A very fine 7.00-carat oval Nigerian spessartite garnet. Note the visually pure orange hue of about thirty percent tone with a slightly darker-toned brownish orange multicolor effect toward each end of the gem. This gem exhibits almost perfect (ninety percent) brilliance.

hue will be even more vivid. This is because, as color science teaches, the orange hue achieves its maximum vividness, its gamut limit, at about twenty percent tone, and yellow slightly lighter at about eighteen percent tone. Thus the yellow secondary hue punches up the saturation. Brown is the normal saturation modifier or mask found in spessartite garnet. Deep and dark hues of orange naturally appear brownish. So a dark-toned orange garnet is a brownish orange garnet. As the stone becomes tonally darker the hue also becomes less vivid. Stones with the least brown mask will exhibit the most vivid key color. Pure spectral hues are always vivid, so a dull orange hue is also a brownish orange hue.

Tone

Given that deep and dark-hued orange spessartite garnets are by definition brownish, the optimum hue in spessartite tends to be quite light. On a scale where window glass is zero percent tone and coal is one hundred percent tone, the optimum tone for orange is about twenty percent.

Clarity

Spessartite garnet is normally sold eye-clean. The only exceptions to this rule of thumb are larger stones and the so-called mandarin garnets from Namibia. Spessartite from this source has a slightly different chemical composition, resulting in a particularly vivid saturation. Namibian spessartite is normally moderately included, containing wispy veils visible to the naked eye. Because of their highly saturated hue, even stones with visible inclusions are highly desirable.

Crystal

Lighter-toned spessartite garnets, those approaching the optimum tone, will tend to have greater transparency. As noted above, gems from certain localities will tend to have a large number of eye-visible inclusions. These inclusions can sometimes be quite small and give the visual impression of dustiness in the interior of the stone.

Cut

Among gemstones, spessartite has the fourth highest refractive index, exceeded only by diamond, zircon, and andradite garnet. When properly cut, spessartite will exhibit exceptional brilliance.

The rarity factor

The largest known faceted spessartite from the Little Three Mine weighs 39.65 carats.[128] The largest mandarin garnet, spessartite from Namibia, weighed just over forty carats. One dealer claimed to have seen a Nigerian stone that weighed over seventy carats. Generally speaking, price and rarity increase at one, three, and five carats. Stones above ten carats are considered extremely rare and command prices to match.

128. E. Gray, personal communication, 1999.

The World of Pearls

The romance of the South Seas! The exotic mystery of the black pearl! It is this combination that has lured me to travel over ten thousand miles to Manihi Island, a remote speck of land in the Tuamotu island group, three hundred fifty miles northeast of Tahiti. It is only in these far-off islands that the natural conditions exist for the culture of this unique gem.[129]

The Manihi atoll is a doughnut-shaped flat ribbon of coral surrounding a central lagoon more than twelve miles across. Several pearl farms are located in the lagoon. This sheltered body of water provides an ideal habitat for the pearl oysters as well as sufficient protection

R. W. Wise

Aerial view of Manihi Atoll, three hundred fifty miles north of Tahiti, French Polynesia.
A small section of the lagoon can be seen in the foreground. Protected lagoons like this serve as a perfect incubator for the black pearl oyster (Pinctada margaritifera).

129. The waters of Tahiti itself are too cold for this oyster to grow. Black pearls can also be found farther north of Tahiti in the Gambier and Cook islands. In earlier times, natural black pearls occurred in both Panama and Baja California. These pearls, however, were produced by a different species of oyster, *Pinctada mazatlanica*. Attempts are currently underway to culture pearls using this mollusk off the coast of Baja California.

for the pearl farmers against the windswept dangers of the open Pacific.

Our expedition gets underway shortly after dawn and consists of a French interpreter, our Tahitian boatman and guide Toputu, and me. Our destination: the pearl farm Kata-Kata.

With an intuitive skill passed down from a thousand generations of seafaring ancestors, Toputu pilots our small wooden runabout through a maze of coral heads that lurk just beneath the surface, waiting to tear the bottom out of our fragile craft.

Crossing the lagoon, we pass several pearl farms. The layout of each is similar. Several small wooden huts face the lagoon. A neatly constructed wooden wharf juts out from the beach approximately two hundred yards out into the lagoon. Perched at the end of the wharf is a small wooden building that serves as the farm's workhouse. Pairs of wooden piers spaced about twenty feet apart extend from the workhouse; connecting the piers is a horizontal gridwork of steel pipes. Suspended by ropes

R. W. Wise

The Kata Kata Pearl Farm, Manihi Island, French Polynesia, is protected by the encircling lagoon. Oysters are implanted inside the building; pearl oyster cages can be seen hanging from the metal grid just visible in the foreground.

from the pipes are slender cages of wire mesh that both house and protect the pearl oysters.

The trip across the lagoon takes a bit over two hours. Upon our arrival at the Kata-Kata farm we are heartily greeted by the farm's manager, Momo Paia, and his wife Tipati. Both are native islanders sporting the natural bronze-tan complexions that Western women would kill for. Both are dressed casually, Western style, but with the relaxed friendly manner that is one hundred percent Polynesian. Responding to my curiosity about the meaning of the farm's name, Momo laughs. From the Polynesian, he explains, "Kata-Kata" translates as "lots of laughs."

Momo leads the way out along the wharf to the headquarter's shack. Inside the one-room unpainted structure, blackboards chart the progress of the cultivation. In one corner is a small kitchen presided over by Tipati. Diagonally across the room is a glistening white enameled lab table where the implanting operation is performed.

Pearl making is an irritating proposition for the pearl oyster. In nature, the pearl nucleus — a grain of sand or small bit of coral — works its way into the soft mantle tissues of the oyster, causing irritation. To combat the discomfort, the oyster secretes nacre. More commonly called mother of pearl, nacre is a two-part calcium carbonate. The nacre covers the nucleus, enlarging it and making the oyster even more uncomfortable. The mollusk responds by secreting more nacre until, layer upon layer, the pearl takes form.

Mr. Sadao Ishi Bashi works at the Kata-Kata pearl farm. He is a slender Japanese man of medium height with a bright smile and an excellent command of English. Mr. Ishi Bashi's job is to implant the nucleus into each pearl oyster. Sadao, as he likes to be called, has been performing this operation for over two decades. A marine biologist by training, he learned his trade at a Japanese-owned company in Australia. Sadao gave me a step-by-step explanation of pearl farming techniques as I watched him perform the delicate operation.

Between October and February, when the waters of the South Pacific are at their warmest, the black lip oyster (Pinctada margaritifera) begins its reproductive cycle. The young oysters begin as "spat," microscopic offspring given off by the parent mollusk by the tens of millions. After several days of free floating in the lagoon, the spat not consumed by predators begin to look for something to attach themselves to. To gather the spat, the pearl farmer simply takes a bundle of miki-miki branches, a scrub bush native to the Tuamotu islands, wraps the bundle in chicken wire, attaches it to a buoy, and drops it into the lagoon in the area where the oysters are breeding. The woody branches of the miki-miki provide an ideal resting place for the spat. The bundles are then gathered and placed in a protected area of the lagoon. After two years, the spat have matured into full-grown oysters, six to eight inches in diameter.

The mature oyster is removed from the water. A worker drills a small hole in the heel of the shell. Using a special tool, another worker gently pries the shell open, sliding a small bamboo wedge between the valves to keep the shell from closing. The oyster is then ready for Mr. Ishi Bashi and the grafting operation.

I watch closely as Sadao slides the oyster into a stainless steel clamp mounted about ten inches above the work surface. The clamp holds the animal in place while the implant is performed. Sadao carefully selects a seven-millimeter mother-of-pearl sphere with a long-handled stainless steel spoon, similar to a dentist's instrument, and slides the spoon between the partially opened valves of the oyster. He then places the sphere, along with a tiny square of mantle tissue taken from another live oyster, in the area surrounding the gonad sac, the oyster's reproductive organ. The addition of this mantle tissue helps stimulate the formation of nacre. He then removes the wedge, allowing the valves to close.

The pearl nucleus, Sadao explains, is cut from the shell of the Pig Toe, a variety of Mississippi River mussel. The size of the implant depends upon the size of the oyster receiving the graft. The black lip can reach a diameter of twelve inches and a weight of eleven pounds. Normally a sphere with a minimum diameter of seven millimeters is used but a very large oyster may take a sphere of up to twelve millimeters.

Once the operation is completed, the oysters are returned to the lagoon. Suspended by a length of monofilament passed through the drill hole, the mature implanted oysters are attached inside a long narrow wire basket and hung between the piers until harvest time.

Kata-Kata will farm an average of sixty thousand oysters. Forty to sixty percent of the oysters will fail during the two-year cultivation period. On average, approximately six percent of the total crop will be finer quality pearls.

Back in Papeete, I ask Ronald Sage, a well-known dealer, about the black pearl's unique color. "It is completely natural," he says. Although it is called black, the color of the pearl varies from a cream color, called poe nono, through gray, poe motea, to a black called poe rava. Sage is referring to the body color of the pearl.

The basic or body color is only one criterion in the connoisseurship of pearls and it is of secondary importance. *Poe rava* or *poe nono*, neither is inherently more beautiful that the other; symmetry, texture, size, luster, and orient are more important. Additional details on pearl grading are provided in chapter five.

History: natural versus cultured

There are two basic types of pearls, natural and cultured. In either case the method of

Chin Cheng Choa, courtesy of Otimo International

producing the pearl is essentially the same. An irritant in the form of a grain of sand, a piece of coral, or a implant introduced by man, is placed or finds its way into the soft mantle tissues of the host mollusk. The oyster in the case of saltwater pearls, or clam in freshwater pearls, secretes a substance called nacre, a calcium carbonate composed of alternating layers of flattened aragonite crystals and concholian, a sort of calcium glue, that acts as a binder.

The first successful pearl culturing was developed in China in the fourteenth century. In the early years of this century, two Japanese researchers, Tokshi Nishikawa and K. Mikimoto, working independently of each other, came up with a process to artificially introduce a nucleus into the oyster. Patented in 1907, this technique made it possible to produce this extremely rare pearl in much larger quantities. In 1908, Mikimoto established the first commercial pearl farm in Japan.

Natural pearls are found in many parts of the world and are produced by a number of varieties of oyster. Historically, the best known pearl-producing areas include the Persian Gulf and the waters of the Gulf of Mannar off Ceylon (Sri Lanka). These waters are the source of the famous oriental pearls, a product of a specific variety of mollusk called Pinctada vulgaris, also known as the lingah shell.

Some of the most famous pearls were not oriental. One famous pearl, La Peregrina "The Incomparable" came from the Americas; it was found in Panama in the late sixteenth century. Originally owned by Mary Tudor, this pearl passed through a series of royal hands, or perhaps bosoms, until it finally came to rest on the most famous bosom of the last century: it was purchased by Richard Burton and given as a gift to his wife Elizabeth Taylor. Another famous pearl, the Tiffany Queen Pearl, was actually a freshwater gem found in 1857 in a stream near Patterson (Notchbrook), New Jersey. This round, highly translucent beauty was once owned by the Empress Eugenie, wife of Napoleon III.

Although a perfectly round pearl is the most desired, historically many of the most important pearls were not. La Peregrina is pear shaped, as was another famous Venezuelan pearl, the Phillip II. During the Renaissance, baroque pearls that suggested the body of an animal or person were used extensively in jewelry.

The cultured standard

Cultured pearls began to appear in force in the market in the late 1920s, causing a dramatic fall in the price of natural pearls. It has taken forty years for the aftershock to subside. It was not until the 1960s that cultured pearls were completely accepted; by that time cultured pearls had almost completely supplanted natural pearls in the world market. This has not happened with any other gemstone enhanced by human intervention.

The cultured pearl is a gem market anomaly. Natural pearls are more expensive than cultured pearls; however, outside the Middle East, there is essentially no market for natural pearls. By the late 1960s a fine natural pearl necklace that had been purchased at the turn of the century was worth roughly one tenth of its original price. Today, despite the depressed market, a single 8mm fine round natural pearl could bring as much as sixty-three hundred dollars whereas a similar 8mm cultured pearl would bring at most four hundred dollars.[130] Synthetic gemstones generally sell for pennies on the dollar when compared to natural stones. Why are pearls so different? Perhaps this is because a cultured pearl is not a synthetic, but is truly a natural product given a leg-up by man.

The three types of pearls that will be discussed in the following chapters — black South Sea, white South Sea, and Chinese freshwater — are all cultured.

130. *The Guide* (Northbrook, Illinois:
Gemworld International, Inc., 2002).

The Japanese akoya pearl, produced by the Pinctada martensii oyster, has been omitted from this discussion. This is not because the akoya is an inferior pearl. In fact, if left to its own devices, Pinctada martensii produces a highly lustrous and superior pearl. However, assembly line methods currently practiced by the Japanese produce a pearl with such thin layers of nacre, and that is so highly processed (bleached and dyed), that it more closely resembles a manufactured product than it does a true pearl.

Chapter 19

The Tahitian Black Pearl

Greenish black pearls are perhaps valued higher than any other colored pearls, if they have the proper orient; this is probably partly owing to their rarity.

G. F. Kunz, 1908

History

The black pearl was not known at all in the West in ancient times. Black pearls first came on the market in 1845.[131] Originally they were not highly esteemed, selling for a fraction of the price brought by white pearls from the traditional sources in the Persian Gulf and the Gulf of Mannar. The Empress Eugenie, wife of Napoleon III, was the person most responsible for bringing the black pearl into fashion. After the fall of Napoleon III, a fine necklace owned by the former Empress was auctioned at Christie's for twenty thousand dollars, the equivalent of several hundred thousand of today's dollars.

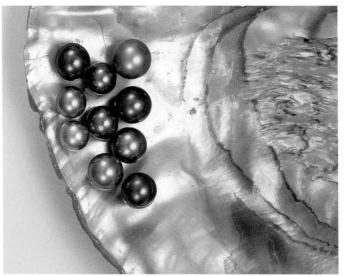

Tibor Ardai; courtesy of Assael International

Round black pearls arranged on the pearl oyster shell (Pinctada margaritifera). These pearls show a range — blue, green, and pink — of the very desirable orient or overtone colors that give the pearl "life."

Body color and orient

The finer examples of black pearl will normally appear greenish, bluish, pinkish, or violetish in tones of gray through black. This appearance is actually a combination of two factors: *body color* and *orient*.

Body color can be thought of as a tonal continuum from gray to black. Orient or overtone is the result of light entering and refracting through the alternating semi-translucent layers of aragonite (crystalline calcium) and conchiolin, a type of calcium that acts as a binder. The result is similar to the effect of oil on water. Orient is the ephemeral fuzzy glow, like sunlight through an early morning fog, that appears to

131. Kunz and Stevenson, *The Book of The Pearl*, pp. 29-30.

emanate from and cling to the surface of the pearl. Orient/overtone can be separated visually from body color by observing the pearl under a light bulb. The orient hue will be seen in the direct reflection of the bulb. The area surrounding the reflection will exhibit the body color. In fine black pearls this test is rarely necessary, as the orient, if present, is normally quite distinct.

It is this distinctive overtone that gives the black pearl its life and its air of mystery, and characterizes the finest of these pearls; it is the defining quality of the Tahitian black pearl.

Specific overtones are given fanciful names. Deep green is called *flywing*. The combination of green and pink is termed *peacock*; a dark-toned body color combined with pink is called *eggplant*. Occasionally pearls have a pure purple or pure blue overtone. Tiffany's famous gemologist G.F. Kunz (see quotation beginning this chapter) held that the green orient, or flywing, was the rarest and most valuable. Writing in 1908, he was speaking of natural black pearls. In cultured blacks, green is the most common orient color. Pink and blue come next in rarity, followed by peacock. Purple is by far the rarest and in my opinion the most beautiful of all.

Luster

Luster, the reflection of light off the surface of the pearl, is essentially the brightness of the pearl. The brighter, the better! In a fine pearl, this reflection is crisp and sharp. As quality decreases, the reflection becomes less distinct. Hold the pearl under a lamp and examine the bright reflection of the lamp on the surface of the pearl. The more distinct the reflection of the light source, the higher the luster.

The luster of the black pearl is somewhat softer than the luster of the akoya or the Chinese freshwater pearl. In the relatively warm waters of the South Pacific, nacre accumulates at a much faster rate than it does in the colder waters off the coast of Japan. However, nacre that accumulates in colder water tends to be closer grained, producing a potentially higher luster than is possible farther south. The luster of both the black and white South Sea pearl is softer than that of "cold water" pearls.

Symmetry

The more perfect the shape, the greater the value of the pearl. Round is the most favored shape, followed by pear, oval, and button. Asymmetrical shapes are classified as *baroque*. Prices of baroque pearls can vary widely. All nuclei implanted in cultured pearls begin as perfectly round and blemish-free; however, nature plays some interesting tricks during the pearl's growth. As a result, the average harvest yields only a very small percentage of perfectly round pearls. Pearls can be found in many unusual shapes.

Texture

Bumps, blemishes, tiny pits, or anything intruding on the pearl's surface is considered a negative. A *silky* flawless skin is the most desirable. Most pearls have slight imperfections; the issue is how much they disturb the eye. Dealers are most concerned with how the pearl will "face up," that is, whether imperfections will still be visible when the pearl is set. Pearls with surface cracks are almost worthless.

The rarity factor

Black and white South Sea pearls are, speaking generally, the largest of all pearls. This is a result of two factors: the size of the mollusk itself and the rate of nacre accumulation. The shellfish, due to its large size, can accept large nuclear implants and this, coupled with relatively rapid nacre accumulation, results in very large round pearls. The larger the pearl the rarer it is and the higher the price that will be asked for it.

Large mollusks can accept either a large number of small spherical implants or a very small number of larger diameters. It takes at least twenty-four months to lay down the two millimeters of nacre required to produce a fine black pearl. Thin-skinned pearls lack sufficient nacre to produce a fine luster and a distinct orient. Thin-skinned black pearls often exhibit a muddy brownish secondary hue or mask.

Since larger pearls command much higher prices, the usual grower's strategy is to produce a smaller quantity of larger pearls. With the increasing production of South Sea pearls, both black and white, this situation has begun to change. Growers are beginning to address market demand for smaller pearls. Prices for round pearls begin at 8mm. Black South Sea pearls under 10mm are very difficult to find for the reasons stated above. Prices increase at a reasonable percentage rate to 12mm. Prices for pearls over 12mm increase at somewhat larger percentages. Above 16mm, prices become negotiable, because, at these sizes, rarity becomes an increasingly important factor in the value equation.

The spread of pearl culturing throughout its growing region is bound to affect prices. Dramatic increases in production in French Polynesia over the past decade have already lowered prices significantly. Although Tahiti has dominated the market for several decades, nascent industries in the Cook Islands and off the coast of Baja California are just beginning to challenge French Polynesia's market dominance. The spread of the pearl culturing industry is likely to continue. The prognosis for the short term is, therefore, a continued softening of prices.

Chapter 20

Freshwater Pearls from China

The finest quality [pearl] that comes from China compares favorably with the finest from Japan

John Latendresse, 1992

China was one of the first to master the art of culturing. The Middle Kingdom began producing cultured pearls in the fourteenth century. In the 1960s a state-controlled industry introduced freshwater cultured pearls to the world market. Originally cultured using the wild *Cristaria plicata* or cockscomb mussel, initial production was of low quality baroque pearls, disparagingly known as rice crispies.

In the early 1980s, Chinese farmers abandoned the cockscomb in favor of the thicker shelled *Hyriopsis cumingii* or "three-cornered shell" mussel. Implantations of this new mollusk resulted in a breathtakingly superior freshwater pearl. By the early 1990s these pearls began to appear in force on the world market. Pearl culturing in China had come of age.[132]

These new Chinese pearls are filling a niche hitherto occupied by Japanese Biwa pearls. Ironically, just as demand for fine freshwater pearls has increased, and the term "Biwa pearl" has come to connote the very finest in freshwater pearls, actual production at Lake Biwa has declined to the point of nonexistence. Pollution is the culprit! Industrialization surrounding Lake Biwa has sounded the death knell for Japanese freshwater pearls.

The Chinese are producing two types of freshwater pearls: tissue nucleated and bead nucleated. Tissue nucleation uses only a thin segment of living tissue from a donor mollusk to stimulate the development of the pearl.[133] Bead nucleation (explained in detail in Chapter 15) is a relatively newer technique in China. Pearls of this type have been available only for about five years.

Tissue-nucleated pearls, which are by far the largest group produced, are mainly baroque pearls and are available in many bizarre and amazing shapes. Bead nucleation, as of this writing, has produced round pearls as large as fourteen millimeters.

Color

Chinese pearls come in a variety of hues including pink, apricot (yellowish orange), peach (pinkish orange), champagne (slightly pinkish yellow), plum (reddish violet), bronze (reddish brown), and every shade in between. Unlike black pearls, these pearls can be bleached white by prolonged exposure to the sun or by soaking the pearl in a bleaching agent for several hours. Natural color Chinese freshwater pearls should be stored in a darkened environment in order to preserve the natural pastel color,

---

132. Richard W. Wise, "The New Face of Chinese Freshwater Pearls," *Colored Stone Magazine*, January 1992, p. 22.

133. The term tissue nucleation is a bit of a misnomer. The tissue implant grows into a sac and does not become the nucleus of the pearl. This type of pearl has, in effect, no nucleus at all. Fuji Voll, personal communication, 2003.

since they may fade with long exposure to sunlight. Color in pearls is not a part of the quality equation. Apricot is not more beautiful than champagne. That is a question of preference and *simpatico* (*see* Chapter 5).

Orient and overtone

Chinese pearls appear to have relatively opaque nacre. In smooth, relatively round pearls, the orient will exhibit itself as a slight darkening of the body color, plus perhaps a bit of pink.

Orient can best be judged if the pearl is viewed against a color that is close in hue and therefore neutralizes the body color of the pearl. Diffused daylight is the best viewing environment. In this lighting the overtone is seen in the actual reflection of the light source; the other color seen is the

Jeff Scovil; courtesy of Freeman Pearl Co.

Chinese freshwater pearl strands of exceptional luster and orient; the orient color surrounds the body color on each individual pearl like a halo.

body color. Incandescent light can sometimes produce the opposite effect, bleaching out the color toward the center of the round pearl. In such cases, the orient may be found in the surrounding halo.

The rainbow effect

Baroque China pearls tend to exhibit a rainbow effect, a quality unique to this type of pearl. This is particularly true of the more baroque tissue-nucleated variety. The more texture, the more pronounced is this effect. Rainbow iridescence must be distinguished from true orient. Though beautiful and desirable, it appears to be a surface effect, not the result of refraction. Rainbow iridescence is probably caused by light reflecting in different directions off the pearl's surface. This phenomenon is called interference; light rays literally bump into one another, resulting in the breakup of white light into various spectral colors.

Symmetry

Symmetry is the least important factor in evaluating a pearl. A majority of Chinese pearls are baroque, occurring in many strange and fanciful shapes. Baroque pearls, like fine abstract sculpture, may assume shapes that in no way detract from (and in fact contribute to) the beauty of the pearl. While it is true that curved surfaces bring out the beauty of the orient in a pearl, and that perfection of form does carry a substantial premium in the marketplace, the requirement that a pearl be perfectly round seems, at least to me, somewhat arbitrary.

Baroque pearls present the flexible aficionado with an opportunity to acquire a beautiful gem at a price which is dramatically less than the price a pearl with comparable luster, orient, etc. would bring in a pearl with perfect symmetry.

Chapter 21

South Sea Pearls

Not a chap among you knows the value of a given piece of pearl. That's how I can help you. I'll undertake to value without any fee for any of you chaps and my valuation stands as an offer too. If none of the big bosses will give you more bring it back to me and I'll pay the fee all right.

Louis Kornitzer, 1900

In addition to black pearls, the sultry waters of the South Pacific also produce white pearls. Three species of pearl oyster are found in southern Pacific waters. The most important of these, the *Pinctada maxima*, is the largest of the pearl oysters. Three subspecies or varieties of *Pinctada maxima* are the white lip, silver lip, and the yellow or golden lip oysters.[134] These three siblings produce pearls that range from a white to silver white through yellow to a distinct golden hue.

South Sea pearls should not be confused with the Japanese akoya pearls, which are a product of the *Pinctada fucata (martensii)* oyster called *akoya-gai* in Japanese. Both these pearls have a white body color. The Japanese oyster rarely produces pearls over 9mm. In fact, 9mm is a very large akoya pearl. The *maxima* regularly grows pearls over 15mm and, if left to its own devices, will produce pearls as large as 20mm.

Pinctada maxima is found throughout the southwest Pacific from the Ryukyu Islands to the Arafura Sea, along a band running within twenty degrees of latitude north and south of the equator. Until the current decade, the vast majority of white cultured South Sea pearls were produced off Australia's northern coast. Recently farms in the Philippines and Indonesia have begun to produce pearls from *Pinctada maxima*, more specifically the golden lip variety. These pearls occur in various tones of yellow through golden.

Body color

The body color of a white South Sea pearl should be white. Pearls, like faceted stones, will sometimes show a secondary or modifying hue. Some of these secondary hues are more desirable than others. Green, for example, is something of a negative factor; even a slight tint of greenish hue to the otherwise white body color will lower the value of the pearl. Gray is a double-edged hue. If it is dull, it is a negative. If it is bright it is called *silver* and adds measurably to the pearl's appeal.

Simpatico

South Sea pearls, as we have seen, are not all white, though white is the most sought after and thus the most expensive. This is because the white body color is *simpatico* (see Chapter 5) with skin tones typical of northern Europeans. People of the developed world simply have more money to spend on pearls; hence demand is greatest

34. The largest known pearl produced by the *Pinctada maxima* oyster is 24mm in diameter.

Courtesy of Paspaley Pearls.

Fine white South Sea pearls from Australia. Note the misty luster and slight pinkish overtone on some of the pearls.

for these colors. The pearl itself occurs in white to golden, passing through various tones of yellow along the way. The actual body color has little to do with quality; s*impatico* is really a measure of compatibility. All other factors being equal, the subtle nuances of hue found in the South Sea pearl are of equal beauty.

Luster and orient:
white South Sea pearls

Luster and orient are the two most important criteria to be used when evaluating the beauty of a pearl. The white variety of South Sea pearl rarely exhibits more than a bit of orient; that is, an overtone of contrasting

A fine strand of South Sea pearls with the signature soft misty luster. Pearls cultured in colder waters such as the ubiquitous Japanese akoya will normally exhibit a harder, brighter luster.

the pearl's skin which lends the South Sea pearl an ephemeral sort of beauty found in no other variety.

Luster and orient: golden South Sea pearls

The golden South Sea pearl produced by the golden lip variety of *Pinctada maxima* shares the softer luster of the South Sea varieties, but will exhibit a distinct orient or overtone. In fact, in finer pearls, the yellow to golden color is part orient and part body color (see the section on connoisseurship in pearls, Chapter 5). It can best be described as a golden glow that seems to cling somewhat tenuously to the pearl's skin and to follow it when the pearl is rotated. In the finest gems, it emanates from the skin and appears to hover over the surface of the pearl.

chromatic color such as that displayed by the finer black South Sea pearls. Occasionally a fine white pearl displays a bit of pink.

The overall luster of these pearls is somewhat softer than that of pearls produced in colder waters. Soft luster coupled with translucency can result in a pearl with a soft misty surface appearance that suggests a lake-bred early morning fog. Thus if one were to apply the luster test described in the discussion on pearl connoisseurship in Chapter 5, the most that could be said is that the luster of the South Sea pearl is, at best, a "good" luster. The misty surface does impart a sense of life to

Size

South Sea pearls are, speaking generally, the largest of all pearls. This is a result of two factors: the size of the mollusk itself and the rate of nacre accumulation. Nacre accumulates up to ten times faster in the warm waters of the southern Pacific than it does off the coast of Japan. The shellfish, due to its large size, can accept large nuclear implants; coupled with nacre accumulation, this results in very large round pearls. The larger the pearl the rarer it is and the higher the price that will be asked for it.

Large mollusks can accept either a large number of small spherical implants or a very small number of larger diameters. It takes at least thirty months to produce a fine South Sea pearl. Since larger pearls command much higher prices, the grower's usual strategy is to produce a smaller quantity of larger pearls. With the increasing production of South Sea pearls, both black and white, this situation has begun to change. Growers are beginning to address market demand for smaller pearls. Prices for South Sea round pearls begin at 10mm. South Sea pearls under 10mm are very difficult to find and pearls under 9mm hardly exist at all. Prices increase at a reasonable percentage rate to 14mm. Pearls over 14mm increase at somewhat larger percentages. At 16mm prices become negotiable, because at these sizes, rarity becomes an increasingly important factor in the value equation.

The spread of pearl culturing throughout its growing region is bound to affect prices. Although Australia has dominated the market for several decades, emerging industries in Indonesia, Burma, Vietnam, and the Philippines are beginning to erode Australia's market dominance. The prognosis for the short term is, therefore, a continuing softening of prices for these fine southern beauties.

RUBY AND SAPPHIRE

The road is narrow and winding, the sky a gunmetal blue and cloudless. The day is hot! A cloud of brown dust hovers over the single lane that is paved only in places. The monsoon rains that will soon turn it all into a muddy quagmire have not yet arrived. The road leads to Mogok and the ancient ruby and sapphire mines of upper Burma.

Riding through the countryside, we pass through villages, seeing houses of plaited bamboo, creaking bullock carts, and peasants, reed-thin and brown as dirt, plodding along the road. The green fields of rice stretch along both sides of the road, like a well-tended lawn, on toward the horizon. Farmers in conical straw hats bend over rice paddies in a tableau from centuries past.

Mogok is a provincial town one hundred seventy miles west of Mandalay, Burma's second largest city. Since antiquity the valley in which the town is situated has been famous as the legendary *Valley of the Serpents*. According to the ancient tale, somewhere in the mystic East was a nearly bottomless valley carpeted with glittering gems. Poisonous serpents stood guard over the gems. Merchants seeking the stones tossed the sticky carcasses of skinned sheep into the valley. The gems stuck to the meat and the great eagles circling the valley floor would swoop down, grasp the meat in their talons, and bring it back to their nests high on the rocks surrounding the valley, thus allowing the men to retrieve the precious stones. Among the stones found in or near this valley were ruby, sapphire, peridot, and tourmaline.

The valley today is still the stuff of legend: deep, enveloped in mist, and surrounded by rocky crags. The Burmese government has kept it closed to foreigners for over thirty years, and in that time the modern world has all but passed it by. Special government permits are still required to travel in this area. Traditionally stones have been found on the valley floor, in the streambeds and catch basins, and in the limestone caves that honeycomb the mountainsides surrounding the town.

It was on the sultry afternoon of our second day in Mogok town that I got my first glimpse of a legend. I was with my friend Joe B., one of Asia's premier gem dealers. We had just finished lunch at an outdoor restaurant where the customer chooses his noodles and condiments. The partially cooked noodles are plunged into a cauldron of boiling stock, ladled into a bowl, and the

R. W. Wise

Kanase women in Moguk, Burma, work the tailings in a stream coming from a large mechanized mining operation. They sieve through the gravel looking for ruby, hoping to find small gems overlooked in the washing process. This privilege, the Burmese version of social security, is restricted to the widows and orphans of miners.

condiments added. The dealer approached our table. He was a thin, dark- haired Burmese in his forties dressed in a Western shirt and the traditional cotton skirt, or *lungyi*. He had a rectangular face and high prominent cheekbones. He apparently knew our agent and they greeted each other with extravagant courtesy. The dealer had heard that we were in town and apparently had something special to show us.

After the introductions and ritual pleasantries, the dealer escorted us to his office, about two blocks along the dusty main street. We passed through an open-fronted food market. At the back of the store, we ascended a staircase of dark teak. The workroom of a bakery was visible below the stairwell and the smell of the baking accompanied us up to the second floor. We entered a room with walls and floors richly paneled in polished teakwood. The market noises and the westering sun filtered through open casement windows overlooking the street.

After sitting down around a low wooden table we were offered tea and delicacies still warm from the ovens below. Two stone parcels were placed before us. My friend opened the first paper and after a brief look handed it to me without comment. Inside was a two-carat cushion-shaped ruby of the finest color I had ever seen. I looked at Joe, our eyes locked briefly, his glance confirmed the insight that had tripped off like a flashbulb in my mind. In my twenty years' experience this was my first glimpse of the Pigeon's Blood!

Asking to see the pigeon's blood is like asking to see the face of God.
                         Anonymous nineteenth-century Burmese trader

The true pigeon's blood red is extremely rare, more a color of the mind than the material world.
                         R. Hughes, 1997

The color was new to me yet somehow I knew it for what it was, perhaps because I had seen everything but! The stone was a primary red, the hue and tone like a rich tomato sauce that has simmered for hours on the stove: a deep-toned pure red with just a hint of blue added to it. I composed myself, breathing deeply to control my rapidly beating heart. My friend reflected for a moment, then asked the price. The asking price was, of course, astonishing! Negotiations continued for about an hour, but in the end our offer was not accepted. The next day proved luckier.

Sapphire comes in many colors. Sapphire is one of two varieties of the gem species corundum. If it is red, it is ruby. If it is any other color it is called sapphire.

Chapter 22

Blue Sapphire

The characteristic color of the Sapphire is a clear blue, very like to that of the little weed called the "corn flower," and the more velvety its appearance, the greater the value of the gem.

W. E.. Streeter, 1879

They say you never forget your first love. Gemologically speaking, blue sapphire was mine. I remember my first date with a Kashmir . . . ah! that velvety blue, that sleepy bedroom glow. It was in Bangkok that I met my first Burmese sapphire, a saucy royal blue, deep hued with just a touch of violet. That vivid saturation gave me a thrill. I didn't know just how lucky I was; it took me ten years to find another as fine.

By the early 1980s sapphires were mostly from Australia, Thailand, and Sri Lanka. Kashmir stones were a fading legend, and except for a trickle across the Thai border, Burma blues just a pleasant memory. Thai stones were available but were dark or black, often opaque. Australians were greenish; Sri Lankans were the best: heat treated, it's true; but the finest– just a step in saturation below Burmese–and with sleepiness, occasionally, almost like a Kashmir.

Beautiful sapphires are still to be found, but the cast has changed. Sri Lankan stones are still in reasonably good supply. Australia is reportedly producing better blues. Thai pro-duction, particularly at Kanchanaburi, is down significantly. Increasingly we hear about new finds in Africa, from places unknown just a few years ago. Madagascar is the new big name in blue sapphire.

Jeff Scovil; courtesy of R.W. Wise, Goldsmiths, Inc.

A 3.05-carat natural Ceylon sapphire with a very slightly purplish "Kashmir" blue key color. Tone is eighty-five percent.

Color: the two standards

Historically, blue sapphire has been judged based on two paradigms: the best stones from Burma and the finest of Kashmir. The best of Burmese sapphire has a pure dark blue primary hue with a secondary hue of ten to fifteen percent purple. This is usually described as "royal blue." Burma sapphire is set apart by its transparency (crystal) and the vivid crispness of its hue. Kashmirs, by contrast, are a purer blue hue of a slightly more open (seventy-five percent) tone, with just five to ten percent purple, a hue often described as "cornflower."[135]

Kashmir stones often have what is described as a sleepy quality, a result of myriad numbers of microscopic inclusions known as *flour* which can be seen under the microscope. Light refracting through this microscopic Milky Way is diffused and this gives the stone an overall sleepy or fuzzy appearance. These inclusions also reflect light, dispersing it throughout the gem and thus reducing extinction. Kashmir sleepiness contrasts with the robust brilliance and transparency of a Burma stone.

Kashmir sapphire was found on one side of one hill in the Indian state it is named for, and was effectively mined out by the 1930s. Burmese sapphire has also been in short supply since the thirties. The new Burma ruby diggings at Mong Hsu produce almost no sapphire, and only a few stones per

year find their way from the old mine areas of Mogok into the Bangkok market. Which is the best? Connoisseurs disagree, perhaps due to rarity, but fine Burmese stones cost at least fifty percent more than Ceylon sapphires, and Kashmir stones more than twice the price of Burmese.

Ceylon sapphire

Ceylon or Sri Lankan sapphire has been the

Courtesy of © Christies Images

The 62.02-carat Rockefeller sapphire, considered to be one of the world's finest Burmese gems, was reputedly purchased from the Nizam of Hyderabad in 1934 by John D. Rockefeller. It sold at Christie's on December 5, 2001, for $3.5 million, almost $57,000 per carat, the highest price ever paid, at auction, for a fine sapphire.

135. The use of terms such as "cornflower" illustrates the problem of comparing the color of a gemstone to another natural substance. Although cornflowers themselves have a violet component, in the gem trade, cornflower is usually used to describe a pure blue hue. Powder blue is probably the more precise term.

quality standard bearer for the past half century. The Ceylon gem may look just like its Kashmir and Burmese brethren, appearing either cornflower or royal blue; some have a Kashmir-like sleepy appearance. However, the relatively larger size of the inclusions causing the effect in Ceylon stones translates into a crisper sort of sleepiness that is qualitatively different, arguably less subtle than the same characteristic in stones from Kashmir. Ceylon sapphires can have a vivid royal blue like a fine Burma blue, but rarely show the crisp velvety transparent crystal and are a touch murkier than the best out of Burma.

When seeking a fine sapphire, the collector-connoisseur is advised to avoid labels and look at the gem on offer. Ceylon sapphire has its own distinct and beautiful look; the natural color stones often have a bit more of a purple secondary hue.

New contenders from Africa

The Tunduru deposit has been described as the most important discovery in fifty years. Tunduru is in southeastern Tanzania hard against the Mozambique border. The best of the Tunduru stones have a deep royal blue color similar to Ceylon; however, in the words of Joseph Belmont, a dealer noted for his fine eye, "Tunduru stones have a much better crystal."[136] The best of Tunduru stones are a step up from Ceylon sapphire and only a half step down from fine Burmese sapphire.

The politics of Tanzania make for sporadic production. Small amounts of Tunduru rough are still finding their way to market in Nairobi. In addition, a few "brilliant blue" stones are to be found in parcels coming into Nairobi from Rwanda and occasionally from Lodwar in northern Kenya.

At this writing blue sapphire from Madagascar is making a major impact on the market. These stones closely resemble Ceylon sapphire with perhaps a bit more of the purple secondary hue.

Australia remains a steady supplier of blue sapphire to the world market. Sapphire is found at a number of sources in Queensland and New South Wales. For many years Australian stones had the reputation of being greenish and overdark with tonal values of ninety percent or more. Sapphire, like ruby, emerald, and tsavorite garnet, is judged by the purity of its primary hue. A little violet is desirable, but green is the bane of blue sapphire. Thai dealers often bought the best of the Australian stones, heated them, and sold them labeled Ceylon in the Bangkok market — and still do. However, with new sources and advanced heating technology, a larger quantity of finer color stones are available today than in the recent past.

America the beautiful

Alluvial sapphire deposits were first discovered in Montana's Missouri River in 1865. Three other sites — Dry Cottonwood Creek, Rock Creek, and Yogo Gulch — were added before the turn of the century. Yogo Gulch, the only hard-rock deposit, was mined steadily until the late 1920s, when it

136. Joseph Belmont, personal communication, 1995.

Jeff Scovil; courtesy of R.W. Wise, Goldsmiths, Inc

A matched pair of oval Madagascar natural (unheated) blue sapphires. The color is a vivid slightly purplish blue, eighty percent tone, fine crystal.

was abandoned; production resumed in the 1980s.

Yogo sapphire is often described as "cornflower" blue, a rich purplish blue hue that has been erroneously compared to Kashmir. Generally, the finest of the Yogo stones have a distinctively crisp "steely" (slightly grayish) appearance. This steely quality is the result of a slight gray mask. These Montana beauties are of uniform color, relatively free of inclusions, and are

not heat enhanced. Unfortunately, rough Yogo sapphire occurs in flat tabular crystals and rarely yields faceted stones in sizes above one carat. Seventy-five percent of current production consists of cut stones under one carat.

Sapphire from the three other sources mentioned has been of little commercial importance until recently. Although huge quantities of sapphire have been taken from the Missouri River and both Rock and Dry

Cottonwood creeks, these areas produced mostly colorless to pale-toned (twenty to thirty percent) stones of little beauty. Advanced heat treating technology has significantly altered the situation. These techniques have raised rough yields from Rock Creek from as little as eight percent to as much as eighty percent facet-grade gem material.

The best of these blue sapphires display a rich (eighty to eighty-five percent) blue primary hue, with a pinch (five percent) of violet and a slight (ten to fifteen percent) gray to gray green modifier. Due to the apparent green secondary hue, Montana stones from these sources never approach the finest sapphire qualities. Blue Rock Creek sapphire most resembles high-grade commercial quality stones from Australia.

The best of the blues: hue and tone

Blue sapphire, like ruby, is a primary color gemstone. The purer the primary hue the better. In practice this means that a dark-toned (seventy to eighty percent) primary blue hue with no more than a ten to fifteen percent secondary purplish hue is most desirable.[137] Some connoisseurs prefer a distinct purplish secondary hue because it adds a velvety richness to the blue; others prefer a purer, more "open" blue of slightly lighter (seventy-five percent) tone. This range of hues is to be considered the finest color in sapphire.

Green is the bane of blue sapphire. Any visible hint of green brings a stone's value crashing down into the commercial range. The problem is that all blue sapphire has a greenish component when viewed at certain angles to the C axis. It is the cutter's job to cut the stone so that this green is not part of the face-up appearance. Often this slight tint of green is difficult to see. Stone-to-stone comparison will often highlight the green secondary hue, as long as the viewer is not looking at a series of slightly greenish stones.

Saturation

Gray is the normal saturation modifier in blue sapphire. Often it will be found mixed with green in lower-quality stones. A slight gray mask will introduce a cool or slightly "steely" quality in the normally warm hue of a sapphire. All pure chromatic hues are vivid. If the key color appears dull and cool, a gray mask is the probable culprit.

Multicolor effect

Since blue sapphire is a primary color gem, the closer it comes to exhibiting a uniformly pure primary blue hue the better and more desirable it is. The face-up mosaic of a gemstone, however, is far from uniform; each facet may exhibit variations in the gem's key color. Some facets may appear bright, some dull; some may display a dark tone, others a medium- or light-toned blue.

Multicolor effect has several causes (see Chapter 4). Sapphire is dichroic, i.e., light entering the gem divides into two rays, one violetish blue, one greenish blue. In addition, the stone may be zoned: colorless

137. C.R. Beesley, personal communication, 1990 and 1998. According to Beesley, the best sapphire in the world would have no more than a seventy percent pure blue hue. The other thirty percent would be a combination of all secondary hues, including some green. Beesley describes this color as "vivid purplish blue." Minor hues are not necessarily visible to the eye. See Beesley, *Colored Stone Training Manual*, p. 15.

zones are juxtaposed against zones of color. Light rays passing through colorless zones lose color. Also, the pavilion facets of the gem cause a light ray entering the stone to reflect at least twice within the stone, absorbing color as it goes. Add to this the effect of light that shifts in color temperature from yellowish to bluish, accentuating or depressing the purplish secondary hue, and you have an idea why the face-up scene may be less than uniform.

In ruby and sapphire a negative type of multicolor effect is traditionally called *bleeding*, manifest as a lightening of tone and a loss of saturation when the stone is shifted from natural to incandescent lighting. At lighter tones, blue becomes pastel, less saturated, and washed out. Bleeding is a good analogy: the color is drained from the stone just as blood is drained from the body. The effect is similar: the stone becomes pallid, and its life, figuratively, is drawn out of it. Bleeding in sapphire may be described as weak, moderate, or strong. The more apparent or stronger it is, the greater the fault.

Kashmir sapphire contains little or no chromium, which appears to be one cause of the multicolor effect. What this means is that Kashmir sapphire, unlike Burma sapphire, for example, will not pick up a purplish secondary hue, but will maintain its hue as the viewing environment is shifted from daylight to incandescent lighting.

Crystal

With gemstones there is one truth: no matter how fine the stone, somewhere there is a better one. Sapphire at its zenith — that is, a stone that seems to have everything: color (hue, saturation, and tone), clarity, and marvelous make — still requires a velvet transparency to reach the very pinnacle of quality.[138] Blue sapphire often will close up in incandescent lighting. This may have little effect on color, so it can't be described as *bleeding*; the *crystal* simply becomes turbid, dark, and murky as the lighting environment is shifted from natural light to the light of the bulb.

Some stones will have the three Cs (color, clarity, and cut), but very few also have the diaphaneity, the good crystal — the fourth C– imparting a quality that is rich, crisp, and velvety all at the same moment. It is this quality that finally separates the very finest from the rest of the herd. Fine stones that fit this description may come from any source. Beauty is its own best pedigree.

Texture

Color in sapphire often occurs in zones that follow the hexagonal outline of the sapphire crystal. Zones of rich color will alternate with colorless areas. This is particularly characteristic of gems from Sri Lanka. Due to zoning, sapphire will often show what experts call texture. This means that the zones are sometimes visible face up, causing the color to appear uneven. Even color is very important in sapphire; it is the cutter's job to integrate the zones so that the face-up color *appears* to be even. What is seen through the side or back of the stone is of little importance. Sometimes the lapidary's attempt to even out the texture by

138. Kashmir sapphire is something of an exception. The diffused *sleepy* effect, together with the tiny inclusions that produce it, reduce transparency somewhat in Kashmir and Kashmir-type sapphire. In such cases, the beauty of this unique phenomenon makes up for some loss of crystal. Although Kashmir sapphires can hardly be described as *limpid*, the best still retain a moderate degree of transparency.

eliminating the effect of the natural zoning in the crystal leads to poor symmetry.

However, stones that appear lopsided below the girdle or that have off-center culets are more tolerated in sapphire than in most other gem species. Symmetry faults that would be considered major flaws in diamond are accepted in sapphire so long as they occur below the girdle and do not create a lopsided girdle outline.

Heat enhancement

No one is quite sure how long heat-enhanced sapphire has been in the market — perhaps a hundred years, probably much longer.[139] Heat treatment, known as burning, was reported in India as early as 2000 BC.[140] However, it was not until the 1970s that the technology to achieve very high temperatures became available, and heat treating began to be practiced on a grand scale. Some lighter Ceylon stones (thirty to fifty percent tones) are unheated. But most of the finer Ceylon and Tunduru stones, as well as a good portion of the Madagascar stones currently in the market, are heat enhanced.

Heating has a negative effect in sapphire. Heat-treated blues have generally poorer crystal than unheated stones. The heating process tends to reduce transparency or muddy the crystal.[141] If all other factors are equal, the very best natural color sapphire will be more beautiful than the very best burned sapphire. For example, of the top ten blue sapphires in the world, two through nine may be heat enhanced, but number one will be natural color. The exact opposite occurs when ruby is subjected to heat treatment. In general, natural color sapphire will sell at a premium of approximately thirty percent above the price of a comparable heat-enhanced stone.

With regard to gemstones in general, all factors are rarely equal. Sapphire, like all other gems, should be considered stone by stone. Heat treatment improves the appearance (hue, saturation, tone, clarity) of a vast majority of sapphires; otherwise, it would not be done.

The rarity factor

Exceptional blue sapphire is rare in any size. Stones over twenty carats are available; however, as with most gem species, stones larger than those readily usable in jewelry on a per carat basis tend to decrease in price.

139. Tagore, *Mani Mala*, vol. 1, pp. 243, 455.
140. Nassau, *Gemstone Enhancement*, p. 25.
141. Joseph Belmont, personal communication, 1997.

Chapter 23

Padparadscha Sapphire

It is GIA's opinion that this color range should be limited to light to medium tones of pinkish orange to orange-pink hues. Lacking delicacy, the dark brownish orange or even medium brownish orange tones of corundum from East Africa would not qualify under this definition. Deep orangy red sapphires likewise would not qualify as fitting the term Padparadscha.

Robert Crowningshield, 1982

Padparadscha is a corruption of the Singhalese word *padmaragaya*, which is composed of two words, *padma*, lotus; and *raga*, color.[142] Thus a padparadscha color sapphire is the color of the lotus, in this case the oriental lotus (*Nelumbo nucifera 'Speciosa'*). As with other cases discussed in this book, such descriptions often create more problems than they solve. What color is the lotus? As a bud it is a beautiful, delicate shade of reddish pink, but as it opens the pink shades into yellow.[143]

As a further source of confusion, some experts believe that only sapphire from Sri Lanka, the original source, may be properly called *padparadscha*. This is another manifestation of the innate conservatism of the gem trade. The experts might be forgiven if the only other possible contenders were the brownish orange pink "African *padparadscha*" sapphires found in the gem gravels of Tanzania's Umba River.[144] However, in recent years, fine padparadscha stones have been found in Vietnam's Quy Chau mines, and more recently still, in newly discovered gem-producing areas of Songea Tanzania and southern Madagascar.[145]

Jeff Scovil; courtesy of R.W. Wise, Goldsmiths, Inc.

This natural 3.09-carat pinkish orange sapphire embodies the essence of padparadscha. The color is pinkish orange, fifty percent tone. Note the delicate blending of hues and the exceptionally limpid crystal.

Hue and saturation

Today it is generally accepted that the term padparadscha may be applied to delicately colored "light to medium tones of pinkish-orange, orangy pink to orange-pink hues."[146] The actual percentages of pink and orange hues cannot be defined

42. Robert Crowningshield, "Padparadscha: What's In A Name?" *Gems & Gemology*, Spring 1983, p. 31. Dealers from Sri Lanka invariably call yellowish orangy pink sapphire "padparadscha."

143. Ibid.

144. Some excellent quality stones have been found at Umba River, comparable to the finest from Sri Lanka. Excellent quality stones can also be found in Vietnam. See Hughes, *Ruby & Sapphire*, pp. 398, 414. The finest I have ever seen were from Songea, Tanzania.

145. Hughes, p. 221.

146 Crowningshield, "Padparadscha," p. 35.

Tino Hammid, © Gemological Institute of America

The Morgan padparadscha sapphire, currently in the American Museum of Natural History in New York, is considered a paradigm of padparadscha gems. Note the distinct yellowish secondary hue (multicolor effect) toward the center of the stone.

generally. It is a question of the individual gem. Additional secondary hues — or, rather, tertiary hues such as yellow or violet — push the definition. Any combination may be acceptable. The key word is "delicate." Padparadscha sapphire may exhibit either a brown or gray mask. In darker-toned gems with an orange primary hue, the orange may shade into brown. This is characteristic of Umba River stones. A gray mask is more prevalent in gems with a primary pink hue.

Tone and crystal

Light to medium tones coupled with a high degree of transparency, or good crystal, translates into a delicate effect in padparadscha sapphire. The tonal range is from thirty to sixty-five percent. Stones with tones above sixty-five percent are too robust to qualify as padparadscha. Stones with less than thirty percent tone may fit the definition, but are too pale of hue to be of interest.

Multicolor effect

Sapphire is a dichroic stone. Since padparadscha is by definition a mixture of hues, multicolor effect is very much present in gems of this type. In many cases, multicolor effect in padparadscha sapphire may include some element of yellow. The most famous gem of this type, the one-hundred-carat Morgan padparadscha, (pictured previous page) in the collection of the American Museum of Natural History, exhibits strong multicolor effect, including a definite yellowish secondary hue.

Ideally the hues should be well mixed. Sometimes an elongated oval or pear shaped stone will show a divided color that is a pinkish orange hue at the center with a darker, more visually pure orange or orangy yellow toward either end. This might be described as parti-colored or a sort of "topaz effect." While this might be a plus in imperial topaz, it is not in a padparadscha sapphire. A uniform pinkish orange to orangy pink is preferable to a stone that is parti-colored.

African bird of paradise

Pink orange to red orange stones from the gravel of Tanzania's Umba River have been marketed for years as African padparadscha sapphire. A majority, though by no means all, of the gems from this source have a marked brownish mask. Umba River stones have poorer crystal and are darker (sixty-five to eighty-five percent) in tone. The combination of hue, saturation, and tone is best described as "robust" rather than "delicate." The true padparadscha express-es itself in a petal-soft visual vibrato. If padparadscha is the color of the lotus, it can be said that most Umba River stones find their floral soul mate in the blossom called bird of paradise (*Strelitzia reginae*).[147]

Rocky Mountain padparadscha

Perhaps the finest and most interesting sapphires produced from the Rock Creek and Gem Mountain deposits in Montana are the medium-toned orangy pink violet to violetish orange sapphires. A majority of these stones are actually tricolor with zones of orange and pink and with a secondary hue of lavender (light violet). When faceted in the brilliant style, the three colors tend to mix into a unique "padparadscha"-type stone that is actually violetish pink orange. The finest of these Rocky Mountain padparadschas are a light to medium tone (forty to sixty percent) with almost no brown mask, allowing an exceptional saturation.

All sapphire from this source is routinely heat treated. Before treatment, Montana stones are extremely light in tone. Sixty percent of the stones heat treat to various tones of bluish green to greenish blue. In 1997 I completed a quality analysis of sapphire from Gem Mountain (part of the Rock Creek deposit outside of Phillipsburg, Montana) commissioned by the American Gem Corporation. At that time approximately two million carats of sapphire rough had been dug, heat treated, cut, and sorted by the company. Of this entire production, less than one hundred stones were graded padparadscha; fewer than ten of these stones weighed over one carat.

147. Richard W. Wise, "The Colors of Africa," *Jewelers Quarterly Magazine*, 1989, Designer Color Pages, p. 7.

Caveat emptor

Padparadscha sapphire is not, strictly speaking, a variety of sapphire. That is to say, there is no scientific gemological test that can establish that a particular sapphire is worthy of the name. With the addition of the Rocky Mountain type, the quote at the beginning of the chapter pretty well sums up the color range of padparadscha sapphire as I understand it. Some gemological laboratories will use padparadscha as a descriptive term on their grading reports. Padparadscha sapphire is also routinely heat treated.

Chapter 24

Ruby

*At a carat there is a price, at two carats that price doubles, at three carats the
price triples . . . at six carats there is no price.*

Jean Baptiste Tavernier, 1676

The Valley of the Serpents is about two miles wide and twenty miles long, and includes the town of Mogok. This area is part of the Shan States, an area controlled by the Shan tribe for hundreds of years. In 1886 the British annexed the Shan States, and in 1888 mining rights were leased to a British company, Burma Ruby Mines Ltd., which worked the mines with sporadic profitability until final bankruptcy in 1922. Following World War II the Shan States were grafted onto Burma in a poorly conceived, untidy little state named the Burmese Federation.[148] In 1962, General Ne Win took power in a military coup, moved the Burmese army into the Shan States, and banned independent mining. Thus began a thirty-year period of isolation which ended only in 1990, with a partial economic reform which allowed the reopening of mining in the Mogok stone tract.

A new strike of Burma-type ruby was found in Mong Hsu, about halfway between Mogok and the Thai border, in 1991. Ruby from this source has a definite violet to purplish cast, much of which can be

Jeff Scovil; courtesy of R.W. Wise, Goldsmiths,

*A ring with a fine 1.56-carat heat-treated Burma ruby from Mong Hsu.
Note the visually pure red primary hue and exceptional transparency
(crystal). The tone is seventy percent.*

148. Richard W. Wise, "In Search of the Burma Stone," *Jewelers Quarterly Magazine*, 1988, Designer Color Pages, pp. 8-11. 149. Adolf Peretti et al., "Rubies From Mong Hsu," *Gems & Gemology*, Spring 1995, p. 4.

removed by heat treatment.[149] As of this writing, a vast majority of ruby on the market in sizes under two carats comes from Mong Hsu.

Burma is better

What makes the re-emergence of Burmese ruby so important is that the Burma stone, clarity and cut being equal, is far superior to the Thai ruby, the standard bearer in the market since Burma was closed in the early sixties.[150] Why is this so? In a word: iron! The Chantaburi-Trat mining district is iron rich. During the ruby's formation, more than one hundred fifty million years ago, trace amounts of iron became part of the gem's chemical composition. Iron lends the Thai ruby its characteristically brownish cast and

Tino Hammid

The 15.97 carat Caplan Ruby. Although tonally lighter than the ideal, this pinkish red beauty exhibits the exceptional color saturation that made Burma-type ruby famous. The stone sold at auction in October 1988 for 3.6 million dollars, the highest per-carat price ever brought at auction. It is a particularly fine example of an old mine (Mogok) stone.

150. Richard W. Wise, "Burma Ruby Making a Market Comeback," *National Jeweler Magazine*, December 1993, pp. 34, 36.

quenches the natural ultraviolet fluorescence of the ruby crystal. This means that Thai ruby is brownish and barely fluorescent under ultraviolet light.

By contrast, the pure white metamorphic marbles of the ruby mining districts of Burma are iron poor. Conditions in Burma are ideal for the formation of ruby crystals (aluminum oxide with trace amounts of chromium) that are an exceptionally vivid red. These crystals fluoresce strongly under ultraviolet light. As any diamond lover knows, ultraviolet fluorescence, while technically invisible to the naked eye, supercharges the saturation of the gem. This causes the color to radiate like the juxtaposed hues of an Op-Art painting or glow like a "blue-white" diamond. Actually the Burma ruby often will fluoresce slightly in visible light. The absence of the diluting effect of iron, coupled with fluorescence, gives the Burma ruby a supercharged saturation.

Ruby of similar appearance also has been found elsewhere, including Pakistan, Afghanistan, and Vietnam. So Burma-type ruby is a better term to use when discussing this ruby. Stones from these areas have small internal differences of little real concern to the collector. Vietnamese stones, for example, may be even more fluorescent than Burmese, and they characteristically have a pinker secondary hue. As always, it is the beauty, not the pedigree of the gem, that is the key issue.

This does not mean that all consumers prefer Burma to Thai ruby. Thai stones generally have a purer red hue. Thai ruby was virtually the only option from the early 1960s through 1991, when Burma reopened and the new mining area was discovered at Mong Hsu.[151] Some ruby lovers who have grown up with the Thai stone prefer it to Burma ruby. It is interesting to note, however, that since the re-emergence of the Burma stone, Thai rubies have almost completely disappeared from the market.

Hue

Although a visually pure red is the most desirable, pure hues are rarely encountered in nature; thus when describing gemstones in this volume we speak of primary and secondary hues. Obviously, in ruby, red is the primary hue; pink, orange, and violet are the secondary hues. In Burma-type ruby the predominant secondary hue is pink. Experts disagree on which of the secondary colors is preferable. Many, of course, prefer a true-red red, others believe a bit of orange frames and pumps up the saturation of the red hue, yet others prefer a slight pinkish secondary hue. The original "pigeon's blood" is usually described as slightly bluish or slightly violet (red and blue, depending on the mixture, may yield either violet or purple). However, poetic terms such as pigeon blood and beef blood are best avoided. A ruby which is approximately eighty-five percent red primary hue and no more than ten to fifteen percent of any of the above secondary hues should be judged as fine color. Stones with secondary hues approaching twenty percent enter the commercial range.

151. In the mid- to late eighties I made several pilgrimages to Bangkok and along the Burma border in search of Burmese gems.

Diligent searches would yield, at most, five or six fine rubies normally in sizes of less than one carat. No Burmese sapphires were available.

152. The only other gems with comparable saturation are the tourmalines of Paraiba, Brazil. Though not available in red, these

tourmalines are at their most vivid in medium tones of blue.

Saturation

Burma-type ruby has been described as a gem of "barbaric splendor." This is largely due to the strong ultraviolet fluorescence typical of the gem. Although it is true that the human eye cannot see light in the ultraviolet range, the fluorescence at times laps over into the visual spectrum, in effect "supercharging" the saturation of the stone. This is particularly true of Burma-type ruby from Vietnam. No other gem achieves the level of saturation of the Burma-type stone.[152] In ruby, the normal mask or saturation modifiers are gray and brown. Thai ruby is distinctly brownish. If the hue of a Burma-type ruby appears dull, a gray secondary (mask) is the most likely culprit.

Tone

Ruby exists in a tonal range between sixty and eighty-five percent tone. Since pink is actually a red of pale saturation and light tone, gems of less than fifty percent tone are by definition pink sapphire. The color red reaches its optimum saturation—what color scientists describe as its *gamut limit*—between seventy-five and eighty percent tone, the ideal tone in ruby. Gems with tonal values below sixty percent appear washed out; those with tones in excess of eighty percent appear overdark (overcolor).

Multicolor effect

Like sapphire, ruby is a primary color gem. The closer ruby comes to exhibiting a visually pure red, the better and more desirable it is. However, like all gems, ruby also can display a multicolor effect. Think of the face-up gem as a patchwork quilt: each facet is a distinct swatch of color and may exhibit variations in the key color.

Multicolor effect has several causes (see the discussion of the multicolor effect in Chapter 4). Ruby is dichroic; i.e., light entering the gem divides into two rays, one purplish red, one orangy red. Also, ruby is often zoned, with colorless zones juxtaposed against zones of color. Light rays passing through colorless zones lose color. In addition, the pavilion facets of the gem cause a light ray entering the stone to reflect at least twice within the stone, absorbing color as it goes. Some facets may appear darker in tone, some lighter; some may show greater or lesser percentages of primary and secondary hues. Add to this the effect of light that shifts in color temperature from yellowish to bluish, and you have an idea why the face-up scene may be less than uniform.

In ruby and sapphire, a negative type of multicolor effect is traditionally called *bleeding*, a loss of saturation and tone when the stone is shifted from natural to incandescent lighting. At lighter tones, red becomes paler (less saturated) and pinkish. Bleeding in ruby may be weak, moderate, or strong. The more apparent or stronger it is, the greater the fault.

Ruby versus pink sapphire

Is it red or is it pink? This is a difficult question, since pink is not a distinct hue, it is a light-toned pale red. In fact, the

Is it pink or is it red? This 5.88-carat slightly purplish pink sapphire shows the highly saturated hue typical of Burmese gems. Note the dramatic multicolor effect, red towards the top and pink at the bottom.

whatever the tone; others prefer to maintain the distinction.

The issue has meaning because the market recognizes a distinct difference between the prices of ruby and pink sapphire. The latter has a price structure close to that of blue sapphire. The former brings a substantially higher price that escalates into the stratosphere as size tops two carats.

Hue: pink sapphire

The connoisseur should pay attention to the primary hue. Is it pink or is it red? Since pink is a lighter-toned red, the assumption might be that a pink stone will be light-toned and pale in saturation. This is not always the case, because the normal secondary hues, purple and orange, achieve their gamut limits, their maximum saturations, at darker tones than does pink. The situation is particularly difficult if the secondary hue is purple. Purple achieves its gamut limit at about sixty percent tone and, of course, can be even darker. A gem with a strong secondary of thirty to forty percent purple may appear quite dark in tone. Stones of this description are often described as *magenta* or *fuchsia pink*.

distinction between ruby and pink sapphire is of modern vintage, and has sparked a lot of debate within dealer circles. Some experts want to call all red corundum ruby,

The distinction is real; the term has a meaning that we all understand. But where does pink end and red begin? This is a question that can only be answered by comparing one stone to another, the path that all true aficionados must tread to become experts. Compare, compare, compare!

Clarity

Eye-flawless ruby, particularly unheated, is extraordinarily rare. Small amounts of threadlike rutile inclusions actually may be beneficial, as they act to break up and scatter the light throughout the stone, reducing extinction. The question is how prominent or disturbing the inclusions are, and how much do they detract from the beauty of the stone. This, finally, is a judgment call. Because of the gem's extreme rarity, the collector-connoisseur may find that otherwise beautiful stones with a few eye-visible inclusions are acceptable.

Texture

Color zoning or texture is another possible fault in Burma-type ruby. A fine gem should exhibit a uniform color appearance when viewed in the face-up position.

Heat treatment

No one is quite sure how long heat-enhanced ruby has been in the market — perhaps a hundred years, probably much longer.[153] Heat treatment was reported in India as early as 2000 BC.[154] However, not until the 1970s was the technology available to achieve temperatures close to the melting point of the material and heat treating began to be practiced almost universally.

Over ninety-five percent of Burma-type rubies currently on the market are heat enhanced. Almost one hundred percent of those from the new mines at Mong Hsu have been heat treated. Generally speaking, a heat-enhanced ruby will have a better visual appearance than an unheated stone. Heat tends to enhance the color, clarity, and crystal of Burma-type ruby. Some of the stones from Mong Hsu, when heated, will assume a particularly pure red hue with very little or no secondary hue.[155] Natural color stones will command a premium of approximately thirty percent over comparable heated stones.

153. Tagore, *Mani Mala*, vol. 1, pp. 243, 455.

154. Nassau, *Gemstone Enhancement*, p. 25.

155. C.R. Beesley, personal communication, 1998.

Chapter 25

Topaz

A topaz presented by Lady Hildegarde, wife of Theoderic, Count
of Holland, to a monastery in her native town, emitted at night, a light so brilliant
that prayers could be read at night without aid of a light. A statement that may
be true if the monks knew the prayers by heart.

Oliver Cummings Farrington, 1903

During the eighteenth century, more than half of the world's supply of gold was removed from the verdant hillsides surrounding the quaint cobblestoned Brazilian town of Ouro Preto. These same hills hold almost all of the entire world's known commercial reserves of "imperial" and "precious" topaz.

Small deposits of low-grade topaz have been found in the northern Brazilian state of Para, and in Mexico, Sri Lanka, Burma, Pakistan, and in Russia's Ural Mountains. Ouro Preto — the name translates as "Black Gold" — is the only location that is currently producing commercial quantities of natural topaz.

Here some clarification about natural color topaz as distinguished from blue topaz is in order. Natural blue — in fact, any topaz in the blue/green color range — is an extreme rarity in nature. The blue topaz that seems to be everywhere in the market is common colorless topaz that has been color-enhanced through radiation and heat treatment.

Harold and Erica Van Pelt; courtesy of Kalil Elawar
Brazilian topaz, in a range of hues from light peach to pink/red.

Imperial versus precious

Natural color topaz is usually divided into two types: precious and imperial. There is some confusion as to the distinction: some experts consider precious topaz to be any topaz in the yellow color range. Others, most notably Richard Drucker, whose gem price

Harold and Erica Van Pelt; courtesy of Kalil Elawar

Dark peach (reddish orange) topaz, gem and crystal from Minas Gerais, Brazil. This sixty percent tone "cocktail" red hue is the darkest, rarest color in topaz.

Faceted topaz is strongly dichroic because the C axis of the crystal is usually darker than the AB axis. When topaz is cut with the AB axis face up, particularly in the long pear, oval, and marquise shapes that insure the best yield from the rough, the darker hue of C axis bleeds into each end of the gemstone, showing a richer, more saturated hue at each tip of the finished gem.

Hue

Natural color topaz occurs on a color/rarity continuum from yellow through orange, cinnamon pink (peach), orange pink (ripe peach), pink, light violet, dark orangy red (hyacinth), and violetish red. Prices follow this same line with yellow hues priced lowest and violetish red ones fetching the highest prices. The peach and cinnamon colors are the most characteristic. Topaz possesses a liquid or soft velvety or limpid brilliance, the result of characteristic refraction coupled with a high degree of transparency.

list, *The Guide*, has become a standard dealer's reference, limits the term precious topaz to stones that do not exhibit the strong multicolor effect. In fact, this is only another example of a distinction without a difference — these labels are purely arbitrary.

Pink or purple

Topaz often occurs in a light-toned violet hue. This hue is difficult to separate from pink and is often lumped under the term pink topaz. Purple, like pink, is a modified spectral hue. Purple occupies a space on the color wheel halfway between blue and red; pink is a lighter shade of red. The distinction is important because true pink topaz, even purplish pink topaz, is much rarer than light purple. The purer the pink hue, the rarer the stone. Thus, the astute collector, who has trained his eye to discriminate between pink and purple, may find a buying opportunity in a parcel of "pink" topaz.

Saturation

Brown is the dominant saturation modifier or mask found in topaz, although gray is also found, particularly in pinker stones.

Tone

Using a tonal scale where window glass is zero percent and coal is one hundred percent tone, the optimum tonal range for topaz is fifty to eighty percent. Below fifty percent, the color begins to pale and wash out; above eighty percent, which is rare, topaz begins to lose the liquid effect and appear overcolor. The optimum tone increases as the hue changes from yellow to peach, to pink and finally red. Twenty percent is optimum tone for yellow, forty to sixty percent for the peach range, and fifty to eighty percent for the pink to red range. Because of the liquid aspect of the key color, gems of lighter than optimum tone may be preferred if the connoisseur favors a more delicate hue.

Nightstone

Topaz is a true lady of the evening, a nightstone, one of the few gems that looks its best in incandescent or candlelight, and holds up well in low-light environments. Topaz tends to bleed a bit; that is, lose both color and tone in fluorescent light and in daylight.

Clarity

Topaz is normally eye-flawless. Stones with visible inclusions are sold at a deep discount.

Treatments

The traditional color enhancement for topaz is heat treatment. This technique, known as "pinking," is performed under relatively low temperatures, at times over the open flame of a miner's campfire. Stones with some pink or bluish pink can be turned a purer hue using this technique. Although experienced dealers claim to be able to separate heated from nonheated stones by eye, pink topaz also occurs naturally, and at the time of this writing, there is no gemological test that can identify "pinked" topaz.

Colorless topaz is run through a linear accelerator that alters the atomic structure of the material, then heat-treats it to turn it blue. Connoisseurs do not take blue topaz seriously as a gemstone. Recently a new process was announced which turns colorless topaz pink through a combination of heat and high pressure. This process is entirely different from the gentle heating that will "pink" a light pink or peach topaz.

Limited production

Most of the topaz currently on the market can be traced to a single mine, Capão,

R. W. Wise

Mechanized mining at the Capão Mine outside the village of Rodrigo Silva, Minas Gerais, Brazil.

large-scale mechanized mines currently operating. The second, Vermelhão, is situated about twelve kilometers to the east.

Capão is an open pit operation with two large pits, each carved over two hundred feet down into the verdant hillside. The mine currently employs forty-seven workers and is highly mechanized. Bulldozers are used to open the pits, and most initial sorting uses German-made hydraulic sluices and sieves, with some final sorting done by hand. The huge amount of water necessary for mining operations is drawn from a nearby lake.

There are a number of smaller mines in the area, including Don Bosco and Garimpo, that are strictly hand operations worked intermittently by independent miners called *garimpeiros*.

The rarity factor

Exceptional topaz is rare in every color and size. Generally stones above twenty carats will decrease in price on a per carat basis.

about five kilometers from the small village of Rodrigo Silva. This village is almost dead center of the two-hundred-ninety-square-kilometer topaz belt running in an east-west direction west of the city of Ouro Preto. Capão, "big lid" in Portuguese, is one of two

OPAL

Life in the outback is hard . . .

We wake before dawn, our bodies glazed in dried sweat. The heat drives us, half asleep, stumbling out the door of the iron-roofed shack. The full moon casts a ghostly film, turning the landscape a gray flannel resembling the dim interior of some forgotten crypt. The desert winds assault us. The bushflies will arrive with the sun to suck the moisture from any exposed body parts; they will be our companions until sunset.

R. W. Wise

View of the outback from the Cragg Mine, Opalton, Queensland, Australia.

Thirsty is not the word — the inside of our mouths are dry as parchment. Water in this part of the outback is drawn from artesian wells drilled three thousand feet into the sandstone. The brownish liquid comes up hot and stinking of sulfur. At this remote location it must be trucked in, a trip that takes ten hours over dirt track. By ten o'clock the temperature passes the hundred-degree mark; by noon it stands at one hundred twenty.

The mining is mechanized at the Cragg Mine. Test holes are dug with a Caldwell drill, a giant, truck-mounted auger which in minutes can drill a thirty-inch hole thirty feet into the red-clay sandstone. This is a job that took days with pick and shovel. The dirt the auger brings up is a dark brick red caused by high concentrations of iron. If traces of opal are found, James Evert, Vince's son and the camp foreman, will lower himself into the hole for a closer look.

We are standing in an area called Mainside, five hundred miles into the Queensland outback. One hundred million years ago, this area, which geologists call the Winton Formation, was an inland sea larger than the state of Texas.

The vista is broken by a series of tabletop buttes, island sentinels in the midst of a rolling plain dotted with trees and bushes. "Trees can be good indicators," says mine owner Vince Evert. "Some blokes dig near gidgee trees — but gidgee grows in the white sandstone. The opal lies under the red." All in one motion, Evert sweeps off his bush hat and wipes his brow with the back of his forearm. "Mallee bush grows in the red sandstone, so it can be a good indicator. Lapunyah, too; its roots grow deep into the faults."

Faults — cracks between strata that run up to the surface — expedite the formation of the gem. Opal begins as water-borne silica that percolates down along the fault lines and is caught between layers of semipermeable sandstone. Over the millennia the water leaches away, leaving a layer of concentrated silica. In some cases the silica hardens into a single layer; in others, it fills fractures in previously formed ironstone nodules.

The Cragg Mine, where the Everts are currently digging, was originally worked in the 1890s. Old timers with colorful names like "Texas Jack" and "Silk Shirt Joe" pioneered

The long road to the opal fields, five hundred miles into the Queensland outback. One hundred fifty million years ago this whole area, called the Great Artesian Basin, was part of a vast inland sea, an area larger than the state of Texas.

these fields with little more than their swag and tucker (bedroll and provisions), a pick, and a shovel. "Nowadays it's D-8 Cats, augers, and backhoes." Vince shakes his head, reflecting on the changing times.

This year they "need a win," as Vince Evert puts it. Last year they found little opal and the cost of the diesel fuel is driving them rapidly towards bankruptcy. A week later the monsoon comes unexpectedly with its driving rains. The rains fill the pits with water and the clay-rich soil turns to glue. The mine area is turned into a series of little islands. The mining stops and many of the miners must be evacuated by air, setting back mining for the rest of the season. Life in the outback is hard. . . .

The discovery of opal

Opal was first discovered in Australia in 1849. The first commercial mine was established in Queensland at Listoral Downs in 1872. With the discoveries at White Cliffs in 1890, Lightning Ridge in 1902, Coober Pedy in 1915, and Mintabie in 1931, Australia has come to dominate the world market and is responsible for more than ninety-five percent of world production of gem opal.

Chapter 26

Opal

A fine opal must have an appropriate ground colour to set off the fire, and this should be milky with perhaps a tinge of blue. The flash or fire must be pure in colour and should be definitely outlined. The pattern should be regular, and the rarest and justly most esteemed, is that in which the pattern is like a mosaic of tesserae cut from a solar spectrum. Such opals are termed Harlequin.

Sydney B.J. Skertchly, 1908

Opal types

Gem opals were traditionally classified by background or body color into seven types. Recently the Australian Opal Dealer's Association has revamped and simplified the classification system. In the new nomenclature, opal body color is divided into four types: light, dark, boulder, and black. Stones that are transparent to semi-translucent are termed "crystal." Thus, under the new system, the categories are light, dark, and black opal, and white crystal, dark crystal, and black crystal opal. However, the older categories are more descriptive so I have used them below, with the new classifications given in parenthesis.

White (light) opal

White opal, the most familiar, has a translucent milky to opaque white background. Most of the current production comes from the fields in south central Australia at Coober Pedy. White opal is the opal normally seen in commercial jewelry.

Crystal opal

Translucent to transparent opal is called crystal opal. Crystal opal may be light, dark, black, or have no discernable body color at all. Crystal opal is found at many sites. Under the new system of classification, any opal that is transparent to translucent when held to the light is called crystal.

R. G. Weber; courtesy of Cody Opal
Fine opal with a white (light) body color.

R. G. Weber; courtesy of Cody Opal
Although somewhat dark, the transparent to translucent body color of the stone classifies it as crystal opal.

Gray (dark) opal

Translucent to opaque opal with a gray body color is termed gray opal. The Mintabe Field in central Australia is the primary source for opal of this type, although much of what is found at Lightning Ridge is properly termed gray opal.

R. G. Weber; courtesy of Cody Opal

Gray or dark opal showing a predominantly green play of color.

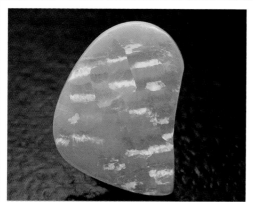

R. G. Weber; courtesy of Cody Opal

Semi-black or dark opal.

Semi-black (dark) opal

Semi-black opal has a body color darker than gray, but not quite black. Semi-black will be semi-translucent when held to the light. Semi-black can be found at Mintabe and in central Australia at Lightning Ridge.

Black opal

Opal that is very dark in body color is called black. According to the old classification system used by the Lightning Ridge Miners Association, opacity is the key that divides black from semi-black. That is somewhat at odds with the more widely held view that the stone should appear opaque but may show some translucency when held directly to the light. The most highly valued blacks have what miners call "a bit of the blue" in a coal-black background. Lightning Ridge is famous for its black opal. A small amount has also been found in the western part of the Australian state of Queensland and at Virgin Valley in the state of Nevada.

Boulder opal

Opal with sandstone or ironstone as part of the cut gem is called boulder opal. The Gemological Institute of America classifies two types: gems with ironstone visible face up, called "opal with matrix," and gems with no visible inclusions called "opal in matrix." Boulder opal is found at a number of fields in western Queensland. Opal in matrix is also mined at Andamooka and has been found in the Brazilian state of Piauí.

Fire opal

Fire opal can be easily recognized by its reddish orange to red body color. This type of opal is normally translucent to semi-translucent with little play of color. Opal of this type is found mainly in Mexico, although a recent strike has been made in Ethiopia. It Is valued chiefly for its highly saturated translucent body color.

A hierarchy of values

There is some difference of opinion among experts about the relative value of the different opal types. Other quality factors being equal, all agree that black opal is the most valuable. This is because the gem's black body color sets off the play of color, resulting in a breathtakingly vivid gem. Boulder opal follows in potential beauty. Boulder-blacks — boulder stones with a

R.G. Weber; courtesy of R.W. Wise, Goldsmiths, Inc.

Millennium, a twenty-five-carat classic harlequin multicolor.

R.G. Weber; courtesy of Cody Opal

Freeform-shaped "opal with matrix" with a red/green play of color. Boulder opals with a black body color are sometimes referred to as "boulder blacks.".

gem that exhibits play of color can be judged in the same way that brilliance is evaluated in a faceted stone. Cut, as well as crystal, is important in the connoisseurship equation.

Play of color

Play of color may occur in any or all of the spectral hues: red, orange, yellow, green, blue, and violet. This phenomenon is the result of light refraction, similar to the effect of oil on water. The internal structure of opal is composed of microscopic silica spheres that are packed together in layers like racks of billiard balls. Opal contains about six percent water, which collects in the spaces where the spheres meet. Light reflecting though the spaces causes the phenomenon called play of color.

Gem of many hues

There is a rough hierarchy of opal colors based on rarity. In descending order the list is red, orange, yellow, violet, green, and finally blue.[156] In the marketplace, there is red — and then there are all the other colors. All would agree that the presence of red, particularly a dark-toned (seventy-five to eighty percent) visually pure scarlet hue, adds dramatically to the rarity and price of an opal.

Opals are named by their dominant hue. A gem with fifty-one percent or more red

black background or body color — can have exceptionally vivid saturation, sometimes surpassing black opal. Boulder, however, occurs in thin layers over ironstone, so this type of opal will rarely have the depth (crystal) of a black, which is solid opal. Depth allows for a more complex visual scene. However, as I have suggested throughout this volume, ignore pedigree and consider each stone individually.

Grading opal

Opal is unique. However, some analogies can be made between opal and faceted gems. Opal does show color, which can be categorized on the basis of hue, saturation, and tone. The percentage of the face-up

156. Purple is actually the rarest hue. Purple occurs in opal only when translucent red and blue patches are layered one on top of the other. Light passing through both patches may on rare occasions produce a purple play of color.

play of color is called a red stone. However, a stone that exhibits a single color is not valued as highly as one that shows several. An opal that exhibits three or more distinct hues is termed a "multicolor." Multicolor gems are the most valuable. *The Guide* reserves its highest rating for an opal with a dominant red (over seventy-five percent of the surface) plus two additional hues. Paul Downing, a respected opal expert and connoisseur, prefers a red-blue multicolor with one or more additional hues.[157]

Saturation comes first

"Opal is like a light bulb: the brighter it is, the better it is." This is how one well-known expert summed up the central truth of opal appreciation. In other words, saturation — not the hue, or the lightness or darkness of the hue, but the vividness of the hue — is the central criterion in opal grading.[158] A simple test: the farther away you can hold the stone and still see the play of color, the better the stone. On the lighter side of connoisseurship you might say that there are four-footers, five-footers, and then there are ten-footers!

Color — hue, saturation, and tone — should be observed in all possible lighting environments. Indirect sunlight (skylight), as always, is the standard, but the gem should be observed in incandescent and fluorescent lighting as well. Standard fluorescent lighting brings out the blues and greens but will often flatten the reds, while incandescent lighting shows off the reds to best advantage.[159]

Daystones, nightstones

The term "nightstone" was originally coined to describe opal that held up well in indirect or shadowed lighting. I like the term so much that I have adapted it to classify any gemstone that looks its best in incandescent lighting. In opal, the criterion is more specific. Opals that look good in intense direct light but dull out in indirect lighting are not as desirable as those that hold their beauty. As always, the aficionado should observe the stone in all indirect lighting environments. Opals that deaden in indirect lighting are called daystones. Stones that qualify as nightstones are beautiful in daylight as well.

Crystal

Generally speaking, in opals with dark or black body color, opacity is preferred and will command a premium. Conversely, in lighter-toned white (light) and colorless crystal gems, the higher the degree of transparency the more the stone will fetch in the marketplace.[160]

Performing the test

If the opal is placed directly under an overhead light source and rotated three hundred sixty degrees, there is a direct analogy with brilliance, the quantity of light reflected from the crown of a faceted gemstone. As with faceted gems, the whole face of the stone is rated one hundred percent. The percentage of nonchromatic or dead areas is deducted from this figure to arrive at the total percentage of brilliance or

157. Paul Downing, *Opal Identification and Value* (Tallahassee, Florida: Majestic Press, 1972), p. 116.

158. Andrew Cody, *Australian Precious Opal* (Melbourne: Andrew Cody Pty. Ltd., 1991) p. 53.

159. Richard W. Wise, "Australia, Thy Name is Opal," *Colored Stone Magazine*, March/April 1991, p. 7.

160. Damien Cody, personal communication, 2002.

play of color. If half of the stone is dead, it can be said to have fifty percent play of color. The greater the percentage of the face that shows play of color the better the stone. This seems simple, but it is just the beginning.

Some opal is highly directional. That is, the play of color is visible only when the stone is tilted steeply away from the perpendicular. This is a fault. It is true that a little directionality can be a plus, as in a rolling flash pattern where the color darts like a prairie fire across the face of the stone as the stone is tilted side to side. However, if the stone shows large areas of extinction when viewed on axis and/or requires more than a twenty-degree tilt from the perpendicular to show its colors, it should be discounted substantially.

Opals are full of surprises! If the stone is to be worn, the stone should be oriented and viewed as it is to be worn. For example, a pin or pendant is worn on the body more or less vertically. This means that the stone will normally be oriented almost perpendicular to a normal overhead light fixture. The stone should be held at the appropriate angle to the light source and observed in a variety of lighting environments. In some cases the opal may actually look better than it looked in the grading position. This doesn't improve the stone's theoretical grade, but it will add measurably to its desirability.

The presence of matrix — that is, ironstone in boulder opal or any other inclusion — is also deducted from the theoretical one hundred percent. The presence of matrix, particularly in the face-up gemstone, is something of a flaw. Its effect can be mitigated, however, by the composition. If the juxtaposition of pattern and play of color against visible matrix is generally pleasing it is less of a negative.

Shape

In opal evaluation the shape of the stone is a factor that has a definite effect on price. Regular shapes — specifically, symmetrical ovals — command a higher price than other shapes and free forms. A cabochon with a high dome is also preferred to a low dome. This may present a real buying opportunity for the collector who is attracted to unusually shaped stones.

The opal as art

A good artwork gives us a glimpse into the mind of the artist. A work of art gives us a glimpse into our own minds as well. In this respect, opal is a work of art. Some might argue that this couldn't possibly be true, that man's only contribution is to shape and to coax the beauty from the rock. But the cutter does more than that. Opal colors occur in juxtaposed layers — like a pile of wet leaves. The lapidary is an important part of the equation: he has to decide when to stop cutting away the layers.

Opals resemble abstract or nonrepresentational paintings more than they do faceted gemstones. Terms such as composition, balance, and depth, terms borrowed from the fine arts, become relevant in the contemplation of opal.[161]

161. Richard W. Wise, "Queensland Boulder Opal," *Gems & Gemology*, Spring 1993, pp. 12-13.

Cubism is an artistic style that views the two-dimensional canvas as an art object rather than simply as a vehicle for a copy of something else, such as a bowl of flowers or a landscape.[162] The cubist approach was the most radical departure in art since the Renaissance. Qualities such as depth are achieved not through the illusion of perspective, but by the juxtaposition of colors, textures, and shapes. Cubism led directly to abstract art, which used color (and to a lesser extent texture and shape) to evoke emotion directly without the aid of any type of representation. In this sense, an opal is very much like an abstract cubist painting.

The psychology of opal

Psychologists have for years used a technique called the inkblot or Rorschach test to plumb the subconscious of their subjects. A series of inkblots are shown to the patient, who tells the doctor what he sees. This technique is used because psychologists have long recognized that these seemingly nonrepresentational shapes evoke certain associations, some of which are subjective and autobiographical, and some of which appear to be objective and universal. Opal patterns evoke similar associations. This explains why opal appreciation is so complex. An opal is a inkblot test combined with an abstract work of art.

This, perhaps, explains why, in my experience, opal aficionados are a distinct class. People either love opal or they hate opal. And those who love opal tend to give their full allegiance to opal to the exclusion of all other gemstones.

The aesthetics of opal

> It gives "atmosphere to the stone," to borrow a painter's phrase, and, like a fine impressionist picture, suggests more than it definitely expresses.
>
> Sydney B.J.
> Skertchly, 1908

If this description is correct, we seem to be left hopelessly mired in subjectivity. Not quite! It is still possible to talk about opal as one would a painting, to consider the stone as a total composition.

Composition

A pleasing composition is largely a question of harmony and balance. In any given stone, how well do the various colors and shapes harmonize and balance one another visually? How well do the areas of color play off against the background and areas of visible matrix? Since the composition of an opal is dynamic — that is, it changes depending on its orientation to the light — what is the effect of that movement? Do the overlay and juxtaposition of shape and color give a feeling of depth? Finally, how do all these factors, combined with the three Cs— color (hue, saturation, tone), clarity, and cut — affect the viewer?[163]

Traditional patterns

In opal grading a number of traditional patterns, based on rarity and collectibility,

162. Douglas Cooper, *The Cubist Epoch* (London: Phaidon Press, 1970), p. 263.

163. Wise, "Queensland Boulder Opal."

are particularly prized by connoisseurs. Pinfire, a pattern of densely grouped points of light much like a neon Milky Way, is the most common. Harlequin, a multicolor pattern of overlapping angular blocks or diamond shapes (resembling the costume of the clown figures made famous in the paintings of Pablo Picasso) is the most sought after.

There are so many variations and types of patterns that the whole question can become confusing and seem needlessly complex. As a rule of thumb, patterns that contain large distinct segments or blocks of color are more desirable than those made up of small patches of color.[164] Thus, pinfire is the least expensive; harlequin will command the highest premium.[165] Rare patterns such as mackerel sky, rolling flash, peacock, flagstone, and Chinese writing are also very collectible and will command a substantial premium among connoisseurs.

164. Damien Cody, personal communication, 2002.

165. Downing, *Opal Identification and Value*, p. 116.

TOURMALINE

Toumaline is possibly the most maligned and misunderstood of all gemstones. Until perhaps fifteen years ago tourmaline was valued chiefly for its resemblance to other gems. Even its name, derived from the Singhalese word turmali, identifies mixed parcels of unknown gems of dubious value. Despised in the East, tourmaline remained largely unknown to both European and indigenous New World cultures until the sixteenth century when Portuguese adventurers discovered it in the Brazilian hinterlands.[166]

Harold and Erica Van Pelt; courtesy of Kalil Elawar

Fine examples of red, blue, and green tourmaline from Minas Gerais, Brazil. Note the distinct multicolor effect in the green oval gem (top left).

One of the most magnificent known green [Mt. Mica] tourmalines is . . . one inch long, three quarter inch broad and one inch thick, and finer than any of the Hope gems.

G.F. Kunz, 1885

When Francisco Spinoza first stumbled upon green tourmaline in the mountains of Minas Gerais in 1554-55 he thought he had found emerald. The green stones were subsequently shipped to Portugal where they were set in the crown of Nossa Senhora da Penha. It took three hundred years before the mistake was corrected and "Brazilian emerald" was finally identified as tourmaline.[167] Once found out, tourmaline was shunted aside and largely ignored until the middle of the twentieth century.

166. The *lyngourion* stone mentioned by Theophrastus (372-287 BC) was almost surely tourmaline. Theophrastus described *lyngourion* as having the pyroelectric "power of attraction just as amber does," a property unique to these two gemstones. He further describes it as "cold and very transparent," stating that "seals are cut from this and it is very hard." The oldest tourmaline gemstone known is a green transparent seal stone carved with a likeness of Alexander the Great, dated between the third and second century BC. (See Ogden, *Jewellery of the Ancient World*, p. 170.) Other known uses in jewelry include a red cabochon set in a gold finger ring of early Nordic origin (1000 AD) and two other red tourmalines set in rings of European manufacture and dated to the thirteenth and fourteenth centuries.

With the advent of World War II, large quantities of mica, feldspar, and lithium minerals were needed for the war effort. Tourmaline was found as a byproduct of the mining. The Germans, who had begun mining in the Brazilian state of Minas Gerais around the turn of the century, were the first to develop an interest in tourmaline as a gemstone.

Tourmaline sources around the world

Tourmaline occurs in almost every color, and the sources of tourmaline are nearly as numerous and varied as its palette. Although Brazil remains the most important source, commercially viable tourmaline deposits have been found in Afghanistan, Pakistan, Mozambique, Nigeria, Namibia, Tanzania, and the United States. The two principal sources in the United States are Maine and California.

Alan Plante

Site of the famous Plumbago tourmaline strike, Newry, Maine (now flooded).

Tourmaline deposits were first discovered at Mount Mica, outside Paris, Maine, in 1820. This deposit produced steadily until the mid-twentieth century. In 1972 a huge pocket of tourmaline was found thirty miles away in Newry, Maine, at Plumbago Mountain. These two mines are part of a single geological formation called a pegmatite that runs in a straight line from Brunswick, Maine, on the Atlantic coast through the towns of Paris and Newry to the New Hampshire border. Approximately seventy-five percent of the gems mined at these two sites were the lovely pastel pink and red gems for which Maine is justly famous. The remainder occurs in various shades of pastel to apple green to dark forest green. Although prospecting continues in the vicinity of Plumbago and throughout the region, little has been found. Attempts to mine at Mount Mica beginning in the summer of 1990 have produced little of commercial interest.[168]

For a short period, starting in the late nineteenth century, California was an important producer of gem

The earliest use of the name *turmale, turmalin* can be found in a 1707 manuscript by Johann Georg Schmidt. F. Benesch and B.

Wohrmann, "Toramalli: A Short History of the Tourmaline Group," *The Mineralogical Record*, vol. 16, September-October 1985, pp. 331-338.

167. Keith Proctor, "Gem Pegmatites of Minas Gerais," *Gems & Gemology*, Summer 1984, pp. 78-81.

tourmaline. The Tourmaline Queen, King, and Pala Chief mines in San Diego County were major producers of fine pink and red stones. Much of the gem material produced from this area in the late nineteenth and early twentieth century was exported to China, where it was coveted as a carving material. The Tourmaline Queen, Pala Chief, and Elizabeth R. mines, all located in the Pala District, recently reopened and currently are producing small amounts of gem tourmaline.

Today, Brazil is the major world source for gem tourmaline. Stones from Brazil come in many hues with green, pink, and red predominant. Brazil is the primary source for the rare blue variety known as indicolite and, of course, is the sole source of the legendary stones of Paraiba.

Most Brazilian tourmaline is found in two roughly adjacent areas in the northwestern part of the state of Minas Gerais. One group of mines is clustered around the town of Govenador Valadares, the other north of Teofilo Otoni in the Araçuaí district.

North of Govenador Valadares, on the east slope of the Serra Safira, is one of the oldest known and most prolific of Brazil's tourmaline deposits, the Cruziero Mine. Cruziero, actually a complex of several mines, produces tourmaline in a range of hues, including a red that rivals the best of Oro Fino as well as the unusual "watermelon" crystals that are pink in the center with a green outer "rind." Cruziero is also the source of the dark, slightly bluish "emerald" green gems first described by Portuguese adventurers.

Tourmaline grading

Traditionally, the three main hues of tourmaline — green, blue, and red — have been evaluated by what might be

Robert Weldon; courtesy of Pala International

Working a tourmaline-bearing pegmatite at the Old Himalaya Mine, Mesa Grande, California.

168. Richard W. Wise, "Oldest Mine in the U. S. Reopens," *Colored Stone Magazine*, July/August 1992, cover, pp. 8-9. Only three tourmaline nodules of note have been found since the reopening in 1990. These cut a 17.56-carat, a 9.40-carat, and a matched pair of 2.5-carat stones. The last two, which I purchased, were of a medium tone (sixty to seventy percent) minty green hue.

R. W. Wise

Tourmaline mining camp north of Teofilo Otoni in the Brazilian state of Minas Gerais, 1990.

called the look-alike standard; that is, by how closely the green variety resembled emerald, the red ruby, and the blue sapphire.

This approach to connoisseurship has continually reinforced tourmaline's status as a second-rate gem. However, tourmaline is a unique gem species (with entirely different chemical composition, crystal structure, and visual attributes) that does not resemble these more famous gem varieties at all.

Tourmaline is found in the broadest range of hues of any gem species except diamond. It occurs in every color of the rainbow and in most intermediate hues as well. Perhaps the only hue that has not been found is a completely achroic or colorless stone. Mineralogists classify tourmaline as a group, like garnet. Tourmaline has a complex chemical formula; the alteration of any part of it can produce a different hue.[169]

Until recently tourmaline hues other than ruby, sapphire, and emerald look-alikes have been ignored. For this reason, tourmaline in the lighter-toned primaries and intermediate secondary hues is one of the best buys in gemstones today.

The perennial daystone

Incandescent lighting is tourmaline's nemesis! The hue may or may not bleed but whatever mask is present will come out in the harsh yellow glow of a light bulb. Green through blue hues will usually exhibit a gray mask that is sometimes so dark as to appear black. Pink through red hues may show either gray or brown. Incandescent lighting will muddy the stone and decrease the transparency (crystal). Nightstones, gems that do not show this tendency, are the super novas in the tourmaline universe.

169. The chemical formula for tourmaline is $X Y_3 Z_6 B_3 Si_6 O_{27} (O,OH,F)_4$ X is predominantly Na or Ca, may also include K, or may be in noteworthy part vacant; Y is predominantly Fe^{2+}. and/or Mg^{2+} or - (Al + Li) or Fe^3 and commonly includes Mn; Z is predominantly Al^{3+}, Fe^3+ or Cr^3 and may also include Mg^2 and V^3 in noteworthy percentages. Cf. Richard Dietrich, *The Tourmaline Group* (New York: Van Nostrand Reinhold, 1985), p. 6

Chapter 27

Paraiba Tourmaline

Asking $1,000 per carat for tourmaline is outrageous—no matter how beautiful it is, groused New York dealer Ary Reith just as prices for Paraiba goods hit $2,000 per carat in Brazil. Rieth refused to stock the gem until its prices came 'down to earth.' They never have.

David Federman, 1992

In early 1989 the discovery of a new type of tourmaline near the village of Sao José da Batalha, near the border of the Brazilian state of Paraiba, entirely altered tourmaline's status in the world of gemstones.

At Paraiba, a new variety of tourmaline was found that derived its color from minute amounts of copper and gold. The combination of these two trace elements yielded a medium-toned (forty-five to sixty percent) blue to green gem of unrivaled saturation.

Traditionally, blue and green tourmaline has been graded using standards borrowed from ruby, sapphire, and emerald. Darker-toned stones (seventy-five to eighty-five percent) have been the most sought after.[170] However, the hottest Paraiba colors are not sapphire-like or emerald-like dark primary hues, but vivid pastel hues in the blue to green range with tonal values between forty-five and sixty percent. Terms like "neon," "Caribbean blue," and "electric green" aptly describe the gems of Paraiba. Within a year of the discovery, prices of Paraiba stones over a carat escalated from several hundred to several thousands of dollars per carat, prices that would have been unimaginable just a year before.[171]

Paraiba produced darker-toned (eighty to eighty-five percent) stones with a seventy-five percent primary hue of blue and a twenty percent secondary hue of green that resembled sapphires from Australia and Thailand. These stones, among the rarest and most sought after tourmaline variety, the so-called sapphire-blue indicolite, were promptly heat treated. Those that turned a lighter-toned neon blue greatly increased in value.[172]

Unfortunately the San José da Batalha mine was mostly exhausted within a few years but not before the tourmalines of Paraiba already had passed into legend. The effect of this discovery was twofold: first, it focused attention on tourmaline and established a tourmaline aristocracy, giving the gem something it had previously lacked: snob appeal. Secondly, attention was shifted from the ruby-sapphire-emerald look-alike standard to a new appreciation of so-called Paraiba look-alikes. That is, medium-toned stones in the blue to green hues earned a new respect. Finally, tourmaline began to emerge from the shadows and to be appreciated for itself, as an important gemstone beautiful and valuable in its own right.

---

170. Richard W. Wise, "Tourmaline: A Modest Proposal," *Colored Stone Magazine*, May/June 1991, pp. 6-7.

171. As of this writing, prices of exceptional Paraiba stones over two carats have approached prices normally reserved for the finest ruby.

172. I held a small parcel of dark blue Paraiba stones for several years before having them heat-treated. The heat enhancement effectively quadrupled the value of the stones. This treatment is carried out under very low heat. In Brazil, I witnessed a Paraiba tourmaline lighten in color in a test tube under the heat of an alcohol lamp. Such low temperature treatment is normally undetectable.

Harold and Erica Van Pelt; courtesy of Kalil Elawar

The most desirable range of colors available in Paraiba tourmaline. Note the exceptional saturation of hue, the defining characteristic of these gems. The three stones at the bottom of the photo exhibit the famous "Caribbean" blue that commands the highest prices in the marketplace.

Hue

Most Paraiba stones are found in hues of green and blue. Caribbean blue, a hue reminiscent of the color of the shallow waters of the Caribbean Sea, is the most sought after. It is a visually pure blue of between forty-five and seventy percent tone. Green stones are found in a similar tonal range from a visually pure green to a slightly yellowish green, a hue similar to iceberg lettuce, with the slightest hint (five percent) of yellow secondary hue. A few reddish purple stones were also produced which, due to their rarity, have not been given much attention.

Blue Paraiba stones, which are more highly saturated and do not have the gray mask, might be described as a sort of "neon-aquamarine." A visually pure blue between fifty and seventy-five percent is the most desirable. Green Paraiba stones resemble a more vivid version of the lighter tones of emerald traditionally associated with the Nova Era area of the Brazilian state of Minas Gerais. Green Paraiba tourmaline, the finest of which is a visually pure green between fifty and seventy-five percent tone, sells for substantially less than the blue variety.

Saturation

Gray is the normal saturation modifier or mask found in Paraiba tourmaline. A large percentage of stones from Paraiba exhibit a distinct grayish mask. This is particularly true of stones with tonal values above seventy percent. Due to the stones' phenomenally vivid saturation, grayish Paraiba can still seem relatively vivid when compared to stones of similar hue from other locations. The asking price for grayish stones is often high because of the Paraiba pedigree. As in all such cases, beauty, not pedigree, should be the aficionado's guide. Tourmalines of similar well saturated pastel hues from other locations can be both more attractive and less expensive than Paraiba stones, and hence a better option for the collector seeking a pastel gem.

The best of Paraiba tourmaline shows no mask in either natural or incandescent lighting, resulting in an extremely vivid saturation. This fact explains why Paraiba tourmaline was catapulted to the heights of the gemstone pantheon in a relatively short space of time. The vivid saturation is found only in one other stone, Burmese ruby. What is even more amazing is that Paraiba stones, unlike the famous rubies of Burma, have achieved this level of saturation without the aid of ultraviolet fluorescence.[173] Paraíba tourmaline is normally inert to both short- and long-wave ultraviolet light.

Research conducted by the Gemological Institute of America indicates that the distinctive chemical properties of Paraiba tourmaline can be positively identified by x-ray fluorescence spectroscopy.[174]

Tone

As stated above, the normal tonal range for Paraiba tourmaline is forty-five to sixty five percent. Darker-toned stones are frequently heat enhanced to a lighter hue.

Clarity

Paraiba tourmaline is usually visually included. Stones that are eye-clean will command a substantial premium. This variety of tourmaline has excellent crystal which tends to lend the inclusions even greater prominence.

Crystal

A high degree of diaphaneity — transparency or crystal — is characteristic of the finest gems from Paraiba.

The Paraiba standard

Paraiba tourmaline has established a tourmaline aristocracy. The Sao José da Batalha mine is mostly played out; but, logically, tourmaline from other localities with a similar range of hues/tones will benefit from Paraiba's ascension. Lighter-toned gems in the blue to green hue range that resemble Paraiba tourmaline will become more sought after.[175] This, in fact, has already begun. Dealers and collectors are paying much more attention to stones of this type and prices have escalated for these gemstones.

The rarity factor

Paraiba tourmaline is rare in any size. Rarity and price tend to increase at one, three, and ten carat sizes.

3. Ruby, specifically Burma type at formed in low-iron vironments, will exhibit strong ak/red fluorescence under raviolet light. This distinct orescence is in part responsible for the characteristically vivid saturation of this type of ruby (see Chapter 15).

174. Emmanuel Fritch et al., "Gem Quality Cuprian-Elbaite Tourmalines from Sao José da Batalha," *Gems &* *Gemology,* Fall 1990, pp. 189-205. Despite the fact that research has made it possible to positively identify Paraiba-type tourmaline, the Gem Trade Lab of GIA does not issue origin certificates.

175. Richard W. Wise, "A Modest Proposal to Reclassify Tourmaline," *Colored Stone Magazine,* May/June 1991, pp. 6-7.

Chapter 28

Green Tourmaline

Green tourmaline is the most widely distributed of the precious varieties of this mineral and consequently is lower in price. It is rarely emerald-green but when this is the case its colour lacks none of the depth of that of the true emerald.

Max Bauer, 1904

Green is tourmaline's most common hue. There are actually two varieties of green tourmaline: elbaite, the most common, is found throughout the world; chrome tourmaline (dravite) is found mainly in East Africa. Elbaite is discussed in this chapter. The chrome variety will be discussed in detail in the next chapter.

Although Brazil remains the most important source, fine green tourmaline is found in Nigeria, Pakistan, Afghanistan, Namibia, and the states of Maine and California.

There are essentially two standards used in the grading of green tourmaline. The traditional standard grades the stone on the purity of its primary green hue; in short, on how closely the stone resembles emerald (see the introduction and overview to this section). The second standard might best be termed the Paraiba standard and is discussed in detail in the previous chapter.

Hue

Tourmaline with a pure green key color is extremely rare, and despite the quotation at the beginning of this chapter, doesn't resemble emerald very much at all. Still, it is a green gemstone and can be compared, at

Jeff Scovil; courtesy of R.W. Wise, Goldsmiths, Inc.

Tourmaline in this handmade ring shows an eighty-five percent green primary hue with a fifteen percent blue secondary hue, seventy-five percent tone.

least superficially, to emerald. Green hue achieves its maximum saturation at about seventy-five percent tone. So, as with tsavorite garnet and emerald, a medium dark-toned visually pure green is optimal.

The secondary hues in the gem are normally yellow and blue. Although a bit of yellow is attractive, more than five percent of a secondary yellow tends to lead the gem toward an unattractive olive or what is often called "camouflage" or "army" green. Most commercial grade tourmaline is exactly this hue.

In lighter-toned gems (thirty-five to sixty-five percent), the impact of yellow can be much more positive, but the stone should have no more than fifteen percent yellow. A bit of blue is a plus — it warms things up a bit. A ninety percent green with no more than ten percent blue runs a close second to the pure verdant gem. This is the look-alike standard and there is no denying that a visually pure green stone is beautiful and desirable. That said, an overly bluish stone is definitely more desirable than an overly yellowish gem. In short, yellow is a discount color in green tourmaline; blue adds value because it adds warmth, beauty, and rarity.

Saturation and tone

The color green achieves its most vivid saturation, its gamut limit, at about seventy-five percent tone. Therefore, like emerald, the ideal tone for green tourmaline is between seventy and eighty percent. Stones with tonal values under seventy percent break through the look-alike standard; stones with tonal values above eighty-five percent are visually overcolor. Lighter-toned, pastel to mint green tourmalines can also be quite beautiful. Many of the stones found at Mount Mica, Maine, and more recently in

Pakistan fit this description and are not to be disparaged.

In the lighter-hued Paraiba-like stones, what the collector should look for is a good balance between hue and tone. Some of the lighter-toned gems have a bright liquid quality that makes them very desirable. High saturation is the key. Remember, beauty is the ultimate criterion.

The mask (saturation modifier) in the green variety is normally gray, which grades to black in darker-toned gems. This mask is greatly enhanced in incandescent lighting, adding a *sooty* quality to the stone.

Multicolor effect

Tourmaline is the most dichroic of all gem species. Multicolor effect is to be expected and embraced. The effect is less prominent in darker-toned (eighty percent) green stones. In lighter-toned gems it can be quite prominent, so much so that occasionally some medium-toned bluish green tourmaline will actually break up the primary and secondary hues and exhibit blue and green scintillation on adjacent facets. This can be a breathtakingly beautiful effect and is in no way a fault.

Before the discovery of Paraiba (see preceding chapter), lighter-toned greens were a real bargain in the marketplace. Post Paraiba, lighter minty hues with tonal values in the Paraiba range (forty-five to sixty-five percent) have been getting more attention and prices have increased. These hues can be extremely beautiful; they are brighter and have better crystal (transparency) than the darker greens. As in the darker varieties, the market values stones with blue secondary hues more than those that are yellowish. In lighter tones, "the bluer the better" is a good rule of thumb.

Crystal

Dark-toned green tourmaline never exhibits the glow, the limpid transparency of emerald. With all due respect to Max Bauer, it is precisely this quality that is often found in emerald but rarely in green tourmaline. Tourmaline is a daystone. Darker-toned green tourmaline tends to be quite turbid; incandescent lighting greatly increases this proclivity. Perhaps smoky or even sooty is a more visually accurate description — it's as if the stone had been blackened over the flame of a kerosene lamp. Transparency is greatly decreased. Gems that exhibit good crystal in incandescent light may be said to be the true "gems" of this gem variety.

Clarity

Green tourmaline is normally eye-clean. Visually included stones, excepting cabochons, are virtually unsaleable, and are of no interest to the connoisseur.

Jeff Scovil; courtesy of R.W. Wise, Goldsmiths, Inc.

Brazilian tourmaline (7.88 carats) exhibits a rich, slightly bluish green hue (seventy to seventy-five percent tone) with excellent crystal. Note the slightly yellowish green multicolor effect along the vertical edges of the stone.

The rarity factor

Though rare in any size, fine green tourmaline is readily available in fairly large sizes. Prices tend to decrease on a per carat basis over twenty carats.

Chapter 29

Chrome Green Tourmaline

Dreaming of tourmaline is supposed to insure success through superior knowledge but there seems to be no evidence that the residents of tourmaline mining areas in Maine or California, where such dreams are particularly common, are any better off as a result.

John Sinkankas, 1971

Chrome is a special variety of green tourmaline that owes its vivid green hue to trace amounts of chromium and vanadium. These are the same elements that also impart to emerald and tsavorite garnet their distinctive pure green hues. It should not be surprising, therefore, that the finest chrome tourmaline tends to resemble the finer examples of emerald and tsavorite. Chrome tourmaline is actually a distinct tourmaline variety called chrome dravite, found in East Africa. Chrome tourmaline is often associated with tsavorite garnet; miners will usually concentrate their efforts on tsavorite, as it fetches higher prices.

Hue

Like emerald and tsavorite garnet, fine chrome tourmaline is a visually pure "forest" green with slightly yellowish to bluish secondary hues. The blue will normally show itself in incandescent light, the yellow will be more visible in daylight. The same criterion applied to tsavorite garnet and emerald is applicable to chrome tourmaline. A blue

Tino Hammid.

A fine chrome tourmaline, a vivid, slightly (five to ten percent) bluish green of about eighty-five percent tone.

secondary hue is preferred to yellow. Chrome tourmaline, unlike emerald, can never be said to be too blue. A visibly pure to slightly (five to fifteen percent) bluish green gem between seventy and seventy-five percent tone is the most desirable.

Saturation and tone

Gray grading to black is the normal saturation modifier or mask found in chrome tourmaline. Due to its chemistry, chrome tourmaline is normally highly saturated. An overabundance of chromium/vanadium appears to be the culprit. A grayish mask is, however, sometimes found. Larger stones tend to be overcolor; that is, so dark in tone as to be virtually opaque. Even though the ideal tone or the gamut limit of green is seventy five percent, chrome of eighty percent tone can be quite beautiful, due to its vivid hue. Stones with tones of eighty-five percent and above are definitely overcolor. Gems of this description will appear to have a virtually opaque black body color punctuated by the occasional flash of vivid green key color.

Multicolor effect

As tourmaline is the most dichroic of gemstones, a strong multicolor effect is to be expected. However, perhaps due to its unique chemical composition and its distinctly dark tone, multicolor effect is rarely observed in the chrome green gemstone.

Crystal

Good crystal is very rare in chrome tourmaline because of its normally dark tone and its behavior in incandescent lighting. Chrome tourmaline, like other members of the species, is a daystone. The stone's crystal has a tendency to close up — to turn sooty like the chimney of an oil lamp — under incandescent light. It seems particularly sensitive to certain kinds of halogen lighting. If the stone tends toward a gray mask, the yellowish light of the light bulb will also exacerbate that tendency.

Generally speaking, chrome tourmaline is simply more opaque than emerald or tsavorite garnet. Its hue is vivid but it is also dense. A chrome tourmaline that meets the criteria discussed above and that exhibits good crystal — that is, one that retains its transparency in incandescent light — is the crème de la crème of this species.

Clarity

Chrome tourmalines are normally sold eye-flawless. Stones with visible inclusions sell at very substantial discounts.

The rarity factor

Chrome tourmaline is quite rare generally, and particularly rare in sizes over one carat. A stone of fine quality over one carat is very rare. Therefore, the collector should expect a large percentage increase in the price of stones in carat-plus sizes. The next jump in rarity occurs at five carats. Stones of fine quality above ten carats are extremely rare, so rare in fact that I have never seen one.

Chapter 30

Blue Tourmaline

Seeing a true blue indicolite is practically a once-in-a-lifetime experience for most jewelers and probably most dealers.

David Federman, 1992

apphire blue tourmaline! Such stones are very rare. The search for such a stone is like the pursuit of the Holy Grail.

Historically, two Brazilian mines, the Manoel Mutuca in Araçuaí and the Golconda Mine northwest of the city of Govenador Valadares, are the source of the fabled "sapphire blue" indicolite. The best of these stones have an intense blue primary hue and a turquoise secondary hue, and are known as *Mutuca Blue*. Stones of this quality are extremely rare. Indicolite is found sporadically throughout the entire region of Minas Gerais.

Jeff Scovil; courtesy of R.W. Wise, Goldsmiths, Inc.

A fine 5.28-carat slightly greenish blue tourmaline from Brazil. Note the absence of multicolor effect and the limpid transparency of the crystal.

Hue

If cut on the C axis of the crystal, tourmaline with a primary blue hue will face-up blue, but not without just a slight hint of a secondary hue of green (ten to twenty percent). Stones cut in this manner will always be dark in tone because the C axis of the tourmaline crystal is itself very dark. In more conventionally cut stones, the primary hue is indeed a rich medium to deep hue reminiscent of sapphire; however, the gem will always show a green secondary hue. Gems with an eighty-five percent blue primary hue with no more than a ten percent green secondary hue should be considered fine.

As with all tourmaline, incandescent lighting will bring out the secondary hue. Stones that appear almost pure blue in sunlight or incandescent lighting will pick up a distinct greenish secondary hue under the light bulb. All other factors being equal, the bluer the stone the better the stone.

Saturation and tone

Indicolite can be found in all tonal ranges. The stone is most attractive as the tone approaches seventy-five to eighty percent, the ideal tone for blue. Gray is the normal saturation modifier found in lighter-toned indicolite. As with most tourmaline, the gray is punched up by incandescent lighting.

Clarity

Tourmaline in the green-blue range of hues is usually visually flawless. However, an exceptional indicolite, given its extreme rarity, may be forgiven a few minor flaws. The presence of any visual inclusions should, however, dramatically lower the price.

Crystal

Indicolite tends to turn grayish, lose transparency, and appear muddy in incandescent lighting. Again, tourmaline is a daystone and puts its best foot forward in natural daylight and daylight-equivalent fluorescent lighting. The collector should always view tourmaline in incandescent lighting before making a purchase. Although the gem is often compared to sapphire, blue tourmaline will almost never exhibit a transparency comparable to sapphire.

As with all transparent gemstones, all other factors being equal, diaphaneity — transparency or *crystal* — will separate the fine from the merely good, the beautiful from the merely pretty. Finer examples of blue tourmaline that hold their hue and that do not close up or turn sooty in incandescent lighting are very rare and are the most desirable examples of this gem variety.

The rarity factor

Blue tourmaline is rare in any size, but the gem is available in fairly large sizes. Prices will decrease above twenty carats.

Chapter 31

Pink/Red Tourmaline

Rubellite may be of various shades of colour, from pale rose to dark carmine red, sometimes tinged with violet. The colour may be so like that of certain rubies that it is difficult, even for an expert, to discriminate between these stones on mere inspection.

Max Bauer, 1904

The Oro Fino Mine in the Brazilian state of Minas Gerais, about ten miles east of the Manoel Mutuca mine, was the legendary source of some of the world's finest red tourmaline, called rubellite. Stones from this source have a pure red primary hue and a purplish secondary hue, yielding a lovely purplish red that has been compared to the color of the Bing cherry. Although Oro Fino has been closed for more than a decade, the term *Oro Fino Red* has come to designate the very finest red tourmaline, regardless of source.

Jeff Scovil; courtesy of R.W. Wise, Goldsmiths, Inc.

Matched pinkish/purplish red tourmaline ovals from Nigeria. Note the 80% brilliance and fine crystal.

Tourmaline occurs in every conceivable hue from pink through red. Despite the misleading appellation "rubellite," red tourmaline looks like red tourmaline, not like ruby at all, although they share the same primary hue. The chief difference in appearance is the multicolor effect. Tourmaline is the most dichroic of gemstones and always exhibits a pronounced multicolor effect.

Hue: "ruby-like" tourmaline

Stones with a pure red hue plus the absolute minimum of secondary hue (normally pink to purple) are, without question, the most valued in the marketplace. However, red tourmaline will always have some mixture of secondary hue, particularly when the viewing environment is shifted from natural or fluorescent to incandescent lighting. Under the light bulb, this tourmaline will almost always appear distinctly pinkish or purplish red. Vividly pinkish and purplish

purplish red. Vividly pinkish and purplish secondary hues of twenty percent or more are characteristic and lend to tourmaline a distinctive appearance that can be quite beautiful though, with apologies to the late great Max Bauer, not particularly ruby-like at all.

Saturation

Though brown is possible, gray is the normal saturation modifier or mask found in red tourmaline. Red, like all tourmaline, is a daystone. The tendency to gray is normally exacerbated by viewing the stone in incandescent lighting. The hue will often appear to close up, losing both saturation and transparency (crystal) under the light of a flame. Some stones will gray only slightly and appear violetish under the light bulb.

Tone

Red tourmaline reaches its most vivid saturation, or gamut limit, at about eighty percent tone, which is, not surprisingly, also the ideal tone in ruby. However, in red tourmaline, lighter tones of red, when combined with a higher percentage of secondary hue, will often result in a marvelously beautiful gemstone. Gems with tonal values between forty and fifty percent will appear rosy; pinkish stones in the fifty to sixty percent range are the color of maraschino cherries. Darker-toned red stones with a purple secondary hue are best described as magenta. This wonderful range of hues provides much latitude for the tourmaline collector.

Crystalline nightstones: the crème de la crème

Diaphaneity — transparency or more commonly "crystal" — is the true fourth C of colored gemstone evaluation. As mentioned, tourmaline is normally a daystone. That is, it looks its best in natural lighting. Incandescent lighting produces a negative affect. A brownish mask shows up under the light bulb, and if it is strong, causes the stone to lose transparency, to "close up" under this type of light. Finer red-pink tourmaline will actually turn violetish or slightly grayish violet. These stones tend to hold their transparency, the violet secondary hue enhancing the overall appearance of the stone. The collector should check any pink-red tourmaline for this property before deciding on an acquisition. Thus, it is important when considering a purchase to observe the stone carefully in incandescent light. This is the crucial test. A stone that is a limpid pinkish red in daylight, but becomes a muddy brownish red in incandescent, is less than desirable.

Tourmaline is one gem species where a contrarian approach to collecting can yield big dividends. It is recommended that the aficionado forget comparisons to ruby and pink sapphire and consider the stone. A strongly violetish to purplish red tourmaline with little or no brownish mask is much more desirable than a muddy ruby-like stone and should be available at the same or perhaps even a lower price.

However, a recent strike in Nigeria brought a large number of eye-flawless stones into the market.

Cut and crystal

Tourmaline, as Max Bauer pointed out in 1904, has a "somewhat feeble" refraction.[176] This is particularly apparent when the gem is compared to ruby. That said, red tourmaline is one of the few examples of this gem variety that can be advantageously cut into round, oval, and pear-shaped mixed brilliants. This is because the C axis of the red crystal is normally not as dark and dense as it is in the green and blue varieties. Red tourmaline potentially may exhibit much better crystal than the green and blue varieties. The pavilion of red tourmaline is often cut with multiple tiny facets. The scintillation produced by this faceting style shows the gem's multicolor effect to great advantage.

The rarity factor

Pink-red tourmaline can be found in large sizes. Although clean red stones of any size are rare, gems over twenty carats tend to decrease in price on a per carat basis.

Jeff Scovil; courtesy of R.W. Wise, Goldsmiths, Inc.

A 6.45-carat pink tourmaline from San Diego County, California. This color is known as "dusty rose," owing to a slight brownish mask that reduces the saturation (vividness) of the hue.

Clarity

Pink-red tourmaline is often visually included. Stones with a few small inclusions that are visible, but affect neither the durability nor the beauty of the gemstone, are acceptable. Eye-visible inclusions have been the norm, particularly in Brazilian reds.

176. Max Bauer, *Precious Stones*, pp. 366-368. Despite his propensity to compare blue, green, and red tourmaline to sapphire, emerald, and ruby, he also takes notice of the tendency of some tourmaline to appear "quite dark and imperfectly transparent."

Chapter 32

Other Colors of Tourmaline

So to the present day, although tourmaline is considerably used in jewelry, it is rarely ever called by that name. The green varieties are often known as Brazilian Emerald, chrysolite--, or peridot, some varieties of blue as Brazilian Sapphire, others as indicolite, and the red as rubellite, siberite, and even as ruby.

Oliver Cummings Farrington, 1903

It is fair to say that tourmaline comes in many other hues — perhaps every other hue. Yellow and orange tourmaline stones are exceedingly rare. I have never seen a stone with a primary purple hue. On the other hand, there is no theoretical barrier to the occurrence of tourmaline in these colors, so sooner or later one will probably be found.

Lemon yellow tourmaline is quite beautiful; however, yellow is usually tinged with green. I haven't seen pure yellow stones above two carats. Most orange is tonally dark and appears brown. Tourmaline of this hue is beautiful in flavors darkening from mocha to chocolate. Brown stones are usually available at very reasonable prices.

The tourmaline crystal will often show distinct zones of different hues. Stones purposely cut to include two or more hues are called bicolors. The most common bicolors are brown/green. The color alteration results from the depletion of certain chemicals during the crystal's formation. This depletion changes the environment and destabilizes the crystal, so that multiple fractures are created within the rough and therefore are in the cut stone. Clean bicolors are rare. An eye-flawless gem that includes a visually pure red and green in approximately equal amounts is the most sought after, and will command the highest price.

It is safe to say that tourmaline which approaches a pure spectral hue — whether red, orange, yellow, green, blue, violet, or purple — will be more desirable in the

Harold and Erica Van Pelt; courtesy of R.W. Wise, Goldsmiths, Inc., and Kalil
This exceptional 120-carat flawless bicolor tourmaline, currently in a private collection, is close to 100% brilliant and is one of the largest and finest of its kind.

market than stones that fall between these pure hues. This is generally true of all gemstones: a pure hue is more desirable than a mixed hue. A pure purple — if and when it is discovered — will be more desired than a pinkish or reddish purple. Likewise, a pure yellow stone is more sought after than a greenish yellow gem. The characteristically strong multicolor effect in tourmaline dictates that stones of this description are truly scarce. The mixture of hues which distinguishes this gem contributes to its distinctive beauty. Tourmalines must be evaluated stone by stone.

Multicolor effect

Tourmaline is the most dichroic of gemstones, usually showing a pronounced multicolor effect. The multicolor effect is considered a fault in sapphire, ruby, and emerald, gemstones that are chiefly valued for the purity of their primary hue. Thus, multicolor effect is considered a fault only in "sapphire" blue, "ruby" red, and "emerald" green tourmalines. In lighter-hued tourmalines and non-look-alike hues, the only issue is whether this particular multicolor effect detracts from the appearance of a specific gemstone.

Connoisseurship in tourmaline: a contrarian approach

Tourmaline does have a traditional grading structure. However, that structure is limited to just a few varieties, or color ranges, of the gem. Historically, stones that fall outside these narrow parameters have been largely ignored. Given tourmaline's propensity to occur in almost any hue, this leaves broad areas open to inexpensive contemplation by the connoisseur. The key issues in evaluating tourmaline are discussed above. I recommend, if the primary/secondary hue is pleasing, that the collector focus on the presence and strength of gray mask, multicolor effect, and crystal when evaluating a specific stone. In addition, if a stone is well cut and earns high marks in both day and incandescent light, it is a fine rare stone and worthy of consideration

Chapter 33

Tanzanite

Tanzanite looks like sapphire wishes it could look.

Barry Hodgin, 1988

anzanite was discovered twenty-five miles south of the dusty frontier town of Arusha, Tanzania, in 1967. A tailor cum prospector named Manuel D'Souza staked the first claim. Two years later a Masai warrior brought a ten-thousand-carat chunk of transparent purplish blue material to Navrottoni Pattni at his office in Nairobi. Pattni, Kenya's first gem cutter, thinking that anything that big had to be glass, dismissed the Masai without purchasing the material. As subsequent events would prove, Pattni had turned away an entirely new gem material. It was eventually named tanzanite by Henry Platt, then vice president of Tiffany's, in honor of the East African country where it was first discovered. Pattni speculates that the piece he was offered could have been cut into a gem in excess of the 220-carat beauty currently in the collection of the Smithsonian. Pattni was offered the stone for fifty dollars. Such are the wages of hesitation.

Tanzanite is the gem variety of the mineral zoisite. Tanzanite is a trichroic gemstone, meaning that it exhibits one of three colors depending on which way the crystal is viewed: blue, amethystine to red, and green yellow to brown. Although some of the stones found on the surface are purple blue because of the heat of the equatorial sun, almost all tanzanite comes out of the ground a gray to root beer brown. Relatively gentle heating will drive off the gray brown, leaving the lovely violet to purple blue behind.[177] Tanzanite may also occur in green and yellow hues, but these colors are so rare that they are not part of this discussion.

Jeff Scovil; courtesy of R.W. Wise, Goldsmiths, Inc.

A 5.55-carat oval tanzanite showing its bedtime color (incandescent light). Note the pronounced purple multicolor effect on one side of the gem, a result of the lighting in the photograph.

177. Peter C. Keller, *Gemstones of East Africa* (Tucson, Arizona: Geoscience Press, 1992), pp. 68-69.

Because tanzanite possessed a passing resemblance to sapphire, Platt decreed that the finest color of tanzanite would be the one that came closest to looking like the finest quality of sapphire. This is another example of the dated look-alike standard. Tanzanite does look like sapphire, or as one of my first mentors in the gem business once put it, "Tanzanite looks like sapphire wishes it could look."

Hue

In daylight, tanzanite exhibits a range of hues from a light-toned violet to purple to a rich dark-toned blue (eighty to eighty-five percent) with a moderate (fifteen to twenty percent) purple secondary hue. The slightly purplish blue color, which Platt defined as the finest, will exhibit a pure blue in daylight, an environment that suppresses the purple. The secondary purple becomes visible as soon as the stone is placed in an incandescent lighting environment. Incandescent lighting will always bring out the secondary hue, be it violet or purple.

The finest stones will show a blue primary hue with just a hint (ten percent) of purple secondary hue by day. By night, under a light bulb, the purple secondary increases to fifteen to twenty percent. Some connoisseurs prefer to see a bit of purple even in daylight. The purple adds a velvety quality to the hue. Some stones will appear almost a visually pure blue — only slightly purplish — in daylight, and change dramatically to a visually pure purple in incandescent. Some connoisseurs, in defiance of the sapphire look-alike standard,

find this range of hues nearly as desirable.

The quality of the secondary hue depends to a large extent on the purity of the red trichroic hue and on the orientation of the crystal prior to cutting. Tanzanite can be violet to purple or violetish to purplish blue depending upon the amount of red. (Remember to distinguish between purple and violet. Purple lies precisely halfway between blue and red on the color wheel. Violet is actually about halfway between purple and blue.)

Sapphire is downgraded if it loses or *bleeds* color when the lighting environment is changed from daylight to incandescent. Tanzanite will always shift color when the viewing environment is switched from daylight or daylight-fluorescent to incandescent lighting. Tanzanite does not "bleed" color, it changes color, losing nothing in the way of saturation. Tanzanite is not sapphire. This hue-shift is characteristic and breathtaking, and partly defines the beauty of the stone.

Saturation

Gray is the usual saturation modifier or mask in tanzanite. Stones without the gray modifier will exhibit an extremely vivid velvety hue. To the untutored eye, the gray mask is quite difficult to see, particularly in daylight. Incandescent lighting will bring out the gray. A gray mask visibly dulls the hue, imparting a cool aspect. Gray is usually more prominent in stones of less than sixty percent tone.

Tone

Like sapphire, tanzanite achieves its optimum hue at between seventy-five and eighty-five percent tone. Although color science holds that eighty-five percent tone is optimum for blue, stones with tonal values of seventy-five to eighty percent have greater transparency (crystal). Stones of eighty-five percent tone appear slightly inky. The difference between blue at seventy-five percent tone and blue at eighty-five percent tone is what separates the finest color from second best. As with sapphire, gemstones of eighty-five percent tone cross the line; they become too dark and are, in fact, overcolor.

Tanzanite versus sapphire

Tanzanite is often compared to Kashmir sapphire.[178] This is not a particularly helpful comparison. Comparisons between two gemstone varieties are usually to the detriment of one of the victims. Each species, each variety of precious gemstone, has its singular virtues. Although the hue of a fine tanzanite, like the finest Kashmir sapphire, can be described as velvety, tanzanite will always have a more distinct purple secondary hue.

Purple sapphire may more closely resemble tanzanite. Most, though not all purple sapphire, behaves almost exactly like tanzanite in changing lighting environments, appearing almost gem blue in daylight and picking up a distinct purple secondary hue in incandescent light.

Most tanzanite is actually purple to purplish blue. Stones with a purple primary hue normally occur in lighter tones, usually no darker than seventy percent. Purple sapphire is normally darker, between seventy-five and eighty-five percent tone. Purple sapphire with tonal values less than seventy-five percent does resemble tanzanite of a similar tone. Such stones may be difficult to separate visually from tanzanite.

Jeff Scovil; courtesy of R.W. Wise, Goldsmiths, Inc.

A 4.38-carat visually pure purple sapphire photographed in incandescent light. This stone would appear slightly bluish purple if examined in daylight.

178. Keller, *Gemstones of East Africa*, p. 72.

Crystal

Tanzanite has a wonderful crystalline character that is hardly affected at all by the heat-enhancement process. Blue sapphire of a similar tone (seventy-five to eighty-five percent) will often appear murky by comparison. Unheated sapphire from Burma will often show excellent crystal, but in fine tanzanite good crystal should always be present.

Durability

If tanzanite has a downside, it is durability. Tanzanite is relatively soft, ranking at six and one half on the Mohs scale. From a toughness perspective, the stone is somewhat brittle. Gems with a hardness of less than seven are subject to abrasion if wiped with a dusty cloth. Dust is mainly a silicate and its hardness is seven on the Mohs scale. Still, six and a half is approximately the hardness of steel and is the cutoff for for membership among the new precious gemstones. Tanzanite is problematic as a ring stone, particularly if worn every day, and should be cleaned carefully using solutions manufactured for the purpose.

The rarity factor

Tanzanite is the single exception to the usual relationship between size and rarity. Most gem varieties become rarer and hence more valuable as size increases. Tanzanite appears to require more mass to achieve its finest quality. For this reason a one-carat gem-quality tanzanite is actually rarer than a five-, ten-, or twenty-carat stone of the same quality; a sub-carat fine gem is rarer still. One would expect that smaller stones would command a higher per carat price. For years, however, this was not the case. Smaller fine quality gems sold for lower per carat prices than larger ones. Only recently have dealers begun to recognize this fact and to adjust prices accordingly.

Tanzanite prices have seesawed wildly over the past decade, due to the fluctuating political climate in Tanzania. Prices seemed to bottom out in 1997, with stones selling for as much as sixty percent off of prices current in the early eighties. In 1998 tragedy struck the mines, all of which are in Merelani. Cave-ins took the lives of a number of miners and choked off rough supplies. As of this writing, prices for tanzanite have stabilized. Still, a fine tanzanite can be purchased for pennies on the dollar when compared to sapphire. Considering the gem's beauty, tanzanite, today, must be considered one of the true bargains in the gem world.

FANCY COLOR DIAMONDS

Fancy color diamonds pose a real challenge for the connoisseur. Unlike their colorless brethren, fancy color diamonds are genuine rarities.

Color in diamond is rare because diamond is composed of a single element, carbon. Diamond is, in fact, the only gemstone composed of a single element. Carbon has an extremely tight atomic structure, the reason for the stone's legendary hardness. It is very difficult for impurities, the atoms that cause color, to make their way into the diamond's crystal lattice.[179] Agents such as vanadium, chromium, and iron, the causes of color in

Courtesy of Stephen Hofer

The "Colour Variety Collection," assembled for a private collector by diamond expert Stephen Hofer, shows each of the thirteen colors of fancy color diamond, including one of the few fancy deep violet diamonds in existence (middle row far right). Previously only twelve colors were known to exist.

9. The crystal lattice is the three mensional arrangement of carbon oms that is the basic unit of ucture in the diamond crystal. The amond lattice is composed of a

tetrahedral arrangement of carbon atoms with one atom at each corner and one in the center.

180. Stephen C. Hofer, *Collecting*

and Classifying Fancy Coloured Diamonds (New York: Ashland Press, 1998). This book is essential reading for anyone interested in collecting

fancy color diamonds. Recently at least one diamond with a violet primary hue has been found.

many other varieties of gemstones, are composed of atoms that are simply too large to replace carbon atoms inside the carbon lattice. In fact, of the one hundred or so known elements, the atoms of only three, nitrogen, boron, and hydrogen, are small enough to work their way into the compact structure of the diamond crystal lattice. Nitrogen, the most common impurity atom, is the cause of yellow and some pink diamonds. Boron is responsible for the gray blue colors. Hydrogen is the coloring agent for some red, olive, violet, and blue colors.

The colouring of diamonds is seldom intense, pale colours being much more usual than deeper shades. Diamonds that combine great depth and beauty of colour with perfect transparency are objects of unsurpassable beauty.

Max Bauer, 1904

Color in diamond has two additional sources: atomic radiation, which is responsible for the color of green diamonds; and the physical deformation of the atomic structure of the crystal, known as plastic deformation. Plastic deformation is responsible for the color in red and pink diamonds.

In his seminal book on fancy color diamonds, Stephen Hofer maintains that fancy color diamonds occur in twelve basic hues: red, orange, yellow, green, olive, blue, purple, white, brown, gray, and black.[180] Also, in fancy color diamonds, white, gray, and black may function as primary hues.[181] Olive, too, has a distinguished lineage. Violet is somewhat controversial. Only about five examples of natural violet diamonds have ever been found.[182] A generalized rarity/price chart for fancy color diamonds follows.[183]

Chapter 4 contains a detailed discussion of the criteria used to grade fancy color diamonds. It is recommended that the reader read this section in conjunction with the essays that follow.

181. The reader will recall that throughout this volume the color of gemstones has been described using just eight hues: red, orange, yellow, green, blue, violet, purple, and pink. Gray and brown are considered masks that dull the brightness of the hue (see Chapter 3). The terminology may be confusing, since GIA classifies as hues all of the above *plus* brown and gray, but excludes olive, which is termed gray-yellow-green. Given the importance of laboratory grading in the fancy color diamond market, it seems appropriate to stay as close to GIA-GTL terminology as possible in this section.

182. Hofer, *Fancy Coloured Diamonds*, p. 612; Harvey Harris, *Fancy-Color Diamonds* (Liechtenstein: Fancoldi Registered Trust, 1994), pp. 60-61. Hofer maintains that instrument measurements of "violet" diamonds

Highest auction price paid
1959–1997

Fancy Color Diamond Rarity/Price Chart						
RARITY	COLOR	COLOR	DESCRIPTION	WEIGHT	PRICE	TOTAL
RANK		GRADE			PER CT.	PRICE*
1	Red	Fancy	Purplish red	0.95	926,313	879,997.00
2	Green	Fancy	Yellowish green	3.02	564,569	1,704,998.00
3	Blue	Fancy deep	Blue	4.37	569,000	2,468,530.00
4	Purple	Fancy	Reddish purple	0.54	122,222	65,999.00
5	Pink	Fancy intense	Purplish pink	7.37	819,201	6,037,511.00
6	White	Fancy	White	3.92	2,933	11,497.00
7	Olive	Fancy	Yellowish gr/grn	7.07	21,937	155,066.00
8	Orange	Fancy vivid	Orange	5.54	238,718	1,322,497.00
9	Yellow	Fancy vivid	Yellow	13.83	238,792	3,302,493.00
9	Brown	Fancy	Orangish brown	8.91	9,259	82,497.00
10	Black	Fancy	Black	46.53	2,418	112,509.00
10	Gray	Fancy dark	Bluish gray	5.54	51,535	285,503.00

*Includes ten to fifteen percent buyer's premiums.

show most of them to be a gray hue with a violetish secondary hue. In his view, violet normally occurs as a secondary modifying hue but never as of 1997) as a primary hue. Harris takes the opposite view, but agrees that gray is a strong component of violet diamonds. Since his book was published, Hofer has documented several violet diamonds, including two from Australia's Argyle Mine. In August 2002 I had an opportunity to examine a violet diamond. The stone, a marquise shape, weighs 0.55 carats and is the first stone ever to achieve a GIA-GTL grade of *fancy deep violet*. Both Hofer and I agree with the GIA-GTL description.

Stephen Hofer, personal communication, 2002.

183. Stephen Hofer, personal communication, 1999.

Chapter 34

Red Diamonds

The true red diamond is valuable according to the glorious beauty of its perfection . . . it feeds the eyes with much pleasure in beholding, and hence discovered to us the Excellencies of super-celestial things.

Henry Nichols, 1651

Red diamond is arguably one of the rarest substances on earth. Certainly it is the most expensive. The concept of a pure red diamond, like the pure red ruby, probably exists somewhere in the Platonic paradise of pure idea and not in this world at all. The Gemological Institute of America (GIA) has documented the existence of fifteen red diamonds. Of these, only four have received the grade of *fancy red*, which classifies them as pure red diamonds with no secondary modifying hue.[184]

Hue, saturation, tone

Red is a deep dark pink and inversely pink is light-toned pale red. In the connoisseurship of red diamonds this is an important fact to keep in mind. Any dividing line between pink and red must be in some sense arbitrary. In the marketplace the distinction is extraordinarily important. Given the tens of thousands of dollars, sometimes hundreds of thousands of dollars in price, the terminology used in the lab report becomes crucial. The red hue achieves its most vivid saturation, its *gamut limit,* at approximately eighty percent tone. Thus, all other C's being equal, a visually pure red

The World Champion Hancock Diamond pictured at the top of the photograph and weighing in at just 0.95 carats, carries a GIA-GTL grade of fancy purplish red. The middle stone weighing 0.59 carats was graded fancy purplish pink. The stone pictured at bottom weighing 0.54 carats was graded fancy reddish purple. This photograph illustrates how subtle the nuances of hue can be and the importance of the wording of a GIA GTL grading report. In this case, purplish pink is particularly difficult to separate from purplish red.

of eighty percent tone, if it could be found, would be the ideal red diamond.

184. King et al., "Natural-Color Pink Diamonds," p. 134. These fifteen stones are described by GIA as being in the public domain," meaning that other stones graded red could not be included due to confidentiality agreements with its clients.

185. Hofer, *Fancy Coloured Diamonds*, p. 315. Hofer, one of the world's foremost experts on fancy color diamonds, has never seen an orangy red diamond, though he maintains that their existence is theoretically possible.

As with ruby, pink and purple are the most attractive secondary hues in red diamonds. Orange would be a third attractive modifying hue, but whether an orangy red diamond actually exists is a matter of conjecture.[185] Of those that exist, pinkish stones are necessarily lighter in tone than purplish stones. The most expensive diamond ever sold, the 0.95-carat Hancock Diamond, is a *fancy purplish red*.[186] As with colored gems generally, chromatic secondary hues are more desirable than neutrals (masks) such as gray and brown. Brown is the normal saturation modifier or mask found in red diamonds. Brownish reds tend to be darker in tone and, of course, duller of hue.

GIA revised its diamond color grading nomenclature in 1994. The new terminology retains the original designations *faint*, *very light*, *light*, *fancy*, and *fancy intense*, adding two additional classifications, *fancy vivid* and *fancy deep*. As of this writing, GIA-GTL has not found the need to use any term beyond *fancy* to describe red diamonds graded in its laboratory.[187]

Multicolor effect

Multicolor effect is a characteristic found in red diamonds. Often this shows up as tonal variations of purple and pink visible in portions of the face-up mosaic of the gem and can be very pronounced indeed. As discussed in Chapter 5's section on grading fancy color diamonds, *pinkish red* is not a term used by GIA-GTL on its fancy color diamond grading reports. Since pink is a lighter-toned paler red, a stone of this description would be graded *fancy red*. This is another example of how the certificate-driven world of fancy color diamonds can leave the budding aficionado scratching his or her head. I examined a 0.52-carat radiant cut diamond with a GIA-GTL report that described the stone as "fancy purplish red." The stone was certainly red, but exhibited strong pink multicolor effect along the edge of the crown.

Clarity

Color in red diamonds is a result of plastic deformation of the crystal lattice. As a result, the color in red and pink diamonds may occur in thin closely packed zones called grain lines. This may result in the stone showing some texture in the face-up position. As in sapphire, texture, or lack of uniformity in the face-up color, is a negative.

It is difficult to talk about negatives with a stone of such breathtaking rarity. As with any colored gem, a brownish mask muddies the hue and should be considered a negative. Texture is a negative. However, it is difficult to conceive of any collector turning down a red diamond, assuming he could afford to purchase it, regardless of the mix of secondary hues. The fancy color diamond market is driven by rarity; beauty is, at best, a secondary consideration.

186. Robert E. Kane, "Three Notable Fancy-Color Diamonds: Purplish Red, Purple-Pink, and Reddish-Purple," *Gems & Gemology*, Summer 1987, p. 91.

187. King et al., "Natural-Color Pink Diamonds," p. 135.

Chapter 35

Pink Diamonds

The first was a stone I came across in the reign of Pope Clement, a diamond literally flesh-coloured, most tender, most limpid, it scintillated like a star, and so delightful it was to behold that all other diamonds beside it, however pure & colourless, seemed no longer to give any pleasure and lose their gratefulness.

Benvenuto Cellini, 1568

Prior to 1985, when pink diamonds from Australia's Argyle Mine began to filter into the market, pink diamonds were an extraordinary rarity. The few pink stones known came from the famous alluvial deposits of southern India, southern Africa, and the Brazilian state of Minas Gerais. A good proportion of those stones were very light in tone and pale in saturation, and were likely to garner designations of *faint* to *light* on the GIA-GTL fancy diamond grading scale. The Argyle pinks changed all that. Of the one hundred fifty or so pinks submitted to the GTL in 1985, almost all achieved the coveted grade of *fancy pink*. Since then, dealers and connoisseurs have awaited with much anticipation Argyle's once-a-year tender of pink diamonds.

Unfortunately Argyle pinks are relatively small. Only two cut stones over three carats have been produced. Famous large pinks are from India, Brazil, or southern Africa. Size, however, does not seem to drive price. In 1995 a 7.37-carat *fancy intense purplish pink* sold at Sotheby's at a per carat record of $819,201 or $6,037,511 for the stone.

The color in pink diamonds occurs in thin, needlelike color zones. Darker zones, closely packed, produce a deeper-toned hue. These zones, commonly called "pink graining," can be visible to the naked eye. Graining is caused by deformation of the diamond crystal while it is in a semisolid state, a process known as "plastic deformation." This deformation of the crystal lattice is the actual cause of color in pink diamonds. Profuse zoning can lend the pink diamond a somewhat fuzzy or hazy appearance, known as "texture." An even face-up color is the ideal, as in all gemstones. Visible zoning is not desirable.

Hue, saturation, tone

Pink is a distinct hue. It is a pale or less saturated light tone of red. Thus the visual

Courtesy of © Stephen Hofer

A "fancy intense purplish pink" diamond photographed next to a colorless (D-color) diamond, from the "Colour Variety Collection."

188. C.R. Ashby, trans., *The Treatises of Benvenuto Cellini on* *Goldsmithing and Sculpture, 1568.* (New York: Dover Editions, 1967), p. 31.

division between red and pink is in some sense arbitrary. Pure pinks are particularly rare. The secondary hues found in pink diamonds are red, purple, and orange. Argyle stones are known for their purplish hues. Light purplish secondary hues are sometimes erroneously described as violetish. In the marketplace, pure pinks and reddish pinks are the most desired, followed by purplish and orangish pink.

Multicolor effect

Isn't a reddish-pink red? In the certificate-driven world of fancy color diamonds, such questions are answered by laboratory analysis, with the most important document by far the one issued by GIA's Gem Trade Lab (GIA-GTL). In an attempt to avoid confusion, GIA-GTL does not use the term *reddish pink* in its grading reports. This is not to say that reddish pink diamonds do not exist — they most definitely do. As discussed in the Chapter 5 section on grading fancy color diamonds, pink stones often have portions of the face-up mosaic of the gem that exhibit a definite red primary hue. The certificate grade, however, will name the hue that shows in the largest percentage of the gem's face, ignoring the multicolor effect.

Based on the 1994 GIA diamond color grading nomenclature — *faint*, *very light*, *light*, *fancy*, *fancy intense*, *fancy vivid*, and *fancy deep* — a majority of pink diamonds will fall into the first four categories of saturation/tone. According to fancy color diamond expert Stephen Hofer, of the three hundred forty-five pink diamonds sold at the major houses since 1959, only three merited the designation *fancy intense*. Hofer further states, "In the last couple of years, a growing number of Argyle stones are being awarded the designations *vivid* and *deep* pink to satisfy the market's fascination with exemplary pink colors."[189] Hofer's statement is a circumspect way of saying that these designations have more to do with politics than with beauty.

Brown is the most common saturation modifier or mask found in pink diamonds. Gray is very rarely present. In fact, brownish purplish pink is considered the "signature" color in pink diamonds from the Argyle mine. In the marketplace, brownish stones are generally preferable to grayish ones. Brownish stones generally appear warmer, and the brown is often prominent enough to rival the pink hue, adding to the overall depth (tone) of the color. Grayish stones read simply as dull-hued pink.

Pink stones are, by definition, pale (light) in tone. Deep-toned pinks approach red. Bright pinks are much sought after by connoisseurs. Dull pinks shade into brown. Light-toned pinks are easily confused with light-toned purples. Lighting is critical. To evaluate color in fancy color diamonds, GIA-GTL uses a special neutral gray box called the Judge II and a 6,500-kelvin daylight fluorescent light source manufactured by the MacBeth Corporation. This kelvin temperature is equivalent to daylight lighting at noon. However, unlike natural lighting, the light box is not subject to the modifying effects of changing latitudes and air pollution.

189. Stephen Hofer, personal communication, 1999.

Chapter 36

Purple Diamonds

Pure purple diamond with no secondary color (modifier) is very rare . . . when such diamonds come on the market they are invariably small — almost never more than 1 carat and usually under 50 points . . . there has yet to be a large, historically important pure purple diamond.

Harvey Harris, 1994

urple is a modified spectral hue halfway between red and blue on the color wheel. Purple is often confused with violet, which is a pure spectral color between purple and blue on the color wheel. Thus, purple teeters on the spectral seesaw, balanced between red and blue.

Purple diamonds are extreme rarities. A number of these stones, lilac in color and mostly less than one carat, appeared in Antwerp in the spring of 1989. Rumor has it that they were Russian in origin. Before the appearance of these stones, fancy purple diamonds were virtually unheard of.[190]

Courtesy of © Stephen Hofer
A "fancy intense pinkish purple" diamond from the "Colour Variety Collection."

Hue, saturation, tone

Color science tells us that the purple hue reaches its optimum saturation, its *gamut limit*, at about sixty percent tone. For this reason, medium dark-toned purples are more visually satisfying, more beautiful. Unfortunately most purple diamonds occur in tones of less than fifty percent and therefore are lacking in saturation, appearing quite pale.

Color in purple diamonds is often uneven. The color occurs in purple zones that alternate with colorless zones. At times the color may be limited to grain lines, which results in uneven or blotchy color, or texture, when the gem is viewed face up. Uneven color is much less desirable than even color, in this and in all gemstone species.

Pink and red are the normal secondary hues found in purple diamonds. Red is obviously the more desirable, as it is rare and by definition a darker tone than pink. Reddish purple is also prized more in the marketplace, even more than a pure purple hue. A touch of red lends the primary hue both vividness and

190. David Federman, "All in the Family: Inside the Diamond Spectrum," *Modern Jeweler*, October 1990, p. 51.

warmth; also, due to its rarity, any time the word red is mentioned, bells start ringing in the world of fancy color diamonds. Pure purple hues are actually rarer, but this is one of the more unusual cases in colored gemstone connoisseurship where a pure spectral hue is not the most desired. Pink is somewhat less desirable as a secondary hue, and it occurs in lighter-hued stones.

At lighter tones, it is extremely difficult for even the trained eye to differentiate between a pink and purple. This problem is exacerbated when the two hues are mixed, as in pinkish purple or purplish pink diamonds. The use of the correct lighting environment is especially critical when evaluating color in diamonds in the pink to purple color range. North daylight at noon is the standard. GIA-GTL uses a 6,500-kelvin fluorescent light manufactured by the MacBeth division of the Kollmorgen Corporation. Given the importance of the GIA-GTL color "cert" in the marketplace, the serious fancy color diamond connoisseur is well advised to invest in one of these lamps.

Either brown or gray can occur as a saturation modifier or mask in purple diamonds. Brown is more common. Experts use the term *smoky* to refer to purple diamonds that exhibit a mask. Many, perhaps most, light-toned purple stones do not show a mask. A grayish mask in lighter-toned purple diamonds will give the stone a cool aspect; brown will appear warmer. If the diamond is pale, dull, and cool, a grayish mask can be inferred. Incandescent lighting will bring out the brown. Daylight and daylight-equivalent fluorescent lighting will bring out the gray. Although noon daylight is the theoretical standard, the aficionado is advised to evaluate the gem in both daylight and incandescent light.

Chapter 37

Green Diamonds

Diamonds of a green color are distinctly rare, only a few examples being known. The most beautiful green diamond known is a transparent brilliant weighing 48 – carats preserved in the 'Green Vaults' at Dresden.

Max Bauer, 1904

The green diamond follows red in overall rarity. According to the records of the major auction houses, just sixty-four natural green diamonds have been offered at auction between 1959 and 1997. Of this total, only twenty-nine were judged to be pure green.[191] During this same period, the major auction houses sold one hundred seventy-five of the next rarest fancy color diamond, natural color blues.

The most famous green diamond of them all resides in the famous Green Vaults of Dresden. Known as the Dresden Green, this forty-one-carat, slightly grayish medium-toned "fancy green" is the largest green diamond in existence.[192] It has lain in the Green Vaults since its purchase in 1741 by Friedrich Augustus II, Elector of Saxony.

There are two types of green diamond: those with a green skin and those with an inherent green body color. Natural green diamonds derive their color from the association with natural atomic radiation. The length of exposure and the type of radiation — alpha, beta or gamma rays — determine the depth of green color. Those exposed to gamma radiation for extremely long periods of time will exhibit a green body color. Green diamonds with inherent green body color are considered much more

Shane F. McClure © Gemological Institute of America.

The legendary Dresden Green diamond; set in its original mounting, a hat ornament made by the Prague jeweler Diessbach circa 1768. Despite the quotation beginning this chapter which states that its weight is forty-eight and one half carats, modern measuring techniques indicate that the Dresden Green actually weighs approximately forty-one carats. Though visually grayish, the diamond would carry a GIA-GTL grade of "fancy green."

233

191. Hofer, *Fancy Coloured Diamonds*, p. 7.

192. Robert E. Kane et al., "The Legendary Dresden Green Diamond," *Gems & Gemology*, Winter 1990, pp. 248-265.

A "fancy deep green" diamond from the "Colour Variety Collection."

© Stephen Hofer

diamonds are yellow and blue. It is difficult, with this degree of rarity, to speak of preferred secondary hues. A yellow secondary produces a brighter, more saturated hue overall. A blue secondary produces a deeper warmer hue. The two highest-priced green diamonds sold at auction (1985 and 1995) were stones with a yellowish secondary hue.

Gray is the normal saturation modifier or mask found in green diamonds. As with blue diamonds, the gray secondary is sometimes added to the green to pump up the grade (see Chapter 4). For example, GIA specialists describe the Dresden Green as "visually grayish", yet its certificate grade in 1990 would have been "fancy green."[193]

Aside from the Dresden Green, there are no large historically important green diamonds. The largest notable fancy green was an 8.19-carat rectangle that sold at Sotheby's New York in 1983 for $48,350 per carat.[194]

desirable than greens whose color is only, so to speak, skin deep.

Hue, saturation, tone

Most green diamonds are pale of hue and light of tone. Due to the gem's rarity, only a small quantity of green (saturation) is required for the stone to make the grade. The normal secondary hues found in green

193. Robert E. Kane et al., "The Legendary Dresden Green Diamond," *Gems & Gemology*, Winter 1990, pp. 248-265.

194. Federman, "All in the Family," p. 49.

Chapter 38

Blue Diamonds

Although writers describe these stones as possessing . . . the beauty of fine sapphires, no comparison can really be instituted, their blue color being peculiar to themselves, dark, verging on indigo possessing a characteristic intensity which differs materially from the mild, soft hue of the Sapphire.

E.W. Streeter, 1879

Blue diamonds are one of nature's great rarities. Unquestionably the most famous blue is the 45.52-carat Hope Diamond on permanent display at the Smithsonian Institution in Washington, DC. The Hope has an interesting history. The celebrated seventeenth-century gem merchant Jean Baptiste Tavernier originally purchased it in India in 1667. Tavernier sold it to Louis XIV in 1668. The stone originally weighed 112.25 carats and was known as the *Tavernier Blue*. It was subsequently recut to 67.12 carats and re-christened the *French Blue*. Stolen in 1792 during the French Revolution, the stone did not resurface again until 1830, recut in its present form. The stone was then sold to the English financier Thomas Philip Hope.

Courtesy of Tino Hammid

The Hope Diamond (photographed under optimum conditions), appears quite a bit darker in normal lighting, and was graded "fancy deep grayish blue" by the GIA-GTL.

Although this famous gem has been described in the literature as "sapphire blue" and "superfine deep blue," these descriptions are a bit wide of the mark. The Hope is of a "fancy deep grayish blue" hue.[195] Visually, the gray modifier is so dark that it appears black, leading to the term which some experts use to describe the Hope: "inky blue." *Fancy deep*–hued stones of this type comprise less than ten percent of all blue diamonds.

The question is often raised as to which GIA-GTL designation — *fancy intense* or *fancy deep* — confers the greatest value on a blue diamond.[196] Were it not for the prevalence of a gray mask in blue diamonds

195. King et al., "Characterizing Natural-Color Type-IIB Blue Diamonds," p. 262.

196. John M. King, "Gem Trade Lab Notes," *Gems & Gemology*, Spring 2002, p. 80. A similar situation exists with green diamonds. *See Connoisseurship in Fancy Color Diamonds, p.62.*

this question would be fairly easily answered, as blue normally achieves its optimum saturation between eighty and eighty-five percent tone. *Fancy deep* is the designation that describes stones that are moderate to dark in tone. As it stands, it is the percentage of gray mask that provides the answer. The gem with the lower percentage will be the more beautiful and hence the more valuable.

Next to red and green, blue diamonds command the highest prices of any substance on earth. Of the ten highest per carat prices paid for fancy color diamonds, six have been for blue diamonds. The current record for blue diamonds was set at Christie's auction house in 1995 when a 4.37-carat diamond graded *fancy deep blue* sold for $2,486,000, or $569,000 per carat.

Courtesy of © Stephen Hofer

A "fancy deep blue" diamond next to a colorless or D-color diamond, from the "Colour Variety Collection." Note the pronounced multicolor effect toward the bottom of the pear. In blue sapphire this would be called color bleeding and considered a major fault; in the rarified world of fancy color diamonds, this gem is extremely desirable.

Hue, saturation, tone

The great majority of blue diamonds are very light in tone and pale in hue. Blue diamonds are extremely rare in nature, so rare that almost any quantity (saturation) of blue hue will be sufficient for a laboratory report to qualify the stone as a blue diamond. As stated above, most blue diamonds are noticeably gray or grayish; so much so, in fact, that many so-called fancy blues are actually slightly bluish gray. At very low tonal levels (thirty percent or less), grading reports issued by the Gemological Institute of America treat this gray modifier as a maximizer, adding the gray to the blue, thus pumping up the grade. Most blue diamonds do exhibit a gray mask, leading to such descriptions as *steel blue,* another term often used to describe the Hope.

This is not to say that pure blue stones do not exist; they do, and a stone with fifteen percent or less of a gray mask is a stone of great beauty and will bring an astonishing price. A few rare examples have a greenish secondary hue. As with most gemstone varieties, a visually pure primary hue is most sought after. After a visually pure blue, greenish blue to green blue are the most desirable combinations of primary and secondary hues. As with other colored gemstones discussed in this book, gray is a negative. Thus, the lower the percentage of gray the more beautiful and more desirable the stone.

Chapter 39

Orange Diamonds

Of the many pure (fancy) orange diamonds reported in the literature most actually have a tinge of yellow. . . . Since yellow and orange colours mix so intimately with each other, this often makes it difficult to decide visually if a subtle yellow modifier is present.

Stephen Hofer, 1998

In October of 1997 a 5.52-carat "fancy vivid" orange diamond sold at Sotheby's for $238,718 per carat or a whopping $1,322,497 for the stone.[197]   Prices like this demonstrate just how rare and costly fancy color diamonds have become. Orange is a spectral hue lying halfway between   yellow and red on the color wheel. Pure orange diamonds are exceedingly rare. Orange diamonds owe their distinct hue to trace amounts of nitrogen in the carbon lattice.

Courtesy of © Stephen Hofer

"Fancy deep brownish orange" diamond photographed next to a colorless (D-color) diamond, from the "Colour Variety Collection."

Jeff Scovil; courtesy of R.W. Wise, Goldsmiths, Inc.

A 0.73-carat "fancy yellowish brownish orange" diamond showing exceptional brilliance and very little multicolor effect.

Hue, saturation, tone

The color orange achieves its optimum saturation or gamut limit at a relatively light tone. Thus, the optimum tone for orange diamonds is between twenty and thirty percent tone. The grading of orange diamonds is further complicated by the fact that the color we call brown is not a distinct spectral hue; it is in fact a deep, dull orange. When grading darker-toned stones, it is difficult to determine where orange ends and brown begins. Is it a fancy orange brown or a brown orange? The difference can mean thousands, even tens of thousands of dollars. Actually there is no such thing as a

197 . "Fancy vivid" is GIA-GTL's highest designation. Vivid, of course, refers to the saturation or brightness of the hue. (See the introduction and overview to fancy color diamonds.)

dark-toned, dull orange diamond: diamonds of this description are brown.[198]

Red, pink, yellow, and brown are the normal secondary hues found in orange diamonds. Green is sometimes found as well. As is true in most gemstone varieties, a visually pure orange is the most desirable hue, followed by stones that are reddish, pinkish, yellowish, greenish, or brownish, in that order.

Brown, as might be guessed, is the most common saturation modifier or mask found in orange diamonds. As was noted above, brown adds measurably to the confusion, particularly in fancy color diamonds, because in the GIA-GTL system of grading fancy color diamonds, brown is classified as a hue rather than as a saturation modifier or mask as it is throughout this book. Thus a dull dark-toned orange diamond is actually a brown diamond and, as will be noted in the following chapter, is graded on a different scale.

Multicolor effect

Orange diamonds often exhibit multicolor effect, usually in the form of alternating flashes of orange and brown. Due to the varying lengths of the light path in both brown and orange diamonds, some light rays will absorb more color than others, resulting in a distinct multicolor effect in the face-up mosaic of the gem. This is further complicated by the addition of yellow, which is, after brown, the next most common secondary hue. It can be hard to decide if the gem is orangy brown or brownish orange. A diamond that has a primary orange hue will, of course, bring a much higher price in the marketplace.

Crystal

Due to an occasional overabundance of nitrogen, orange stones, particularly stones that fall into the range of intense to vivid in saturation, will often have a cloudy appearance. This is clearly a fault. Stones with vivid saturation and a high degree of transparency are much sought after.

198. Hofer, *Fancy Coloured Diamonds*, p. 325.

Chapter 40

Brown Diamonds

A diamond when brown, unless of a deep and pleasing colour, is very undesirable, as it absorbs much light and appears dirty by daylight and dark and sleepy by artificial light.

Frank Wade, 1918

rown is not a unique spectral color; it is a dark-toned dull hue of orange. This, as noted in the foregoing chapter, complicates the grading equation. Light-toned brown diamonds create an additional complication. Brown-"ish" diamonds, like yellowish diamonds, are considered *off-color* and are graded on the Gemological Institute's colorless diamond scale. This scale could also be called the colorless to light yellow, brown, and gray scale, as it views brown in almost exactly the same way as it does yellow. This is based on a tradition that historically has considered brown stones to be of little value as gems.

Still, there are a number of famous brown diamonds, most of them from South Africa. The Earth Star, a 111.59-carat pear-shaped orangy brown, was cut in 1967 from a 248.90-carat piece of rough found at the Jagersfontein Mine in South Africa. This stone was sold to a collector in 1983 for $900,000, or $8,065 per carat.[199] Other famous brownies include the 104.15-carat pear-shaped bronze called the Great Chrysanthemum and the 55.09-carat emerald-cut Kimberley.

Market resistance to brown-hued diamonds began to break down in the 1980s

© Stephen Hofer

An illustration of the jeweler's dictum that if you can say it in French you can always charge more for it. The Argyle Mine's "champagne" diamond grading scale, with tonal values from five to ten percent called light champagne (C-1 and 2), twenty to forty percent termed medium champagne (C-3 and 4), fifty to seventy percent dark champagne (C-5 and 6), and fancy cognac (C-7). Note the tonal jump from forty to sixty percent between C-4 and C-5. C-7 is approximately eighty percent tone.

199. Harris, *Fancy-Color Diamonds*, p. 142.

as fancy color diamond prices began to escalate; it changed forever in the late 1980s when a 4.02-carat fancy brown brought $4,925 per carat at auction in 1986 and a 8.91-carat fancy orangish brown diamond sold at Christie's for $82,497 or $9,259 per carat in 1987.[200]

When Australia's huge Argyle Mine came on line in the early 1990s, brown diamonds became more available in the market. In fact, fully one third of Argyle's production is brown stones. The mine's owners initiated a brilliant marketing program to sell its brown diamonds. Rechristened "champagne" and "cognac," these formerly despised colors became the new darlings of the diamond market.

A brown is a brown is a ...

Diamonds with a faint brownish body color to a light brownish body color are graded L through Z on the colorless diamond scale. Brown diamonds that are graded K through M *are termed faint brown*; those graded between N and R are called *very light brown*, and stones graded S through Z are termed *light brown*. Brown stones that are considered fancy color diamonds begin with the grade *fancy brown* at about thirty to thirty-five percent tone. Diamonds carrying letter grades on the colorless scale are not considered fancy color diamonds; they are off-color colorless diamonds and will carry a negative premium.

It is important to remember that the letter grades on the GIA colorless scale reflect the body colors, not the key color, of the stone.

A diamond with a Z grade should face up brownish rather than brown. GIA uses master stones to grade diamonds on this scale. For a yellow, gray, or brown diamond to achieve fancy status, its key color must be more saturated than the key color of the GIA Z-grade master stone viewed face up. The aficionado is advised to examine diamonds graded X through Z on the GIA colorless scale closely. They may face up with more color than the actual grade would suggest.

Hue, saturation, tone

Any hue except green is possible as a secondary hue in brown diamonds. In fact, red followed by orange, pink, purple, and yellow are the usual modifying hues and, in descending order, are the most desirable in the marketplace. Reddish brown is distinctly beautiful. Diamonds of this hue have the quality of fine old wine aged in oak casks. Orangy, along with yellowish brown, is the most common. A visually pure chocolate brown is also quite desirable and difficult to find. These are followed by the non-spectral, or mask, hues of gray, white, and black. As is the case with other gems, gray tends to mask or dull the color, reducing saturation.

Multicolor effect

Brown diamonds often exhibit multicolor effect, usually in the form of alternating flashes of orange and brown. Due to the varying lengths of the light path in both brown and orange diamonds, some light rays will absorb more color than others,

200. Harris, *Fancy-Color Diamonds*, p. 142.

resulting in a distinct multicolor effect in the face-up mosaic of the gem. This is further complicated by the addition of yellow, which is the next most common secondary hue. It can be hard to decide if the gem is *orangy brown* or *brownish orange* or, for that matter, a *yellowish orangy brown*. A diamond that has a primary orange hue will, of course, bring a much higher price than a stone with a pure brown hue.

Tonally, brown can occur in light to dark tones. Brown diamonds will often appear both darker of tone and deeper of hue in incandescent lighting. As with all gems, the aficionado is advised to view brown diamonds in both daylight and incandescent lighting.

In the world of diamonds, brown diamonds are not particularly rare. Although rarer than colorless diamonds, they are, along with yellows, the most common of the fancy color diamonds. However, beautiful browns are rarer than fine-quality colorless diamonds, and they sell at lower prices.

Chapter 41

Yellow Diamonds

Equally unfortunate for the cape yellows is that they have often been described in the literature as "off-colour" or "byewater" diamonds, especially by gemologists who fail to appreciate these delicate pastel colour tones in favor of the more saturated "fancy" cape yellows promoted in the marketplace.

Stephen Hofer, 1998

Yellow diamonds are among the most beautiful of the yellow gems. They are unquestionably the most expensive. In April 1997, a 13.83-carat "fancy vivid yellow" diamond sold at Sotheby's for $3,302,493 or $238,792 per carat. Pure yellows can be found in a number of other gem species, including sapphire, topaz, and citrine. Yet nowhere else can be found the unique combination of pure hue and exceptional brilliance that are possible in a yellow diamond. Yellow diamonds are relatively common in nature, but due to strong demand they are rare in the marketplace.

Almost all diamonds have a hint of yellow in the body color. When diamonds were first found in southern Africa in the late nineteenth century, it was noted that most of these stones, when compared to Indian and Brazilian diamonds, were yellowish. Quality grading in colorless diamonds is all about the elimination of yellow. Beginning with the letter H and proceeding to Z, the body color of the stones becomes progressively more yellowish. This is not always reflected in the face-up view. Dealers may be heard to say that a stone "faces up white," meaning that it has a slightly yellowish body color that is not visible in the key color. This is the result of cutting. The inverse is also possible! A stone with a light body color may show more color face up. This is another good reason to examine the stone carefully and avoid "buying the cert." Speaking generally, diamonds graded H through Z are yellowish, not yellow. Dealers use the term "off-color" or "byewater" to describe a yellow hue that lacks the saturation and tone for the yellow to be truly present.

Courtesy of © Stephen Hofer

A "fancy vivid yellow" diamond from the "Colour Variety Collection" shows a slightly brownish/greenish secondary hue not mentioned on the certificate. "Fancy vivid" is the highest, most sought after grade.

Hue, saturation, tone

Yellow is a primary spectral hue lying between green and orange on the color wheel. Green and orange are the normal secondary hues found in yellow diamonds. Of the two, green is the more prevalent, orange the more desirable. Greenish stones may appear murky. A visually pure yellow hue is more desirable still. Yellow diamonds are unusual in that they may show either a brown or gray mask. Brown is the more common and the more desirable. Grayish yellow stones appear cool, dull, and listless, compared to the warmth of brownish stones.

Color science tells us that the yellow hue achieves its maximum saturation in transparent media at about twenty percent tone. The vividness of the yellow hue tends to drop off dramatically over forty percent tone. This is the lightest optimum tone of any gem hue. Translated into terms useful to the aficionado, this means that in yellow-hued gemstones, a lighter (twenty to forty percent) tone is a brighter stone, and a brighter stone is a better stone. Stones of this description fall into the coveted GIA-GTL categories of *fancy intense* and occasionally *fancy vivid* (see p. 63), the highest accolade.

Pure dark-toned yellows do not exist. As tonal values increase, yellow becomes either brownish or greenish, usually the former.

Yellow diamond will often appear more saturated under the light of the light bulb. That makes yellow diamond something of a nightstone. It is recommended that the aficionado view yellow diamonds in both daylight and incandescent light before considering an acquisition.

Given the low optimum combination of saturation and tone, stones in the last few color grades on the colorless scale, i.e. X through Z, are often quite attractive face up. These are called "cape" colors, a reference to the fact that diamonds found in southern Africa (Cape of Good Hope) often have a yellowish tinge. Pure yellows in these grades display a delicate hue that goes beyond the designation off-color; that is, it is a lovely light yellow.

GIA-GTL grades yellow diamonds as *fancy* if the key color is darker in tone and deeper in saturation than the GTL *Z*-grade master stone (when examined face up). Stones in these grades are very low in price because they are considered off-color. But, as previously noted, diamonds can face up either darker or lighter than their body color would indicate. The aficionado is advised to examine carefully the key color of yellow diamonds in these last three grades.

Chapter 42

Lapis Lazuli

In ancient times the lapis-lazuli was the blue stone par excellence, because of its beautiful color and the valuable ultramarine dye derived from it.

G.F. Kunz, 1904

Lapis lazuli: the name evokes a sense of mystery and has a Biblical ring. This is simply because the gem has an ancient lineage. Lapis lazuli, like carnelian,

© 2001 Christie's Images
Sumerian lapis lazuli bull amulet from the Early Dynastic period (2650-2350 BC).

was one of the "precious" gems of antiquity and was highly esteemed through the Middle Ages, though it has fallen into relative disfavor in modern times. Lapis was almost certainly the sapphire mentioned in the Bible. The Roman historian Pliny described what he called sapphire thusly: "Sapphiros contains spots like gold. It is also sometimes rarely blue tinged with purple. It is never transparent." Obviously this is not an accurate description of sapphire; it is, however, a straight-on description of lapis lazuli.

Lapis lazuli — the name means blue stone — was highly regarded by the great civilizations of ancient Egypt and Sumer. The main source of both ancient and modern lapis is in the far northeastern reaches of Afghanistan, north of the Hindu Kush, in the remote province of Badakhshan. Archeological evidence suggests that these mines were worked as early as 8000 BC.

The earliest known worked lapis can be traced to the site of the ancient city of Mehrgarh in the Indus Valley, but the finest collection of ancient lapis was unearthed at the site of the royal tombs of Ur. Jewelry in the form of elaborate beaded necklaces and carvings of the finest lapis, the property of a Sumerian queen, has been dated back approximately forty-six hundred years.

Russia and Chile are the two other major sources of lapis. Russian lapis has greater amounts of pyrite and Chilean lapis is rich in calcite. Some of the very finest Chilean and Russian material is said to rival the Afghani. However, I have never seen material from either source that even comes close.

Hue, saturation, tone

Lapis is an opaque mineral, actually a rock with a varying composition of lazurite, pyrite, calcite, and diopside. Except that the stone is opaque rather than translucent, lapis lazuli is directly analogous to blue sapphire in hue, saturation, and tone. *Crystal* is,

obviously, not part of the equation in the evaluation of lapis. From a connoisseur's perspective it might as well be called opaque sapphire. Lapis was considered by the ancients to be the stone of heaven and in its finest qualities resembles the night sky. The finest lapis, like sapphire, is a visually pure (ninety percent) royal blue hue, sometimes modified, as Pliny noted, with a secondary hue of about ten percent purple.

Tone is a critical part of the quality equation, as lapis is opaque and, unlike sapphire, lacks transparency (crystal) to mitigate its deep tone. As in sapphire, the finest lapis teeters on the edge of overcolor. The optimum tone in lapis is between seventy-five and eighty-five percent. At ninety-percent tone it loses saturation and becomes decidedly dull and blackish. Usually a darkish stone (ninety percent tone) will be a bit too purple; pure blue stones tend to be lighter (seventy-five percent) in tone. Close your eyes and picture the night sky at midnight under the light of a full moon. That is the finest color in lapis lazuli.

Tino Hammid

This polished slab shows the rich midnight blue hue that characterizes the finest color in lapis lazuli.

Inclusions

Calcite and iron pyrites are the normal inclusions found in lapis lazuli. Calcite occurs as either whitish veins or as tiny dust-like particles. In either case it is considered a flaw. Lapis from

Chile is known for its distinctly dull and dusty appearance caused by concentrations of small calcite particles.

Pyrite, though considered a flaw by some, may sometimes materially contribute to the beauty of the gem. The slightly yellowish pyrite, commonly known as "fool's gold," when sprinkled throughout the stone gives the appearance of golden stars scattered across the evening sky. An artful dusting of golden flecks of pyrite can be very desirable. Lapis with pyrite inclusions is highly sought after, particularly by collectors in the United States.

Cut

Lapis lazuli is almost always cut *en cabochon*, although lapis beads are sometimes faceted. This sort of faceting has nothing to do with creating brilliance; it is simply a decorative effect. Since the gem is opaque it is never cut into traditional faceted shapes. The shape of the cabochon has little impact on value, except that a domed stone is usually preferred to one that is flat.

Treatments

The aficionado should beware of color-treated lapis lazuli. Lapis simulants date back to the ancient Egyptians, who made imitations using faience or frit, a type of fused glass (see Chapter 1). Today the stone is often dyed. Another simulant is reconstituted lapis. In this case lapis dust is mixed with an adhesive, allowed to harden, then polished to mimic the solid stone. Given the relatively low cost of even the finest lapis lazuli, these sorts of imitations are rarely seen in the United States and any of them can be readily separated from the genuine article by a seasoned gemologist.

The rarity factor

Fine lapis is available in large sizes. Stones over twenty carats tend to decrease in price on a per carat basis.

Chapter 43

Spinel

The connoisseur seldom confuses ruby and red spinel. The great clarity of this color of spinel, together with its lack of dichroism and the evenness of its color, differentiates it from ruby.

GIA Colored Stone Course, 1980

Spinel has endured a mostly downhill slide on the rocky road to popularity. Spinel might be called "the dealer's stone" because so many gem traders have fallen in love and tried, with little success, to promote it to the public. In the Western world red spinel was, up until the nineteenth century, often confused with ruby.

Spinel was first synthesized in 1919. Colorless synthetic spinel was then introduced as a diamond substitute. Because of its superior hardness, synthetic blue spinel was also used as a substitute for both natural aquamarine and blue sapphire. It seems almost as if a sort of negative cachet has attached itself to this beautiful natural gemstone. For whatever combination of reasons, spinel is one of the least appreciated of all precious gemstones. This was not always the case.

The gem was highly regarded in the ancient East. Spinel is often found associated with ruby; for millennia the *balas ruby*, as spinel was known, was consistently mistaken for true ruby. It is almost as if, given its history, spinel and ruby should share the name.

An old and venerable tale told by the seventeenth-century traveler Jean Baptiste Tavernier describes a Hindu merchant who sold a large stone represented to be a ruby for 95,000 rupees to Ja'far Khan, uncle of Aurangzeb, the Great Mogul of India. The stone was then presented as a gift to the monarch. The emperor regarded the gift with suspicion, because he could not tell if the red gem was a true or a *balas ruby*. He sent the stone to Shah Jahan, his father, the former emperor, whom he had overthrown and imprisoned. The deposed emperor, and builder of the Taj Mahal, identified the stone as spinel, stating that it was worth no more than 500 rupees. At which point the mogul demanded his uncle's money be returned.[201] Shah Jahan, alas, remained a captive and subsequently died in prison. With the birth of modern scientific gemology in the mid-nineteenth century, many famous large "rubies" have been identified as spinel; these include the 140-carat Black Prince's Ruby, the 352.50-carat Timur Ruby, and the 398.72-carat Catherine the Great's Ruby.[202]

Red spinel versus ruby

Spinel and ruby form in tandem in the identical geological environment; they are often found together. Spinel actually crystallizes first and ceases only when the magnesium in the immediate environment is

201. Tavernier, *Travels*, vol. 2, p. 127.

202. Hughes, *Ruby & Sapphire*, p. 247. New evidence confirms that the Arabs, at least, were aware of the gemological distinction between ruby and spinel as early as the thirteenth century. Ahmad ibn Yusuf al Tifaschi, in his *Best Thoughts on the Best of Stones*, comments that spinel is a distinct gem, can be scratched by ruby, and is worth only about half the value of ruby. See Huda, *Arab Roots of Gemology*, p. 112.

exhausted. With a refractive index of 1.71, spinel is very close to ruby in its refractive qualities.[203] Spinel, however, is singly refractive and rarely exhibits the dramatic multicolor effect or color bleeding normally seen in ruby (see Chapter 4). Spinel is a tough and durable gemstone. At eight on the Mohs scale, its hardness is slightly less than that of ruby. For this reason it takes a slightly inferior polish. In ancient times, a comparison of the surface luster was one method used to separate the two gemstones.

Although spinel occurs in a full spectrum of colors, the pink to red variety is the one that is commercially important. The Arabian scholar Al Tifaschi, writing in the thirteenth century, recognized four categories of red spinel: *mu'aqrabi* or scorpion (deep red), *atash* (of lesser red), *inari* (the color of the pomegranate), and *niaziki* (of lesser red, possibly pink).[204] As was true in ancient times, most of the other hues, with the possible exception of the "cobalt blue" gems, are really quite unattractive and of little interest to the connoisseur.[205]

Jeff Scovil; courtesy of Clark Gem and Mineral

A 7.24-carat fine red spinel. This gem shows a red primary hue with little or no secondary hue, eighty percent tone.

Hue: red spinel

Comparison with ruby is, in this case, unavoidable. Like ruby, spinel occurs in a tonal continuum of hues from light pink to a rich deep visually pure red. The "ruby red" spinel is extraordinarily rare and almost unobtainable. In my own career I have seen only two. The pink normally has a light purple (twenty percent) secondary hue while the reds almost always show a distinct orange secondary hue. True reds, those gems with ten percent or less orange secondary, are without question the rarest and most sought after of all spinel.

Hue: flame spinel

"Flame spinel," a red stone with a distinct orange secondary hue, is second to red in overall availability and price. In fact, it is the rare spinel that does not show some admixture of orange. The flame variety is relatively available in sizes under five carats.

203. The refractive index of ruby is 1.76-1.78.

204. Huda, *Arab Roots of Gemology*, p. 112.

205. Eduard Gubelin and Franz-Xavier Erni, *Gemstones: Symbols of Beauty and Power* (Tucson, Arizona: Geoscience Press, 1999), p. 108. According to Professor Gubelin, "The cobalt spinel can be expected to develop into a cult gemstone for collectors."

Jeff Scovil; courtesy of R.W. Wise, Goldsmiths, Inc.

A finely cut 2.53-carat pink spinel showing a lovely pastel pink of about forty percent tone. Note the slight multicolor effect toward the bottom edges of the gem.

The orange secondary hue can be prominent, usually between fifteen to fifty percent of the total hue. The distinctive color of flame spinel is found in no other gemstone.

Pink spinel

The hue we call pink is simply a lighter-toned red; therefore the demarcation between a pink and a red spinel is in some sense arbitrary. The boundary tends to move up and down, depending on whether it is the buyer or the seller who is making the decision. In pink spinel, due to its pronounced light-toned purple secondary hue, the decision is easier to make. The hue of pink spinel is often quite pure. What I am calling a "secondary hue" manifests itself as an unusual phenomenon known as *transmission luminescence.* The purple shows up as an ethereal glow that emanates from the stone like a pearl's orient or the billowing sheen (adularescence) seen in moonstone. This phenomenon is typical of pink spinel from East Africa.

Saturation and tone

Red reaches its ultimate saturation or its *gamut limit* at about eighty percent tone. As with ruby, a fine red spinel tends to be medium dark in tone. Reds over eighty percent tone rapidly lose saturation and are generally considered overcolor. Gray is the normal saturation modifier or mask found in spinel. In fact, most of the other hues of spinel (blues and greens) are undesirable simply because they are distinctly grayish and quite dull.

With pink stones, the darker the tone, the more saturated the hue will become. Thus, a darker-toned pink hue is a more beautiful pink. Because of the light tone and purple secondary hue, the gray mask is often difficult to see in pink stones. The key color of a fine pink spinel is a highly saturated "hot pink." A dull cool pink is the result of a grayish mask.

Crystal

As the quote at the beginning of the chapter suggests, spinel can be quite transparent and crystalline, particularly when compared to ruby. A true red spinel, due to its exceptional crystal, will compare in beauty to even the finest ruby.

As previously mentioned, pink spinel, even when faceted, will often exhibit a fuzzy almost moonstone-like lavender mist (adularescence) that is considered a fault by some connoisseurs. This sleepy glow affects the gem's crystal. It resembles a similar phenomenon that is found in the finest Kashmir sapphire, where it is considered the hallmark of the most beautiful sapphires from that region. In the case of pink spinel, however, it is the secondary hue that actually glows. The effect is unique and charming. Why it should be a plus in sapphire and a minus in spinel is difficult to understand.

The rarity factor

Pink, pink red, and orangy red spinel is fairly available in sizes up to five carats. Above five carats the gem is rare, and it becomes exceptionally rare in sizes above ten carats. A visually pure red with ten percent or less of an orangy secondary hue is rare in any size.

achroic Without color; a colorless gemstone.

achromatic As above

adularescence A phenomenal effect; e.g., the billowing "moonglow" effect in moonstone.

akoya pearl A pearl from the saltwater *akoya-gai oyster* (Pinctada martensii); "Japanese pearl."

baroque Any pearl that is not symmetrical, round, or teardrop, oval, or button shaped.

bead nucleation The use of a shell bead, usually spherical, implanted in the oyster to stimulate the growth of a cultured pearl, and forming the center of the pearl.

bellied Describing a stone purposely cut with extra weight around the girdle, yielding a bulbous outline.

bicolor A stone with two distinct, separate hues, common in tourmaline.

bleed color The loss of saturation and tone when the viewing environment is shifted between natural and incandescent lighting.

body color The color of light transmitted through a gem, as distinguished from key color, the color of refracted light.

brilliance The total quantity of light refracted and reflected (from a gemstone) back to the eye of the viewer.

brilliant cut Usually refers to a full-cut brilliant of fifty-eight facets, with thirty-two facets and table above the girdle, twenty-four facets and a culet below; used almost universally in cutting larger round diamonds.

byewater Off-color; poor color and transparency; see also *water*.

"buying the cert" A purchase based not on an analysis of the beauty of the stone, but on the language of the grading report (certificate).

cabochon, en cabochon Gem with a rounded top, without facets. French, "little head."

carat Unit of weight in gemstones, one-fifth of a metric gram.

cat's-eye Phenomenal effect in cabochon cut gemstones resembling the iris of a cat's eye.

clarity One of the "four Cs" of quality grading, referring to the presence or absence of inclusions or flaws.

color See *body color, key color.*

crown The top half of a faceted gemstone; the portion above the girdle.

crystal One of the "four Cs" of gem connoisseurship, coined by author, referring to the transparency and diaphaneity of the gem. See also *water* and *transparency.*

culet The point at the very bottom of the pavilion of a gemstone.

cut The style in which a gem has been fashioned; e.g., emerald cut, brilliant cut. Also refers to a gem's proportions; e.g., well cut.

daystone A term coined by the author to describe a gem species or variety or single stone that looks its best in natural daylight.

diaphaneity The property of being transparent or translucent.

dichroic Of two colors; the characteristic of a transparent substance to divide refracted white light into two distinct rays.

diffraction The modification of white light as it breaks up into the color spectrum.

dispersion The division of white light into its constituent components as in light through a prism; the rainbow effect.

dog A poor quality gemstone in a parcel.

drusy Tiny quartz crystals growing on the surface of a gemstone.

en cameo. Cut in relief. Opposite of cutting *intaglio.*

enhancement Any process applied to a gemstone to improve its color or clarity; also heat enhancement, burning, cooking; see also *treatment*.

extinction The dark gray to black portion of a face-up gemstone that does not refract light; usually caused by off-axis refraction.

eye The finest gemstone in a parcel.

eye-clean, eye-flawless Describing a gem with no inclusions when viewed with the naked eye (assumes 20/20 vision).

eye-visible Inclusions visible to the eye without magnification.

face up The view of a gem from the top or crown.

fancy color In diamond, any color other than colorless viewed face up; in diamond any color is a fancy color.

fish-eye A dark gray to black (achroic) spot at the center of the gem caused by improper proportions from poor cutting; see also *extinction*.

flawless Describing a gemstone with no visible inclusions under 10X magnification.

flour Tiny inclusions that cause a "sleepy" effect in the key color of a gemstone.

fluorescence A glow or color visible under ultraviolet light.

fortification The technical term for stripes of color in chalcedony.

"four Cs" The four factors used to analyze and discuss the beauty of a gemstone: *color, clarity, cut,* and *crystal*. Altered by author. Traditionally, *color, cut, clarity and carat* (weight).

gamut limit The point on the tonal (light to dark) scale at which a given hue produces the most vivid saturation.

girdle The outer edge of a faceted stone, the area of greatest diameter, usually the part where the prongs are placed when the gem is set.

"holding the carat" A cutting strategy designed to produce a finished gem above a certain whole carat weight.

hue The descriptive technical term for color; e.g., red, pinkish orange, and chartreuse are hues.

ideal cut A specific set of proportions discovered by Marcel Tolkowsky in 1919 thought to produce the greatest brilliance and maximum dispersion in a round brilliant cut diamond.

imperial Archaic term used to describe certain hues of topaz.

incandescent Light produced by a flame, candle, campfire, or light bulb.

inclusion Anything visible to the naked eye or under magnification in a gemstone, such as a foreign body or crack. A stone with an inclusion is described as *included*. See also *eye clean, loupe clean*

intaglio Designs cut in a gemstone that appear in relief when the stone is pressed into a soft substance like clay. Opposite of cutting *en cameo*.

iridescence The exhibition of prismatic (rainbow) colors on the surface of a gem. See also orient, *overtone*.

kelvin A unit used to measure light temperature.

key color The color of the light refracted out of a faceted gemstone; the color of the gem's brilliance or sparkle.

loupe clean Describing a flawless gem; no visible inclusions under 10X magnification.

luster Reflections off the surface of a gem or pearl.

mask A modifying color, usually brown or gray, that diminishes the saturation (brightness or vividness) of a gem's hue.

master stone Stone of a known color and quality used for comparing other gems of the same species or variety; also a diamond of known color grade used to determine the grade of other diamonds.

modifier A color that changes the appearance (hue) of another, e.g., a primary hue such as red can be modified by a secondary hue such as orange, yielding an orangy red hue. Saturation modifier, see *mask*.

Mohs scale A relative scale of gem hardness; talc is 1, diamond is 10.

mosaic The complex visual scene in the face-up gem. See also *multicolor effect*.

multicolor effect The display of divergent colors or tonal variations of the same color on a gem viewed in the face-up position.

nacre The mother-of-pearl secretions of the mollusk; pearl essence.

nailhead Dark center in a gem; see *fish-eye*.

native cut A poorly proportioned gemstone supposedly fashioned by primitive means; considered pejorative.

nightstone A term adapted by the author to describe a gem species or variety that looks its best in incandescent light, showing its most saturated hue. Traditionally, an opal that retains a strong play-of-color in low light environments.

nonchromatic Without color; a colorless stone, without chroma; see also *achromatic*, *achroic*.

off-color Insufficient color, or saturation, in a diamond to be considered good color. Used to describe colorless diamond with a strong tint of yellow.

opaque Impenetrable by light; neither transparent nor translucent. *Opacity* is the quality of being opaque.

orient The iridescent effect visible in finer quality pearls; also called overtone.

overcolor A stone with a hue that is overly dark in tone, usually above eighty-five percent.

overtone See *orient*.

padparadscha Color of the lotus; a light to medium-toned pinkish orange to orangy pink sapphire.

pair Two gems matching in color, cut, clarity, crystal, and diameter.

parcel Gems sold as a group.

pavilion The portion of a faceted stone beneath the girdle.

Peruzzi cut An early brilliant style cut, the first brilliant.

phenomenal stone A stone that exhibits a phenomenal effect, such as a star, cat's-eye, or adularescence.

pick A selection from a parcel of gemstones.

pink To heat topaz at a low temperature to turn the hue to pink.

play of color The iridescent effect in opal.

precious An archaic term used to describe certain hues in topaz.

primary When referring to hue, the dominant hue in a gemstone; a pinkish red gem has a red primary hue.

reflection Light reflected from a surface.

refraction The bending or deflection of light passing from one transparent media to another; e.g., from air to water, from a gem into the air.

refractive index A measure of the angle of the deflection of light as it passes from one substance to another.

reinforcement Coined by author to describe a memory aid used to recall the color of a specific gem, i.e. using taste to reinforce sight.

rutile A crystal (inclusion) that forms in golden hairlike masses.

saturation The quantity of color in a gem which translates into the color's vividness or dullness.

scintillation The breaking up of light into tiny constituents, a function of the facets of a gem.

seal stone A gem carved in intaglio producing a design in relief, when pressed into clay, usually the owner's signature or emblem.

secondary When referring to hue, the second or modifying color; an orangy red gem has an orange secondary hue.

simpatico An affinity between a certain color pearl and the skin of the potential wearer.

skylight Light diffused around the body of the viewer with the back turned to the sun.

sleepy Having a fuzzy or misty quality in the brilliance of a gem, a lack of crispness. Defining quality in Kashmir sapphire

smoky Dirty or sooty looking. Also refers specifically to grayish fancy color diamonds.

sooty Blackish and fuzzy or smoky, refers to the crystal or transparency of the gem.

star A phenomenal effect in some gemstones, appearing as a six rayed figure.

suite Three or more matched gems.

super-d A misnomer used to describe an ultra-transparent diamond. A noted characteristic of Golconda diamonds.

texture In transparent gems, a description of color zoning visible face up. In pearls, a reference to any indentations or imperfections in the pearl's surface.

tint A hint of color, not sufficiently saturated to be a hue.

tissue nucleation The use of mantle tissue from a donor mollusk to stimulate the growth of a pearl. A tissue-nucleated pearl is a non-nucleated cultured pearl.

tone The third constituent of color, defined as lightness to darkness.

translucent Allowing light to pass through, but preventing the clear viewing of images.

transmission luminescence Emission of light effect by a substance caused by the excitation of light rays.

transparent Allowing light to pass through so that objects may be clearly seen.

treatment, heat treatment The heating of a gemstone to improve its color or clarity.

trichroic The breaking up of light into three constituent rays, each containing a portion of the visible spectrum (rainbow).

water An archaic term that refers to the combination of color and transparency in gemstones; used hierarchically: first water (gem of the finest water), second water, third water, byewater.

window The center of a gem cut too shallow. Produces a read through effect that lacks brilliance; also called *lens effect*.

zone, zoning Alternating sections of color inside a gemstone.

BIBLIOGRAPHY

Books

Aidonia Treasure (The); Seals and Jewellery of The Aegean Late Bronze Age. Demakopoulou, Katie ed., Athens: National Archaeological Museum, May 30 – September 1, 1996.

Bauer, Max. *Precious Stones.* Translated by L.J. Spenser. 2 vols. 1904. Reprint. New York: Dover Publications, 1968.

Beesley, C. R. *Color Scan Training Manual, Part 1, The Systematic Analysis of Color Quality in Gemstones.* New York: American Gemological Laboratories, Inc., 1985.

Berge, Victor, and Lanier, Henry W. *Pearl Diver: Adventuring Over and Under Southern Seas.* New York: Garden City Publishing Company, 1930.

Berlin, Brent and Kay, Paul. *Basic Color Terms; Their Universality and Evolution.* Berkeley: University of California Press, 1969.

Conklin, Lawrence H. *Notes and Commentaries on Letters to George F. Kunz, The Tiffany Edition.* New Canaan: Matrix Publishing Co., 1986.

Cox, Christopher R. *Chasing the Dragon: Into the Heart of the Golden Triangle.* New York: Henry Holt, 1996.

Dietrich, R. V. *The Tourmaline Group.* New York: Van Nostrand Reinhold Co. Ltd., 1995.

Downing, Paul. *Opal Identification and Value.* Tallahassee, Florida: Majestic Press 1972.

Dubin, Lois Sherr. *The History of Beads.* New York: Harry N. Abrams, 1987.

Epstein, David S. *The Gem Merchant.* Self-published, 1995.

Epstein, Edward J. *The Rise and Fall of Diamonds: The Shattering of a Brilliant Illusion.* Simon & Schuster, 1982.

Federman, David and Hammid, Tino. *A Consumer's Guide to Colored Gemstones.* Lincolnshire, Illinois: Vance Publishing Corporation, 1990.

Greenbaum, Toni. *Messengers of Modernism: American Studio Jewelry 1940-1960.* New York: Flammarion, 1996.

Gubelin, Eduard and Erni, Franz-Xavier. *Gemstones; Symbols of Beauty and Power.* Tucson, Arizona: Geoscience Press, 1999.

The Guide. Northbrook, Illinois: Gemstone International, Inc., 2002-2003.

Harris, Harvey. *Fancy-Color Diamonds.* Liechtenstein: Fancoldi Registered Trust, 1994.

Hofer, Stephen C. *Collecting and Classifying Coloured Diamonds.* New York: Ashland Press, 1998.

Huda, Samar Najm Abul. *The Arab Roots of Gemology: Ahmad ibn Yusuf al Tifaschi's Best Thoughts on the Best of Stones.* London: The Scarecrow Press, 1998.

Hughes, Richard W. *Ruby & Sapphire.* Boulder, Colorado: RWH Publishing, 1998.

Kanfer, Stefan. *The Last Empire: De Beers, Diamonds, and the World.* New York: Noonday Press, 1993.

Kant, Immanuel. *The Critique of Pure Reason.* Kemp-Smith, N., ed. & trans. London: St. Martins Press, 1966.

Kautilya. The Arthashastra. Rangarajan, L. N., ed. & trans. India: Penguin Books, 1987.

Keller, Peter. Gemstones of East Africa. Tucson, Arizona: Geoscience Press, 1992.

Kessel, Joseph. Mogok: The Valley of Rubies. London: Macgibbon & Kee, 1960.

Kornitzer, Louis. Trade Winds: The Adventures of a Dealer in Pearls. London: Geoffrey Bles, 1933.

Kunz, George F. The Curious Lore of Precious Stones. 1913. Reprint. New York: Dover Publications, 1971.

Kunz, George F. Shakespeare and Precious Stones. Philadelphia: J.B. Lippincott Company, 1916.

Kunz, George F., and Stevenson, Charles H. The Book of the Pearl: The History, Art, Science, and Industry of the Queen of Gems. 1908. Reprint. New York: Dover Publications, 1998.

The Treatises of Benvenuto Cellini on Goldsmithing and Sculpture (1568). Translated by C.R. Ashby. New York: Dover Publications, 1967.

Moholy-Nagy, L. Vision in Motion. Chicago: Paul Theobold, 1947.

Nassau, Kurt. Gemstone Enhancement: History, Science and State of the Art. London: Butterworths, 1984.

Ogden, Jack. Jewellery of the Ancient World. New York: Rizzoli, 1982.

Raabe, H.E. Cannibal Nights: The Reminiscences of a Free-lance Trader. New York: Payson & Clarke Ltd., 1927.

Rose, Gustav. Humboldt's Travels in Siberia, 1837-1842: The Gemstones. Translated by John Sinkankas.

Edited by George Sinkankas. Phoenix, Arizona: Geoscience Press, 1984.

Roskin, Gary. Photo Masters for Diamond Grading. Northbrook Illinois: Gemworld International, 1994.

Shipley, Robert M. Dictionary of Gems and Gemology. Sixth edition, Santa Monica: the Gemological Institute of America, 1974.

Sinkankas, John. Emerald and Other Beryls. Radnor, Pennsylvania: Chilton Book Company, 1981.

Sinkankas, John. Gemstones of North America Volume III. Tucson Arizona: GeoScience Press, 1997.

Smith, G. F. Herbert. Gemstones. 9th edition. London: Methuen & Co.,1940.

Sperisen, Francis J. The Art of the Lapidary. New York: The Bruce Publishing Co., 1961.

Streeter, Edwin. Precious Stones and Gems. London: Chapman & Hall, 1879.

Tagore, Souindro M. Mani Mala; A Treatise on Gems. 2 vols. Nairobi: Dr. N. R. Barot publisher, 1996.

Tavernier, Jean. Baptiste. The Six Voyages To India. Translated by V. Ball. Edited by V. Ball. New Dehli: Oriental Books Reprint Corporation, 1977. Originally published in 1678.

Themelis, Ted. Moguk, Valley of Rubies and Sapphires. Los Angeles: A&T Publishing, 2000.

Villiers, Alan. Sons of Sinbad: Sailing with the Arabs in Their Dhows. London: Hodder & Stoughton, 1940.

Ward, Fred. Pearls. Bethesda, Maryland: Gem Book Publishers, 1994.

Ying-yai Sheng-lan. Ma Huan. The Overall Survey of the Ocean's Shores [1433]. Bangkok: White Lotus Press, 1970.

Zucker, Benjamin. Gems and Jewels: A Connoisseur's Guide. New York: Thames and Hudson, 1987.
Articles:

Benesch, F., Wohrmann, B. "A Short History of the Tourmaline Group." The Mineralogical Record, vol. 16, September-October 1985, pp. 331-338.

Crowningshield, Robert. "Padparadscha: What's in a Name?" Gems & Gemology, Spring 1983, p. 31.

Federman, David. "All in the Family, Inside the Diamond Spectrum." Modern Jeweler, October 1990.

Hammid, Mary Murphy. "Golconda Diamonds." Christie's Magnificent Jewels, October 23, 1990, catalog, pp. 301-302.

Hemphill et al. "Modeling the Appearance of the Round Brillliant Cut Diamond: An Analysis of Brilliance." Gems & Gemology, Winter 1998, pp. 158-183.

Reinitz, Ilene M. et al. "Modeling the Appearance of the Round Brilliant Cut Diamond: An Analysis of Fire, and More About Brilliance." Gems & Gemology, Fall 2001, pp. 174-197.

Kane, Robert E. "Three Notable Fancy-Color Diamonds: Purplish Red, Purple-Pink, and Reddish-Purple." Gems & Gemology, Summer 1987, pp. 90-95.
Kane, Robert E., et al. "The Legendary Dresden Green Diamond." Gems & Gemology, Winter 1990, pp. 248-265.

King, John M., et al. "Characterization and Grading of Natural-Color Pink Diamonds." Gems & Gemology, Summer 2002, pp. 134-147.

King, John M., et al. "Characterizing Natural-Color Type II-B Blue Diamonds." Gems & Gemology, Winter 1998, pp. 246-268.

King, John M., et al. "Color Grading of Fancy Color Diamonds in the GIA Gem Trade Laboratory." Gems & Gemology, Winter 1994, pp. 22-242.

Kjarsgaard, B.A., & Levinson, A.A. "Diamonds in Canada." Gems & Gemology, Fall 2002, pp. 208-237.

Levinson, A.A., et al. "Diamond Sources and Production: Past, Present and Future." Gems & Gemology, Winter 1992, pp. 234-253.

Liu,Yan; Shigley, J.E.; and Hurwit, K.N. "What Causes Nacre Iridescence?" Pearl World, December 1999, pp. 1, 4.

Moses, T. F. "A Contribution to Understanding the Effect of Blue Fluorescence." Gems & Gemology, Winter 1997, pp. 244-259.

Piretti, Adolf, et al. "Rubies from Mong Hsu." Gems & Gemology, Spring 1995, pp. 2-25.

Procter, Keith. "Chrysoberyl and Alexandrite from the Pegmatite Districts of Minas Gerais." Gems & Gemology, Spring 1988, pp. 26-28.

Procter, Keith. "Gem Pegmatites of Minas Gerais." Gems & Gemology, Summer 1984, pp. 78-81.

Stockton, Carol, and Manson, Vincent. "A Proposed New Classification for Gem-Quality Garnets." Gems & Gemology, Winter 1985, p. 205.

Tashey, Thomas E. "The Effect of Fluorescence on the Color Grading and Appearance of White and Off-White Diamonds." The Professional Gemologist, Spring-Summer 2000, p. 5.

Ward, Fred. "The Wisdom of Pearls." Pearl World, The International Pearling Journal, vol. 11, no. 2, July/August/September, 2002, p. 11.

Wise, Richard W. "Burma Ruby Making a Market Comeback." National Jeweler Magazine, December 1993, pp. 34, 36.

Wise, Richard W. "The Colors of Africa." Jeweler's Quarterly Magazine, 1989, Designer Color Pages, pp. 7-8.

Wise, Richard W. "Diamond Cutting; New Concepts, New Millennium." Gem Market News, March/April 1998, 3-4.

Wise, Richard W. "Garimpeiro Dreams." Gemkey Magazine, May/June 2000, pp. 42-44.

Wise, Richard W. "Light Up Your Life." Asia Precious Magazine, Guide to Industry Services, 1998, pp. iii-iv.

Wise, Richard W. "A Meditation on Pearls." Pearl World, July/September 2001, pp. 10-11.

Wise, Richard W. "The New Face of Chinese Freshwater Pearls." Colored Stone Magazine, November/December 1992, pp. 30-31.

Wise, Richard W. "Oldest Mine in the U.S. Reopens." Colored Stone Magazine, July/August 1992, cover-p. 8.

Wise, Richard W. "Queensland Boulder Opal." Gems & Gemology, Spring 1993, pp. 4-15.

Wise, Richard W. "In Search of the Burma Stone." Jeweler's Quarterly Magazine, 1989, Designer Color Pages, pp. 8-11.

Wise, Richard W. "Tourmaline: A Modest Proposal." Colored Stone Magazine, May/June 1991, pp. 6-7.

X

x-ray fluorescence spectrophotometry, 203

Y

yellow
    gamut limit for, 22
    as primary color, 18
    stones, viewing, 38
    symbolism of, 135
yellow diamond, 225, 243–244
yellowish-diamond, 243, 244
Yerilla (Northern Territory, Australia),
gemstones from, 80, 117
Ying-yai Sheng-lan, 40
Yogo Gulch (Montana), blue sapphire
from, 165–166
Yogo sapphire, 166
Yusuf al Tifaschi, Ahmad ibn, 108

Z

Zambia, gemstones from, 77, 108
Zimbabwe, emerald from, 77
zoisite. *See* tanzanite
Zonari, Paulo, 99–100
zoning
    blue sapphire, 168–169
    pink diamonds, 229
    ruby, 179–180
Zucker, Benjamin, 40, 85